# THE BIG BOOK OF

# PAGAN

# PRAYER

# AND

# RITUAL

## CEISIWR SERITH

WEISER
BOOKS

*For Hope,*
*who gives so much joy.*

This edition first published in 2020 by Weiser Books, an imprint of
Red Wheel/Weiser, LLC
With offices at:
65 Parker Street, Suite 7
Newburyport, MA 01950
*www.redwheelweiser.com*

ISBN: 978-1-57863-692-1
Library of Congress Cataloging-in-Publication Data available upon request.
Cover design by Kathryn Sky-Peck
Typeset in Times New Roman
Printed in Canada
MAR
10 9 8 7 6 5 4 3 2

# CONTENTS

# Part Three: PETITIONARY PRAYERS

# ACKNOWLEDGMENTS

Many people helped in the writing of this book. Those who have willingly suffered through the various rituals I've written while I honed my skills have gone above and beyond. Of these, I especially thank the members of my grove, Nemos Ognios. It was Neal Levin who, by suggesting the book's structure, gave me the idea of writing from the point of view of a ritual.

I gladly thank my wife Debbie and my daughter Elizabeth for encouraging me and for providing me with an environment in which I could allow my thoughts to turn to religious matters. My time with two women who are so good with words has increased my own skill, and from the most personal point of view, most of what I know about the concerns of real people has come from them. Most especially, my wife has worked hard through the years, allowing me to take the time to discover that I could write. I couldn't have done it without her.

# INTRODUCTION

I hope this book is only the first in a long line of books of Pagan prayers that will come out of Paganism as it grows. Prayer is a subject that can never be exhausted. It's a conversation between us and the numinous. As long as there have been people, they have conversed with one another, and still they find things to talk about. Why should we expect sacred conversation to be any different?

I wrote this book with several goals in mind. First, to encourage others to use them, I wanted to explain why prayers and offerings matter. Second, I wanted to show people how they could write their own prayers. Third, I wanted to provide the Pagan community with a selection of prayers to use.

There are short commentaries to some of the prayers in which I try to explain the Pagan deities, images, and myths and to indulge in a little theology. These commentaries also show the connection between myths, images, theology, and prayer, thereby helping you in the construction of your own prayers. I decided to forego an explanation of neo-Paganism itself, however. There are already enough books out there that do that; I don't have much new to say on the basics. I will say, however, that I believe that Paganism is defined by its rituals rather than its beliefs, so readers will find my thoughts on the subject in the prayers. If you aren't familiar with the basics of neo-Paganism, don't worry; if you read the prayers and my commentaries, you will find the explanations you need.

Although I've tried to be very careful with words in this book, I've sometimes used "gods" instead of "deities" or "gods and goddesses" when the flow of the language seemed to require it. I have even used the politically incorrect phrase "gods and men." For this transgression, I can only ask you to put it beside "deities and people" and see which scans better.

The order of prayers in this book follows that of my second book rather than the first. I've found it to be more user friendly, one from which it's easier to form one's own rituals.

The categories into which I have divided the prayers are not hard and fast. For instance, you can use a prayer of praise as an introduction to one of thanksgiving. Because of this, you shouldn't feel bound by the chapter titles. Feel free to mix and match, to change and edit, and indeed to make these prayers your own. It is you who will be talking to the gods, and you are the one who will have to answer to them for what you say. Be clear. Be careful in how you pray. Take care how you come before the gods. Give them your best.

Most forms of Paganism are unashamedly polytheistic, believing in a multitude of deities. I myself believe in an effectively infinite number, although I personally worship only a few. With so many gods to choose from, it is obvious that I will only be able to address some. For those deities not represented here, some of these prayers can be adapted—or, at least, serve as models or inspiration for your own.

A critique of my previous books has been that I didn't have enough prayers to deities from certain cultures, in particular Baltic, Slavic, and Near Eastern. This was a legitimate criticism that I've tried to correct in this version.

There may, however, be deities I give prayers to that some don't consider deities at all—or, at least, Pagan ones. For instance, I give prayers to *numina* who in Zoroastrianism are considered Yazatas, who aren't exactly deities. I hope I don't offend any Zoroastrians by this, but the Yazatas I've written prayers to come, in a historical sense, from pre-Zoroastrian Pagan deities, and it is to them that the prayers are directed, not the Zoroastrian figures.

I've chosen to use the standard spellings for deity names. In some cases, this results in scary things like "Tvaṣṭṛ." Some of these are probably obvious, like "Kriṣṇa," but others not so much. In the glossary of deities at the back of the book, I've included alternate spellings that are sometimes found that, while not completely accurate, are good enough. For Proto-Indo-European deities, for which there are only the acceptable spellings, pronounce the vowels as in Latin or Italian. The Proto-Indo-European "x" is the sound at the end of Scottish "loch," and accents simply mark accented syllables. The superscript "w" in "Gʷouwindā" and "Perkʷūnos is a little trickier (and scarier), but you won't be too far wrong if you use "gw" and "qu." The letter "š," found in several languages, is pronounced like English "sh," "č" like English "ch," and "ž" like the "s" in "measure" (French "j").

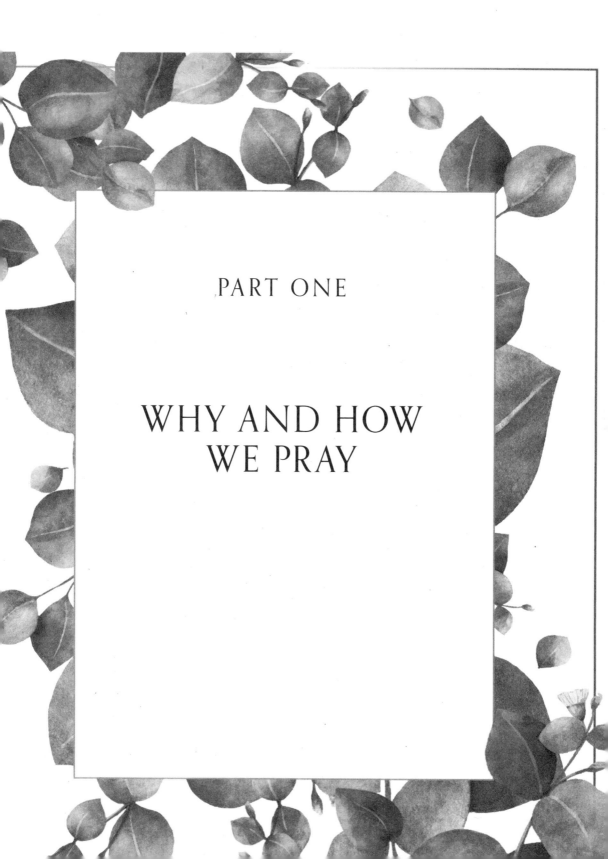

PART ONE

# WHY AND HOW
# WE PRAY

*Chapter 1*

# THE ROLE OF PRAYER–
# YESTERDAY AND TODAY

Those of us who call ourselves Pagans owe a debt to all those who came before us. Before trying to define our own modern Paganism, therefore, we should find out as much as we can about what the ancient Pagans did. To do that, we'll look at their prayers. Then we can either follow their lead, or, if we choose to be different, we can at least choose from knowledge rather than from ignorance.

## *Ancient Prayers*

The most reliable sources on how the ancient Pagans prayed are the prayers recorded by the Pagans themselves. There are several types of sources of ancient Pagan prayers, such as the literary and the epigraphic. There are quite a few literary sources for Greek and Roman Paganism, even more for the Egyptian tradition, and a great wealth of material from India. Anthropologists in modern times have supplied us with large amounts of material from all over the world. We most certainly do not lack information.

We also have stories written down in the Middle Ages by monks. These present both problems and benefits, however. When people in Irish stories swear "by the gods my people swear by," is this repeating an ancient Irish oath, or just the sort of thing that the monks figured Pagans would say? We don't know. This sort of reference is inspiring, however; if not in substance, at least in style. Maybe these monks were on to something.

The epigraphic evidence comes from inscriptions on offerings, temple walls, etc. Offerings sometimes have a short prayer inscribed on them that gives the name and intent of the one making them. Inscriptions found on Egyptian temple walls are particularly rich in information.

Even in areas from which information is otherwise scanty, we find examples, such as in travelers' reports and late versions of myths. Whether we can rely on these sources has long been debated. Even if this type of evidence does not accurately reflect the culture it claims to depict, however, it can at least tell us how the culture that recorded the stories and reports saw prayer. And this, in turn, can inspire our own prayers.

Two very different sources of information on ancient Pagan prayer are the local styles of modern prayer and surviving folk customs. Many people think that when Christians pray in a particular way in a particular culture, the practice must come from the pre-Christian days of that culture. There is a tendency to act as if Christians had no creativity of their own. It's very possible, however, that local prayer styles, no matter how ancient they may seem, were invented by local Christians rather than Pagans. This doesn't mean we can't use these styles in our own prayers, of course. Never ignore inspiration. Just don't assume you are following some ancient Pagan tradition when you use this sort of source.

Folk customs often contain prayers and songs. But these can present a similar problem. We can rarely know how much of the customs come from a Pagan culture and how much from other sources. To make the situation worse, sometimes the person who recorded the folk material "improved" it, further obscuring its Pagan roots.

So what is a poor Pagan to do? We must educate ourselves as best we can, using all the sources we can find. We must look carefully at what has been passed on to us from ancient times, weighing its possible antiquity and Pagan nature carefully. Most important of all, however, we must have an active prayer life. We must ask the gods for guidance on how they wish to be prayed to, and we must listen carefully for their answer. Then we can share the results with our fellow Pagans, so that the stock of prayers we hold in common will grow.

## Prayers and Offerings

Almost all religious people pray and most make offerings. Yet a search through the literature of neo-Paganism turns up only a small number of prayers, and even fewer references to offerings. There is much ritual material, to be sure, but the sort in which the worshiper stands before their deities, addresses them with respect, and offers them gifts is in short supply. Invocations, declarations, and spells are found in great number, but acts of praise and devotion, or simply requests rather than demands for help, are not.

This is a modern development, though. If we look through the writings of the ancient Pagans, we find huge numbers of prayers. We have inscriptions left by the ancient Celts. We have many prayers from the Greeks; characters in their tragedies were wont to pray at the drop of a corpse. The most ancient Hindu texts, the four Vedas, are essentially long prayer books. From the Americas, from Asia, from Africa, from Oceania, from Australia, we find more and more prayers, building up higher and higher, until we are crushed beneath the obvious: the most common form of Pagan religious expression is prayer.

Closely allied to prayer is the offering—the second most common form of worship. This makes sense; prayers and offerings are the same thing. They both present gifts to the gods—one of words and time, and the other of objects. Prayers usually accompany offerings, and offerings frequently accompany prayers. A line between them cannot be drawn, and I have not tried to do so. When we come before the numina, it's wise not to come empty-handed. We should come bearing words if not objects; if not objects, then words. And how much better if we bring both!

# Why Do We Pray?

The ancients may have prayed and made offerings, but what is the point in this modern day and age?

When we pray, we talk to sacred beings. They are like our spiritual friends, or our parents, or our cousins. We talk to our human friends and parents and cousins, so it only makes sense to talk to their divine counterparts as well.

Why do we need to talk in the first place? Don't the gods already know what we want or how we feel about them? Let's go back to the human equivalent. Do you talk to your friends, or do you just assume they know how you feel and what you want? Do you send notes to your grandparents thanking them for gifts, or do you figure that they'll understand how thankful you are, even if you don't tell them? If Cousin Harry does something great, do you give him a call and say, "Nice going," or do you decide his own feeling of self-accomplishment should be enough? Surely the gods deserve at least as much consideration as Cousin Harry.

Maybe the problem is the way you see the divine beings. Pagan gods aren't omniscient. Unlike Santa Claus, they don't see you when you're sleeping, or know when you're awake. They have to be invited into your life. Give them a call and tell them how much you've missed them; tell them how wonderful you think they are; and, while you're at it, maybe ask for a favor or thank them for favors done. You might find you like talking to them.

# Why Make Offerings?

While the "why" of prayer may be pretty obvious, the "why" of offerings is a bit harder to see. Why would the gods need, or even want, our gifts? What can a spiritual being do with a bottle of wine or a piece of art?

The various Pagan religions give a variety of reasons for making offerings. Each justifies the practice according to its own theology and social structure. Neo-Pagans, with their lack of common theology and without a distinct society, have to review the many reasons given by other traditions to decide which ones are acceptable. When we do this, we may find our beliefs regarding the gods changing. A god we make offerings to is different from a god we don't. Since Paganism is a religion of action rather than belief, this is to be expected. What matters is that we do the right thing.

Why do the gods demand material gifts from us, then? Why aren't they satisfied with prayer and a sincere heart? In part, it's because there's no sharp line to be drawn between the material and the spiritual. By asking for material offerings, the gods remind us that the material is sacred, too.

Offering material gifts also ensures sincerity. Anyone can give words, and anyone can pretend sincerity, but to offer something shows we care for the gods at least as much as for our material possessions.

When we make offerings, we take part in the way of nature. Just as there's a mystery in the natural order of eating and being eaten, so, too, there's a mystery in the natural dynamic of giving and receiving gifts—not in the sense of "you wash my hands and I'll wash yours," but rather, the same hands that reach out to give also reach out to receive.

We enter into this reciprocal relationship with the gods so that they may become active in our lives. They long for this, waiting for us to approach them with gift-laden arms. This is, quite likely, the origin of the sacred nature of hospitality. The gods are the ultimate hosts, inviting us in when we knock. We must be the best of guests, returning their generosity by acting as hosts in turn. It is the bonds of hospitality that tie people together and communicate the truth that they are not so separate after all.

The giving of offerings is hospitality toward the gods. We invite them into our lives and, as their hosts, we give them gifts, and they give us gifts in return. This is no different from our everyday rules of hospitality. I invite you to my house for dinner, and now you have an obligation to invite me to yours. If I'm always the one doing the inviting, our chance for friendship will fizzle out.

It's the same with the gods. We offer to them, and the gods have a social obligation to repay us. Since the divine beings can't invite us over for dinner, they repay our invitation in other ways—prosperity, health, success, etc. By this exchange, we become friends with the gods.

## The "Politics" of Prayers and Offerings

An offering is an act of completion. So many things come to us from the gods. If we keep them, the flow ends there. By holding tightly to the gifts of the gods, we create an interruption in the natural rhythm of the world, a dead end into which the universe flows and then stops.

Neo-Pagans, though, are dedicated to the idea of circles and cycles, of things changing and transforming. There are no dead ends in nature. Even if we hold tightly to our possessions, in the end, of course, we will lose them. We will die, and they will go to others. The gods will not allow a dead end to persist; they will not permit interruptions of their cycles.

This is not something we can take comfort in, as we grasp our goods ever more tightly. If we are indeed Pagans, then we must live the way the gods want us to live. While we are alive, we must not be "dead ends." We must give freely of what we have, to each other and to the gods. When we make offerings, we tell the gods that we know this, and we remind ourselves of it, so we will be less likely to do the wrong thing in the future. Such a wonderful return from so small a gift as a glass of milk, a bowl of grain, a painted stone!

Writing neo-Pagan prayers presents special difficulties. The prayers of many religions incorporate mythical themes, either making reference to myths or actually telling them. Although neo-Paganism has embraced many ancient myths, Wicca, the most widespread form of neo-Paganism, has few myths of its own. I've dealt with this in several ways.

First, not all prayers incorporate myths. Second, there are indeed *some* Wiccan myths—the most obvious being the Legend of the Descent of the Goddess and the myth of the year implied in Wiccan rituals. Third, there are the myths told about ancient deities. Although not actually absorbed into Wicca, these deities find devotees among neo-Pagans, who might therefore be expected to be interested in prayers to their favorite deities.

In this book, I have also taken elements that are found in a number of myths and applied them to the Wiccan God and Goddess. Essentially, what I am doing here is writing new myths for Wicca. I think it best to be honest about this. Of course, the divine beings to whom these prayers are addressed are not just the Wiccan God and Goddess. Worshipers from many of the modern Pagan religions will find prayers to their deities here. I hope that those who encounter deities from traditions other than their own will be inspired to pull out some mythology books and learn more. Learning is never a waste of time.

Prayers are often accompanied by offerings. These have traditionally included animal sacrifices, libations, food, incense, and just about anything else. Because of its importance in ancient times and because what is subtle in other kinds of offerings is clear in it, I will begin with sacrifice.

The why of sacrifice has been argued over by scholars for many years with no resolution. I think one reason for this is that scholars have seen sacrifice through their own ideology, the culture they've studied the most, or their own culture. A Freudian will find a Freudian meaning, an anthropologist who spent his career studying the Nuer will apply Nuer theology, and a member of PETA will find the whole thing offensive.

But the major problem is seeing sacrifice as a single thing. It is one only in the sense that a raised hand is one thing. Is it raised in greeting? To strike? To swear an oath? There is no one meaning to an upraised hand, and there is no one meaning to sacrifice—there are several.

One of these is that something is being given to the sacred. This is the origin of the word "sacrifice"; it is "making sacred." This is usually seen as giving something up, and that's how we tend to use the word in everyday speech. A religious sacrifice, however, is not so much a giving *up* as a giving *to*. It isn't, "Aren't I great for depriving myself?" but, "Isn't it great that the deities are getting what they want?" The gods aren't impressed by how much you suffered by making your sacrifices.

The giving by ancient Pagans was not one-sided, though. Just as people gave gifts to the deities, so the deities were expected to give some back.

Something like this on a human scale was found in many societies, such as early Germanic ones. There, warriors gave service to their chieftains, who in turn gave them riches, to the point where "ring giver" became a kenning for "chieftain." A significant aspect of this is that the socially superior was expected to give more than they received. This was how they maintained their status and was a form of noblesse oblige.

This operated on the divine scale, too. The deities were seen as superior and were therefore expected to return more than what was offered. The sacrifice of a single ram might be expected to increase the fertility of an entire flock. This theory could lead to a certain amount of "manipulation" of the deities by varying the size of the offering. If a single bull was expected to bring certain blessings, how much greater the blessing from the

Greek hecatomb, in which a hundred animals were sacrificed? A certain one-upmanship was initiated, in which the gods, because of their superior status, would give greater gifts than they received.

This is sacrifice in terms of reciprocity. Bonds are established and maintained through reciprocal giving. These can be seen as the bases for all relationships.

Sacrifice can also be seen as hospitality. We find this in what was, in fact, the point of most sacrifices—that they involved a shared meal with the deities. Almost all of the edible parts of the animal (except for a small portion burned for the gods) were cooked and eaten by those present; sacrifices were like sacred barbecues. Through them, humans acted as hosts to the gods, providing them with hospitality and drawing them near.

Since so many ancient deities were fond of sacrifices, it's good to do them; since modern sensibilities may be offended by them, it's good *not* to do them. There is a way out of this dilemma, a way that has been used by Pagans both ancient and modern: the use of symbolic substitutes. Something else is named an animal, then treated as one.

Bread has always been the most common substitute. Under the influence of vegetarian Hinduism, for instance, Zoroastrians in India took the bread and butter that had accompanied sacrifices (Jamaspasa 1985) and used it to replace the sacrifice itself (Modi 1922, 296–8). A modern example is the replacement of goats with rice wrapped in banana leaves in a 1975 celebration of the Vedic *agnicayana* ritual (Staal 1983, II:464–5).

Bread can be more strongly identified with an animal by forming it into an animal shape. Baking pans in such shapes are available for use as molds for forming bread or to make a cake (another possible substitute) in the proper shape.

Other substitutes are possible and were made in ancient times as well, possibly by those unable to afford an actual animal. Clay animals have been found in ritual contexts and make good sacrifices. They do, however, make sharing with the deities impossible. A piece of meat taken from a meal is another possibility. Butter, especially when clarified, is a great substitute for cattle. It comes from cows, can be part of a shared meal, and burns well.

I don't want to give the impression that animal sacrifice is the most common form of offering, especially in this book. Traditionally, the libation was. The Greeks, for instance, poured a libation before drinking anything. You can again see a shared meal.

Libations are therefore the most common form of offering you'll see here. They can be of any drink, although alcoholic ones and milk are the most traditional, and certain deities may prefer certain ones. For instance, a goddess connected with cows, such as Brigid, would prefer milk; whereas deities from Egypt, where beer was an important part of the diet, might like that. Here is another meaning of sacrifice: both milk and alcoholic beverages are offerings of life.

Distilled drinks make especially good offerings into fire, since they burn so well. If you use them, though, be careful; they flare up suddenly. (I once came close to a nasty accident with Drambuie.) Also, when the alcohol burns away, you're left with what's essentially water, which may extinguish the fire, never a good thing in a ritual. Butter and vegetable or olive oil also burn well and are far less dangerous.

Don't pour anything with a lower alcohol content or with none at all (such as milk) directly onto a fire. It will put the fire out. Instead, pour it at the base of the fire.

Bread isn't just a good animal substitute but a worthy offering in itself. It is the "staff of life," a representative of food in general. By sharing it with the divine beings, we are therefore sharing part of all our meals. Bread burns pretty well, too, especially when it has been buttered.

Some offerings can't be burned or poured. No problem; coins can be cast into rivers, jewelry can be buried, etc. We thereby give something over to the gods.

Do you see now why I brought up sacrifice? Its meanings reverberate throughout other forms. What applies to sacrifice applies to all other offerings—with the appropriate changes.

There are many other kinds of offerings, the only requirement for which is that they are seen as being valuable to the being to whom they are offered. I've included an appendix with general advice on what kinds of offerings are appropriate to what kinds of deities, but individual ones will have their own preferences. These can be found out only by research and/or experimentation.

Of course, a prayer of praise can be an offering. In fact, it always is, and the more beautiful the better.

## To Whom Do We Pray?

One way to divide the types of beings Pagans pray to, the numina, is to split them into three categories: the High Gods, the Ancestors, and the Spirits.

The High Gods fall into two categories: the God and Goddess of Wicca (the archetypal male and female) and the gods of the ancient Pagan pantheons—Brigid, Mitra, Isis, and so on. I obviously couldn't write prayers to all of the ancient deities, so I wrote to those who are popular among other neo-Pagans, as well as to those who appealed to me personally. There is a short glossary of the deities in appendix 2. Maybe one you've never heard of before will strike your fancy.

The Ancestors may either be those of a particular family or those of us all—a genetic ancestor or a cultural one. For instance, George Washington has no genetic descendants, but he is a cultural ancestor of all Americans. When I use the term "Ancestors," I usually mean genetic ancestors, but there are always cultural implications as well. After all, we are, in the end, one family.

The Spirits are a miscellaneous category identified primarily by their limits. Instead of being the gods of a people, they are peculiar to a locale or an object. They may be associated with a tool or a weapon, or they may be connected to a place. You may wish to pray to the Spirit who inhabits an impressive tree near your house or those who live in the woods you visit on a camping trip.

Let me illustrate the differences between the High Gods and the Spirits with an example. One of the early Norse settlers in Iceland was a worshiper of Thor. When he emigrated, he took with him the pillar from his temple. As he approached the coast, he threw the pillar overboard and allowed it to float to the shore. In this way, Thor himself chose the settler's landing spot. As a High God, Thor came to the new land with his worshipers.

The Land Spirits, on the other hand, had been left behind to dwell in the places with which they were associated. In the new land, the Norse discovered new holy places and established relationships with the Spirits of these new places. Having left behind the Spirits who lived in the burial mounds, stones, and forests of their old home, they sought out those who lived in their new one.

In general, the divine beings like us. This is one of the reasons they want our prayers and offerings; if they didn't care about us, they wouldn't care about our prayers. That's why they respond well to petitionary prayers: they want to help us. They really do.

Some are ambivalent, though. Why should the Land Spirits feel warmly toward us when we cut down their forests and pave over their meadows? Don't feel too smug when you've protested against logging in old growth forest. Where do you think the land your house is built on came from? What kind of land was there before it was plowed under to grow your food?

Dealing with Land Spirits can be difficult, then. We have to show them we are grateful for their sacrifice. As I hope I have shown earlier in this book, we do this by giving something back.

All three types of numina are worthy of prayers and offerings, however. I guarantee that if you give them a chance, if you talk to them and give them gifts, your life will be greatly enriched.

*Chapter 2*

# PRAYER STRUCTURE

At their simplest, prayers are just talking to the gods. You think about them, and you talk. But the gods are different from us. Talking to them is, therefore, different from talking to people. You can show this by using a different style of speech when addressing them. Just as you have set aside time and space for this sacred conversation, you set aside your normal way of speech to make your prayers special.

Because prayer is communication with a divine being, and because Pagans are polytheistic, Pagan prayers must identify the being to whom they are addressed. Whether the gods need this or not is not the question. If you reach out to deities, it is only polite to call them by name. No sense starting out on the wrong foot.

## *Identifying Your Gods*

The gods you recognize help to define the universe as you see it. Do you recognize a deity of government? The name of this deity can tell you a lot about what you think of government. Most people don't know that the Roman god Mars was not just a god of war but was also connected with agriculture. The Romans saw a connection there, and by calling on Mars, they recognized that connection. Even if the gods don't need to be identified exactly, it is a good thing for you to do so.

Gods don't have to be identified by name; they can frequently be identified by title or function. The hearth goddess Brigid may be addressed, for instance, as "Lady of Fire." Dionysos may be called "You who watch over our vines, who flow with the sap." Isis might be called "You in whose wings we find safety." Just as good thank-you notes do not have to start with the words "thank you," so a prayer does not have to start with the name of the deity. You might start with something like, "I who stand before you, I who come into your presence, I who am your worshiper, call out to you, Mitra." The name should come relatively early in the prayer, however. No sense building up too much suspense.

In most cases, though, it is best to start with the deity's name or a title. This is good both for you and for the deity. For you, it serves to focus your intent. For the deity, it serves to bring you to his or her attention. There is no sense making all the deities listen to all our prayers on the off chance that they might be involved. They are not unlimited, even if they are vastly greater than we are.

Deities are frequently named more than once in a prayer, although not usually by the same name. Repeating the same name can make the prayer tedious and one-dimensional. Moreover, you risk getting only a partial understanding of a deity if you use only one means of identification. Divine beings are far more complicated than that. It is more effective to give your deities titles that describe their attributes or relate myths associated with them. For instance, Apollo might be addressed in this way: "Sweet-songed Apollo, hear me. I come before you, Lord of the Bow, whose arrows bring healing. I ask that you help me, Leto's son: heal my own child."

Some ancient prayers are essentially long lists of such titles. Such lists are very useful for calling or praising a deity. They can become boring, but boredom can be a good thing; it can turn off your mind and release your spirit. Besides, when a prayer works, and the presence of the deity becomes obvious, it quickly stops being boring. The piling up of title after title can build to a level of ecstasy, as the person praying becomes more and more aware of the deity's power and presence. A tension is created as each title reveals a new piece of the deity's identity, until the tension is released, and the prayer goes on its way, an arrow loosed from the bow of your words.

The defining of a deity may also be done through relating myths. A god is what he does and what he has done. Mentioning these myths not only honors him by telling of his wondrous deeds, it also prepares him for the sort of request (if any) that is to follow. A prayer to Indra might begin, "Wielder of the vajra, slayer of Vṛtra." This calls upon Indra as the keeper of the thunderbolt, the *vajra,* both the symbol and the means of operation of his power. Describing him as "slayer of Vṛtra" defines Indra as the one who killed the great serpent at the beginning of time, removing the obstruction that kept the world from growing. This may hint at what you are about to ask for; perhaps there is some obstruction in your life that you would like removed. If you're praying to praise the god, it becomes something for which he should be honored. If you're praying out of gratitude, it expresses in a metaphor the kind of thing you are thanking him for.

Germanic literature uses an interesting means of relating these myths and titles called "kenning." In kenning, short descriptions can take the place of names or nouns, expressing a whole myth in a few words. For instance, Thor, who is to kill the wolf Fenrir in the battle at the end of time, would be called "Fenrir's Bane." This sort of allusion can bring in many myths in a short time, making a prayer multilayered and sending the worshiper's mind soaring outward into the divine realm by filling it with more than it can hold and forcing it to expand into a new spiritual reality.

In fact, it may not even be necessary to use the deity's name. Sometimes a myth or title is enough. There is no other deity who can be described as "Wielder of the vajra, slayer of Vṛtra" except Indra. Remember, too, that what we think of as the names of the gods are sometimes titles by which they have become commonly known: Cernunnos is "The god with antlers," Epona is "The horse goddess," Mitra is "Contract." Sometimes these names are transparent to the worshiper, and sometimes they were devised so long ago that their meaning has been lost to their worshipers. I doubt that there was any ancient Greek who knew that Zeus meant "Bright Sky." But I'll bet Zeus knew, and when he was called upon by name, he knew that name was originally a title. Of course, a name and its meaning, expressing a title, may coexist in one prayer. You can mix them together to get something like, "Great Mitra, Lord of Contract."

While it is true that myths can be used to identify a deity, it is also true that a prayer can actually relate a myth. The Homeric Hymns do this; they are, for instance, the main source for our knowledge of the myth of Demeter and Persephone. The telling can be the whole point of the myth, serving as praise, since everyone likes to have their deeds remembered. It can also teach both the person praying and anyone else present something about the deity addressed. Even if the story is known to all present, a good myth reveals something new each time it is told.

Titles can express the many sides of a deity. Most of us learned the job descriptions of the Greek and Roman gods when we were young—Venus was the goddess of love, Mars was the god of war, Mercury was the messenger of the gods. But gods are not that simple. Apollo, for instance, whom most of us learned to identify as the god of the Sun (and then we wondered how Helios could also be the god of the Sun), is god of music, beauty, order, and healing as well. Calling on him under these various areas of expertise rounds him out, makes him more real to us. For instance, a prayer to Apollo can begin, "I pray to the one whose arrows bring health and illness, to Apollo the beautiful one. From your lyre come tunes of harmonious enchantment, and I listen enraptured, sweet-singing Apollo."

Names, titles, their meanings, myths—you can mix them all together to define the recipient of your prayer more precisely: "Athena, Goddess of Wisdom, Protector of the crafty Odysseus." With each descriptive element, the deity becomes clearer in your mind, and you become more ready to open yourself to the holy presence.

From the fact that gods are deeply three-dimensional comes one of their most important characteristics: ambiguity. They come to us at times that are neither one time nor another, such as dusk or dawn. They come to us in space that is neither one place nor another, such as tidal regions. And they come to us through actions that are neither one kind nor another, such as holding out our hands—are we giving, receiving, or both?

Thus we arrive at a seeming contradiction. Should you be precise in whom you call, taking care to invoke just the right aspect of your chosen deity? Or should you take care to preserve the ambiguity of the divine beings? There is really no problem here. Prayers have the same primary goal as other forms of communication—accuracy. What exactly are you trying to convey? Do you have one particular goal in mind? Then be precise. Are you interested in experiencing deities in all of their subtleties? Then be ambiguous.

Some deities are more ambiguous than others, of course. Cernunnos may be said to have ambiguity as his very nature, for instance. All gods have something about them that cannot quite be defined, however. If we could define them completely, we would limit them to such an extent that they would no longer be gods.

Prayers may effectively use ambiguity to express the nature of the gods. For instance, "Worthy are you of sacrifice," may mean either that the deity is worth sacrificing to or worth being sacrificed himself. The Wiccan God may appropriately be addressed in this way. Ambiguity is also useful for economy of language. It is the nature of symbols that they can have more than one meaning, and a prayer in which all of a symbol's meanings are used can be, in essence, several prayers at once.

Finally, the world is not simple. We do not always know the precise meaning of things, especially when the gods are involved. By speaking to our deities in ambiguous language, we remind both them and ourselves of this fact.

## Prayer Formats

After naming your deities, mentioning their titles, and linking them with their myths, you can expand your identification by bringing up past favors, given either to you or to others: "Indra who slew the serpent, whose vajra has been ever my aid, who has been my steadfast companion." This links your identification with what comes next—petition, praise, or thanksgiving.

You should do one last thing before you bring up the purpose of your prayer. You should honor your deity. (Of course, that might be the whole point of the prayer and, if so, good for you.) This is, at the very least, the polite thing to do. It also puts you into a proper relationship with your deity. The gods are more powerful than us—more glorious, possessing more wisdom—and this should be recognized. In my own prayers, I prefer a simple: "I offer you my worship," or "I do you honor," or "I praise you, I honor you, I worship you." If your prayer is one of praise, this pattern can be repeated over and over, building praise upon praise, until an ecstatic state of awareness of the deity is achieved. This can be followed by a period of silent contemplation, ending with a statement of gratitude.

Only after you have identified your deities, described them, linked yourself with them, and done them honor is it time to bring up your own intentions. If your prayer is one of thanksgiving, now is the time to offer your thanks. This is a good time to make an offering, either one promised earlier or one built into the prayer out of sheer gratitude: "I pour out this wine, Asklepios, for you have cured my illness."

If the offering is in payment of a vow, that should be mentioned. A touching statement of faith from ancient times comes from the Roman practice of vowing to set up an altar when a prayer is answered. Hundreds of these have survived, each inscribed with a prayer of thanks, such as, "[Name] dedicates this to [deity's name] willingly and deservingly in fulfillment of a vow." In fact, if your prayer asks for something, it is a good idea to either offer something at its end or promise something upon the receipt of that which is asked. A gift demands a gift.

Exactly what gift to give will vary with the deity. An appropriate offering for a storm god like Indra might be an axe, either actual or in miniature. Offerings can be based on your deity's culture; Roman gods like wine. If you can't decide what to give, stick to the basics: bread and a drink.

This is the standard structure of prayers to Indo-European deities, those of most of the cultures from Europe to India, and it is a good one to use in general. Other cultures have other traditional structures. Typical Egyptian prayers, for instance, are structured like this (Redford 2003, 313–4):

First is praise, often with many titles: "Isis, throne of kings, mother of gods and men, whose name was praised in Egypt and Rome."

Then comes a description of the one praying, often self-deprecating. "I who am poor in goods, and weak in power, and in need of aid, pray to you."

Next, a mention of a specific transgression, especially if it is seen as having caused the problem the prayer is about. "I, who in my weakness have violated the commands of heaven."

Then follows the request, especially in terms of the violation. "I who am weak from transgressing the holy way, who have become ill from my transgression, ask for healing from the disease I suffer."

Now comes a promise of future praise, especially in a public way. "I who have prayed to you will make your power well-known to those I encounter."

Finally would come a description of the request as if already granted. "I say this, I who have been healed by you, Isis, queen of heaven."

So we have:

Isis, throne of kings, mother of gods and men, whose name was praised in Egypt and Rome,

I, who am poor in goods, and weak in power, and in need of aid, pray to you,

I, who in my weakness have violated the commands of heaven,

I, who am weak from transgressing the holy way, who have become ill from my transgression, ask for healing from the disease I suffer.

I who have prayed to you will make your power well-known to those I encounter.

I say this, I who have been healed by you, by Isis, queen of heaven.

Another structure, to the *kami,* beings or things of numinous power, is found in Shintoism (Nelson 1996, 108–13):

A call to those present. "You who have gathered here to pray to these kami on this day, hear me."

A statement of purpose. "I pray that all might be made as pure as it is proper to be, as it is proper to do."

An historical precedent, expressed as a myth. "As it was indeed pure when the land was made. It was then that Izanagi no Mikoto and Izanami no Mikoto formed it. Then the spear was dipped in the sea, stirred it into foam; then from the foam came the land, pure and shining."

The reason the prayer is required. "Yet we have done impure deeds. We have broken divine laws. We have violated familial obligations. We have supported the wrong."

A description of what is to be done. "When these are done, the people pour out sake, they dance in the ancient way to please the kami. Best of all things, and before these things, they purify themselves, washing in pure water. They wash the hands which offer, they wash the mouth that prays."

Next the way the kami will respond. "With our purification of ourselves, the kami will be inspired to purify perfectly. With the performance of proper rites, the kami will be inspired to purify all. Izanagi no Mikoto and Izanami no Mokito will impart the purity of the new land to each and to all, for now and for the future."

Finally, an end. "This is what I say today."

And so:

You who have gathered here to pray to these kami on this day, hear me.

I pray that all might be made as pure as it is proper to be, as it is proper to do.

As it was indeed pure when the land was made. It was then that Izanagi no Mikoto and Izanami no Mikoto formed it. Then the spear was dipped in the sea, stirred it into foam; then from the foam came the land, pure and shining.

Yet we have done impure deeds. We have broken divine laws. We have violated familial obligations. We have supported the wrong.

When these are done, the people pour out sake, they dance in the ancient way to please the kami. Best of all things, and before these things, they purify themselves, washing in pure water. They wash the hands which offer, they wash the mouth that prays.

With our purification of ourselves, the kami will be inspired to purify perfectly. With the performance of proper rites, the kami will be inspired to purify all. Izanagi no Mikoto and Izanami no Mokito will impart the purity of the new land to each and to all, for now and for the future.

This is what I say today.

There are other formats. One I use a lot is to go from the mundane to the sacred. First, I describe the situation—the season has changed, I am sick, I lack inspiration. I then bring to mind a deity or an aspect of divine reality with which this might be linked by myth, function, or imagery. This gives the situation sacred meaning; I link the present with the eternal. In a sense it's like a haiku.

This is enough for praise or for observance of an occasion. For petitions, once I have connected the situation with a deity, I have gained contact with someone from whom I can ask a favor, so I add a line or two expressing that.

The basic idea is the same, though: what deity is prayed to, what the request is, why the deity should respond, what the worshiper will give in return. The order of the elements may vary, and what each consists of may vary, too, but the concepts are found in most prayers.

As you read through the prayers in this book, you'll find that I don't stick to the patterns described here very strictly. I generally use a few lines to set up the prayer, then I describe the situation addressed by the prayer. Only then do I begin to work within this pattern. I do this for a number of reasons.

First, there is not much point in using the pattern over and over. The suggestions given above and a few examples should be enough to enable you to write your own prayers. Second, prayers written in this other way have a built-in sacred space-and-time element. Before getting to the main purpose of the prayer, you define just where and when the prayer is being said. In that way, even if you have not established sacred space or time through ritual, you are nonetheless there. This can be a great help if you are in a situation where a full-fledged introductory ritual cannot be performed. It can even be useful if you do perform an introductory ritual, because that ritual is general. The first few lines of your prayers can then make the time and space more specific, focusing on the actual purpose of your prayer.

Not all prayers, or even all parts of a given prayer, are necessarily expressed in the first person: "I praise you," "I pray to Sarasvati." Third person prayers are also common:

> Inanna rules over the gods.
> She descends to death,
> she ascends to life.
> Neither death nor life can hold her.

This sort of prayer is great for praise, since you keep yourself out of the prayer, speaking only of the gods, describing them and their great deeds. By remembering them, you grow closer to them. This pleases them. Everyone wins. After speaking in the third person, you can then switch to the more expected format:

> The Spirits of the mountain exist in strength.
> Their roots are deep in the Earth,
> their heads pierce the air and mount to the sky above.
> They dance from flat to peak
> and, spiraling, descend again.
> Good Ones, when I come under your trees and upon
> your stones,
> guide me.

In this case, you can think of the section spoken in the third person as both calling and praise. The gods come to hear of their deeds, delighting in them as a lord in a hall enjoys hearing his exploits sung before assembled guests. Then, when they have been pleased and are in a good mood, you can feel free to ask them for something. Or you can praise or thank them, shifting from an impersonal account of their greatness into a description of why they mean something to you, or how they have helped you. This sort of prayer recognizes both that the Holy Ones have concerns other than you and that you are concerned with them.

When you finish a prayer, you may feel a need to say something to cap it off—an "amen." Something seems necessary, if only to keep the prayer from drifting off into nothingness. In public prayer, a firm ending also gives those present who may not have said anything a chance to add their own prayer by assenting to the one that has already been made. This can be shown simply as a drop in your tone of voice. It can also be written into the prayer itself, as in a technique Shakespeare uses that I'll talk about a bit later on.

This is especially useful in group rituals, where it is seen as an affirmation by the group of what has been prayed by a particular person. It can be used as a punctuation point, separating prayers in a ritual. It can be used more than once in a prayer, as if prayer were piled upon prayer. If you do this, though, you will need the final ending phrase to be more emphatic, by saying it more than once, for instance. A final line might be more elaborate, to put a seal on the prayer: "May it be so, may it be so, may it truly be so."

Those who grew up in a Christian or Wiccan environment might feel that a prayer is unfinished without an "amen" or "so mote it be." This kind of ending can be in the language of the person praying (e.g., "so be it") or the language associated with the deity prayed to (e.g., "Bíodh sé amhlaidh" for an Irish deity). Many Wiccans use the Masonic "so mote it be." Many Pagans use the American Indian "Ho." Each has its own disadvantage. The first is ponderous, and the second can be seen as "playing Indian."

How about "amen"? It's Hebrew for "so be it," and, with the deep associations it has within many of our psyches with prayer, it is a fine ending. The objection will, of course, be made that it is Judeo-Christian. That may be so, but the phrase long ago made its way into our culture in a manner that transcends its original religious meaning. "God," "deity," and "heaven" all come from non-Christian roots, yet these words have been enthusiastically embraced by Christians. We can do the same with this lovely little word—amen.

## *Set Prayers and Spontaneous Prayers*

Prayers can be spontaneous, read, or memorized. There is a certain bias among modern Pagans toward spontaneous prayers. We are supposed to be creative and inspired. The feeling is that if we "speak from the heart," all will be well. To be perfectly frank, though, Pagans aren't more creative than most people, until we have trained ourselves to be. I'm sure we have all suffered through halting performances of rambling spontaneous prayers from people "speaking from the heart."

This goes with a search for authenticity, for truth in all things. That is a principle I can get behind. I just don't think it has anything to do with the legitimacy of set prayers.

In many cases, this attitude is, itself, not authentic. Neo-Paganism is cursed with a number of problems that have their roots in the childhood practices and beliefs of its members. Since they belong to a religion formed mainly of converts (a situation that is, fortunately, now changing), neo-Pagans have a bad tendency to react against their early religious background, which, in most cases, is Christianity. They seem to believe that Christianity is a religion of rote repetition, whereas Paganism is, by nature, spontaneous.

This does both Christianity and Paganism a disservice. The repetition of a memorized prayer is not necessarily a mechanical thing. It involves a relationship between the one praying, the prayer, and the one prayed to. This relationship is expressed through the words of a prayer, perhaps, but each prayer event is no more identical to those before than each performance of a particular piece of music is the same as another.

Now, I do not think that even the most hard-nosed proponent of set prayers would be opposed to spontaneous prayer. The techniques given in this book are meant to teach you how to compose your own prayers. Once you have mastered them, you can compose prayers anywhere, anytime. If you follow these rules, your prayers will be no less spontaneous than your normal speech is when you follow the rules of grammar. They may even help to make your prayers *more* spontaneous, since having some order to rely on sometimes opens us up creatively. On the other hand, even if you don't use these techniques, you can impress the gods with your sincerity by speaking what you truly feel.

The disagreement arises when people oppose set prayers on principle. Their attitude seems to be that a prayer must come from the heart; it must be completely unique to the moment, expressing what the person praying feels at just that point in time. Anything else is thought to be insincere. I understand this position.

Ancient Paganism, for its own part, had set prayers. The Rig Veda is a collection of prayers that acquired canonical status. In Pagan Rome, following set prayers was so important that an assistant with a prayer book stood next to priests, whispering the proper words to them. There is, thus, definitely a strong Pagan tradition of set prayers.

And why shouldn't there be? Our circumstances aren't that much different from those of others—we mourn, feel gratitude, desire to praise, want to make requests. Why should each of us have to compose a prayer each time we need one? I happen to be good at writing prayers. I'm a lousy plumber. If there is a plumber out there who isn't good at writing prayers, why shouldn't we avail ourselves of each other's talents?

Most important of all, there are times when we want to pray, but words fail us. I think here of mourners at a Catholic funeral praying the rosary. Locked in their grief, they fix their minds on words they know by heart. They no longer need to think; they give themselves over to mourning and are comforted. It would be a shame for Pagans not to have the same gift.

Moreover, it is impossible for people to pray spontaneously as a group. They need to know what to say, so they can say it together. Prayer is not just a private matter. Sometimes a group will be drawn together by circumstances—anything from a funeral to a seasonal celebration—and they will want to pray together. Sometimes, the whole point of praying will be to practice religious acts as a group. Prayer can be used to unify people; those who say the same words are, in a sense, one. The Catholic mourners described above can know that the other mourners are feeling the same thing they are and be comforted by that.

The most important rationale for set prayers, however, is a phenomenon I call "deepening." The more often a prayer is said, the deeper it sinks into your consciousness.

Eventually, it sinks into your unconscious mind. When this happens, it can be said that the prayer prays you. It becomes part of who you are. It changes you in a way that would not have been possible with a prayer said once and forgotten.

It should come as no surprise, of course, that I like set prayers. This is, after all, a book of them. I have given you quite a few to work with here. I have also shown you how to write your own. If you do write your own prayers, don't discard them after use. Work with them more than once. Chew them over in your mind; let them grow in you. You will discover an amazing thing—you have written better than you had thought. As the prayer is said on each new occasion, you will discover insights in it that you didn't even know were there. It is an amazing feeling. I would hate for you to be deprived of it.

When you feel as though nothing will do but to burst forth with a prayer, go right ahead. Don't feel as if you're cheating either the gods or yourself, however, if what comes forth is a pre-learned prayer. Sometimes set prayers can carry meaning even better than those you come up with on the spur of the moment.

As you write and perform more and more prayers, you will get better with spontaneous prayers, like a jazz musician learning their scales and then learning to improvise. I'm not saying that your early spontaneous prayers will be ineffective (out of tune), mind you, simply less beautiful and less precise than you will eventually be able to compose. And I am *definitely* saying that to be good at improvising you need to learn your scales.

Previously written prayers can be memorized or read, and may be written by yourself or by others. Besides being easier to write well (editing is a wonderful thing), they allow you to concentrate on performance rather than production. This allows you to think about tone of voice, pauses, gestures, and other stylistic touches that add to the beauty of performance. Don't underestimate the value of pre-planning and rehearsing these touches.

Some people have problems memorizing. Someone reciting an insufficiently memorized prayer will stumble over words, pause at inappropriate points to remember, go back to forgotten points automatically, or without thinking say, "wait," before redoing a poorly recited part. A poorly memorized prayer isn't as good as one read well.

Reading prayers is okay, and even expected in certain occasions. Weddings and funerals that are attended by non-Pagans are examples. We have become so used to an officiant reading from a book that people might take a memorized prayer less seriously (and a spontaneous one not at all). It is very important to read a prayer over a few times before the ritual to become familiar with it. Otherwise you will find yourself tripping over the words.

One of the great strengths of prepared prayers is that they can be repeated. Repetition can have great psychological effects. It's especially nice for prayers for comfort; familiarity can bring peace all on its own. Also, each time a prayer is said, you may discover new meanings in it, new connections with the divine, new understandings of the deity you are addressing. This can be true even if you have written the prayer yourself. You may have touched on an aspect of the divine you had not understood but now, through the continued reflection brought about by repetition, becomes clear to you.

*Chapter 3*

# PRAYING WITH WORDS

Now it's time to talk about how we pray.

If prayer is communication with a divine being, and if we usually communicate in words, our prayers will consist primarily of words. There are many ways to say a prayer. You can speak loudly, proclaiming to everyone (even if you are alone) what you have to say. You can speak softly, indicating a desire for intimacy with the divine being to whom you pray. You can pray in a singsong voice, perhaps accompanied by a rocking motion. This adds a rhythm to your words that may express the rhythms of nature you are trying to express. You can even pray silently, in your mind. In public, this may be your only option. In private, however, it may express a desire for an intimacy even greater than that which you get from speaking softly. It may even be that the state in which you find yourself makes your voice seem shocking and disturbing.

Whatever voice you use to pray, speak distinctly. If you pray the same prayer over and over on one occasion, you may eventually start to slur your words. That is fine; what happens is that you begin to go beyond words. You should start out in a clear voice, though, making sure that you and the one to whom you pray know exactly what is being said.

It isn't necessary to pay attention to each word. Sometimes too much attention can get in the way of feeling; you focus on the mental side of things, letting the emotional and spiritual elements fall away. Sometimes, however, a word jumps out of your prayer to shock you, making you realize something about it that you'd never realized before. This is one of the truly wonderful possibilities of prayer. This kind of insight can help you to understand just what it is you are saying to the being you are praying to. In fact, this insight may very well be a gift from that being, a gift of understanding that will affect your prayer life from that moment on. Don't just listen to the words you are saying then; listen for any answer to them.

As a form of speech, prayer, like speech in general, can be divided into marked and unmarked. Unmarked speech is informal. It can be called "conversational," since it is the style we use in conversation. It's a prose style, friendly, using everyday words in everyday arrangement: nothing fancy here. In prayer, this style is most appropriate for deities with whom you are on very good terms and who are close to people in general. An example would be hearth goddesses, homey deities who live with us and with whom we interact daily. Prayers to other kinds of beings can be in this style, as well; Ancestors, who were people like us, might enjoy it, as long as it is respectful. High gods such as Zeus, on the other hand, might not appreciate being treated on chummy terms.

Conversational prayers are almost nonexistent in what we have from ancient times. In general, then, marked speech is most common in prayers. This is simply any form that is out of the ordinary. At one end is elevated prose. One form of this is what might be called "newscasters' speech." Grammatical niceties are observed, and the sort of words more common in written speech than spoken are used, but the interest is clarity and precision rather than decoration. There are more formal types of elevated prose. These may include technical terms; a good example is legal speech. Elevated prose may include sentences that have become ritualized: "I now pronounce you husband and wife." It may contain archaic terms, such as "thou," or words that still exist but are used with archaic meanings, such as "suffer" for "allow."

Grammatical rules such as word order might be played with; for instance, "For this I pray" rather than "I pray for this." This sort of speech requires a lot of practice and skill, careful planning and editing. The style may be magisterial; it conveys, without pointing out, that the occasion is an important one. Words are used not just for their basic meanings but also for their psychological and social implications. Fancy words are seen as equaling fancy thought.

We are seeing the beginning of poetry, with the way something is expressed becoming as important as its bald meaning.

A very formal type of speech is found in the King James Bible. Contrary to what many think, this is not the English of the time of translation. It was a consciously archaic form, looking back toward Elizabethan England but formalized to create a language that no one had ever spoken. So, even at the time, it was marked. It was also designed to be spoken rather than read, and careful attention was paid to flow, ease of pronunciation, and meter (Nicolson 2003). It was most of the way to poetry.

And it is poetry that is the most marked form of speech. It was always the most common form for prayers in ancient times; even many prayers that seem at first to be prose have been shown to be structured like poetry (Watkins 1995). It's therefore useful to have a good knowledge of how poetry works when you are writing prayers.

It is difficult to define poetry, and the line between it and elevated prose is not always easy to draw. The definition given on *Wikipedia.org* as "a form of literary art in which language is used for its aesthetic and evocative qualities in addition to, or in lieu of, its apparent meaning," could be applied to some other forms of elevated prose. In poetry, however, this definition is more intensely applied. Poetry, then, pays careful attention to beauty; it is decorative. This decoration, however, carries part of the meaning.

Although in recent years the rules of the type of compositions considered to qualify as poetry have loosened, there are traditional formats. These might limit the number of lines, the meter, and the rhyme scheme. We all know about sonnets and haiku, for instance.

The grossest level of a poem is its overall structure. Is there to be one verse or more? If there are more than one, are they to be separated by a chorus? A verse/chorus structure is possible whether a prayer is sung or spoken. In either case, it works well in groups; a main celebrant sings/says the verse, and everyone joins in on the chorus.

You need to decide how many lines you want. If you are using a set format, such as a sonnet, this may be determined for you. (The English sonnet, for instance, has fourteen.)

You also need to consider syllable count. Each line can consist of a set number of syllables. (In English sonnets, it is ten.) Lines may also have differing numbers of syllables, even with some set formats. The most familiar pattern of this is probably that of the haiku, with three lines in a syllable count of 5-7-5.

Haiku traditionally present a stripped-down description of nature that is then related to an emotional state or the transcendent, making them very suitable for Pagan prayers. A haiku prayer can end in a call to or praise of a divine being:

> Winter snow lies thick
> on the frozen ground beneath:
> Hail, Winter Spirits!

The structure can be modified to suit your purpose. For instance, sometimes I use an extended haiku format. Instead of three lines, 5-7-5, I might use 5-7-5-5 or 5-7-5-7:

> Winter snow lies thick
> on the frozen ground beneath:
> Hail, Winter Spirits!
> Hail all of you here!

Or I might extend the number of syllables in the last line, 5-7-6, or truncate the last line, 5-7-4, or combine extended line length and truncated syllable count, 5-7-5-4 (or the reverse):

> Winter snow lies thick
> on the frozen ground beneath:
> Hail, Winter Spirits!
> Hail in the cold!

A final line with an unexpected number of syllables gives a strong feeling of completion; it sticks out as important. (It's marked.) An extra word in a final line, for instance, makes the prayer feel complete. A shorter line, on the other hand, might feel as if a new line has been started but left unfinished; the connection with the sacred is open.

The first is good for a petitionary prayer, and the second for a calling or prayer of praise. Try them out and see what emotional response each evokes in you.

Lines of the same length, on the other hand, can create peace and contentment:

> Winter snow lies thick
> covering the ground.
> Hail, Winter Spirits!

Lengthening or shortening the last line in non-haiku poems (5-5-6 or 6-6-5) can have a similar effect as in haiku:

> Winter snow lies thick
> covering the ground.
> Hail, bright Winter Spirits!

And so on; play around with syllable counts, and they may become the unifying principle of your prayer style.

Another thing to consider is meter. This is the pattern of long and short syllables, or of accented and unaccented syllables, or open and closed syllables. These overlap somewhat, with a closed syllable being longer than an open one, and long syllables tending to be accented. An open syllable is one that either is just a vowel or ends with a vowel (V, CV), whereas a closed one ends in a consonant (VC, CVC).

Meter is what drives a poetic line. Does it rush on or take its time? Does it come smoothly to a stop or end with a crash? It is a skeleton on which to hang words; it creates order from chaos. This was an important part of ancient religion, so doing it within a prayer makes that prayer into a reflection of one of the goals of religion itself.

Meter also gives a beauty to a prayer. This is in large part the response we have to a good structure. It may also come from our strong connection to rhythm.

There are a variety of meters, each with a different feel. The famous iambic pentameter, in which each line has five groups of unstressed/stressed combinations of syllables, is a natural meter for English and is therefore the easiest to write and the easiest on the ear. "We wish that you might come to us today." More exotic meters can make a prayer more marked but also are more difficult to write well and may seem a bit stilted. For instance, the trochee, which is made up of stressed followed by unstressed syllables (the reverse of iambic), may have been the meter followed by the great Finnish epic the *Kalevala*, but it is also that of "Hiawatha," making it hard for those raised on Longfellow to take seriously.

Repetition within a prayer is similar to meter, giving it a structure around which the rest of the prayer turns. Some parts can be repeated and others not, as in a song with verses and choruses. This gives a combination of order and change that might well express the nature of a deity or aspects of the divine reality in which they operate.

Further, each time the repeated part is said, it drives itself deeper, and the differing parts fall into the hole dug by it. The message of the repetition is manifested in different ways, increasing your understanding of it.

Finally, we get to word choice. All of the considerations of elevated prose apply here— archaisms, alliterations, and so on. These are more important in poetry than in prose. "Thou" sounds silly outside of the most elevated prose, but can fit in well with certain types of poems.

Word choice can follow a pattern. The best known is rhyme. This is very common in modern poetry (so much so that many incorrectly see it as poetry's defining characteristic), but it was rare in the ancient world. A big reason for this is that many ancient languages are highly inflected. This means that the endings of words changed with their use. For instance, the usual Latin ending for a first-person plural verb (the "we" form) was -mus. This makes rhyming so easy and boring that there wasn't much point in it. The endings don't rhyme so much as they are identical. It is harder to rhyme in modern English, and rhymes can be both more subtle and more complex and, therefore, more marked and more beautiful.

Rhyme schemes are as varied as meters. The easiest to write are couplets, two lines that rhyme. These are then stacked together to make the poem, aabbcc, etc.:

> Demeter, blesser of women and men,
> as was done of old we call you again,
> Holy Queen and Mother of Earth
> bring life, and laughter, and birth.

Couplets can become boring in a long prayer, but you can use that to lull the consciousness into an altered state. Couplets can also be used to good effect in litanies, with the response changing each time, but rhyming with the call.

More complicated is an abab structure, where the first line rhymes with the third, the second with the fourth, and so on:

> Demeter, blesser of women and men,
> Queen and Mother of Earth,
> as was done of old we call you again,
> bring life, and laughter, and birth.

Still more complicated schemes exist. For instance, as well as end rhymes, where the last syllable of each line rhymes with others, there are internal rhymes, where words inside each line rhyme with those inside others. One of the prayers in this book contains both end and internal rhymes:

> With rain, he brings us the greening,
> with grain, he brightens our days,
> with might he drives away falseness,
> with right he opens our ways.

Note that I've combined couplets, formed by the internal lines, with an abcb pattern formed by the end rhymes. This sort of poetry is hard to write, which is one reason there is only one prayer like it in this book.

Shakespeare often used rhymes in an interesting way by ending unrhymed soliloquies with them. After a number of unrhymed lines, there is a couplet. Take, for instance, *Henry IV*, part 1, act 1, scene 2, where, after twenty-one unrhymed lines, we find:

> I'll so offend as to make offense a skill
> Redeeming time when men think least I will.

Using a couplet in this way would provide a clear ending to a prayer, without having to carry a rhyme scheme for the whole prayer. It can be especially useful in groups, to tell everyone the prayer is over.

Rhyme has the same advantages as meter. It provides a structure, beauty, and ease of memorization. It also has the disadvantage of being more difficult to do well. There are many truly bad rhymed prayers out there. The most common fault is using clichéd rhymes, the Moon-June-spoon problem. Other times, the words don't rhyme exactly, such as "mine" and "time." An unrhymed prayer is better than a poorly rhymed one.

Another type of word choice is alliteration. This is when two words begin with the same sound: "bright and beautiful," "great and glorious," "dewy dawn." Note that it is sounds, not spellings; "carefully" alliterates with "kill," not "celebrate." In some systems, all vowels alliterate, so that "easy" doesn't alliterate just with "even" but with "aisle."

Alliteration is the base of Germanic poetry. This form of poetry is made up of lines that are divided in half by a slight pause:

Holy in heaven, / we hail you, Tyr.

In each half, there are two accented syllables, or "lifts." The main lift is the first one in the second half. One or both of the lifts in the first half must alliterate with it, but the second lift in the second half must not. This is a very appropriate style for prayers to Germanic deities, and it's a natural and powerful style for English. There is more to Germanic poetic rules (see Tolkien 2009, pp. 45–50), but this will do for now.

Synonyms help with word choice. One of the glories of English is its large vocabulary, and this can be used to great advantage. Synonyms can be useful if you want a word of a particular meter, or are looking for a rhyme, or for a word to alliterate. They rarely have *exactly* the same meaning, though. Their meanings can overlap in some ways and diverge in others. "Cease" implies a complete ending, "halt" is abrupt (Hayakawa 1968, p. 593).

Even if the meanings are the same, they often differ in level of formality. English has many synonyms in which one word is Germanic—simple, friendly, everyday—and one is from Latin, French, or Greek—longer, formal, marked. Compare "ask" and "request." Even Germanic words can differ in level of formality; "ask" is a very different word from "beseech."

The use of synonyms in succeeding verses is called parallelism. This is a form of repetition in which it is the idea that's repeated, not the words. For instance:

I pray to you for help,
I ask you for your aid.

In this case, each line has two words that have synonyms in the other. This can be done with even more lines:

We give praise to the Shining Ones.
We honor the High Holy Ones.
We worship them, as is right.

This example shows how you can combine different techniques for effect. "Give praise to," "honor," and "worship" are parallels that tie the three lines together, as do the number of syllables (eight per line) and the "we" at the beginning of each. The last line differs from the others, however. The first two have a second parallel, "Shining Ones" and "High Holy Ones." This is missing in the final line, replaced by the pronoun "them," which has been shifted toward the beginning. This leaves a hole, into which something new has been dropped, a reason for the action(s) that already existed.

Thus this prayer, short as it is, has been tied together, while providing a clear end. We've seen the same clear ending in syllable counts and final couplets, and here we see how you can use more than one technique to cap off a prayer.

Other techniques can be used, of course; the two last words could alliterate, for instance. Don't use too many at once, though, or the prayer will seem fussy. Don't feel as if you always have to have a hard-hitting end, either. Sometimes a prayer can be effective when it just trails off.

A prayer should be beautiful, and there are many ways to achieve this. It can be a gothic cathedral, lacy and strong. It can be a Japanese tearoom, sparse and balanced. It can be a Picasso, showing different sides of an idea all at once. Pick a way, and stick with it for the length of the prayer. Otherwise, you will have a mess on your hands.

There are many other techniques of poetry that can be used to good effect in prayers, to increase both their beauty and their depth. This book is threatening to become a handbook of poetry, though, so I will simply recommend that you consult any one of a number of introductions to poetry. *Wikipedia.org*'s entry on "poetry" is a good place to start.

You should at least read poets, especially the greats. You probably read them in school but read them again. Read Whitman and Frost and Yeats; yes, Shakespeare, too, both his poetry and his prose. Read over your favorites; they're your favorites for a reason. Read other people's poetic prayers, ancient and modern, even non-Pagan ones. *The Book of Common Prayer* is good.

While you are reading, allow yourself to absorb. See what turns of phrase are used. Get a feel for how one word flows into another and for how sentences are ordered. Pay attention to how two words that are supposed to mean the same thing can still feel different.

Immerse yourself in poets, pick up their style, and try to write like them. Write hymns to the Greek gods in the style of the Homeric Hymns and to the Vedic gods in the style of the Rig Veda. Don't worry that you aren't being original in this; you are trying on styles to find your own. Try out the styles of modern poets, too. Try to write a prayer like Frost, for instance. Eventually you will find a style or styles that appeal to you. You will then find it easy to write in that style and to respond to prayers written in it.

There is no shame in adopting another's style. If it is beautiful, if it speaks to you, then why not? No sense reinventing the wheel. But maybe your survey of other people's styles will lead you to realize that you don't like *any* of them, and that will cause you to create your own style or styles. Great, go for it.

Do all this, and you will find a style that works for you. Do that well enough, and your style will work for others. At the very least, though, do it well enough that it will work for those to whom it is addressed. Don't be so afraid that your work isn't good enough that you abandon the effort; be just afraid enough to want to write the best you can.

One thing that will help you in this is to remember that prayers are meant to be spoken aloud. You are writing for speech, not for sight. Speak your prayers, either as you compose or afterward. You need to learn not just how words fit together but also how they sound.

Good poetry is easy to say. A good structure keeps the tongue from tripping over words; one follows the other in a natural way. The beauty of structure makes possible a beauty of performance.

This overlaps with another function of specific forms—that they are comfortable by being familiar. For instance, even though the haiku wasn't designed for prayer, its format is well-enough known that the format is comfortable to hear and say.

A nonintuitive function of structured form is that the work involved in creating a prayer can be balanced by the ease with which it can be said. The form does a share of the work. Well-structured prayers, no matter how much sweat has gone into them, can be easier to say than conversational ones.

*Chapter 4*

# PRAYING WITHOUT WORDS

As with all conversation, prayer can involve much more than words. Making an offering, for instance, is praying with an object. The gods may be prayed to with dance, or music, or gestures. Even when words are involved, any of these other methods of prayer may be used as well.

When you assume a posture, you pray with your body. When you speak, you pray with your mind. When you pray with your mind, objects, and your body, you pray with your soul. It rises up into the presence of the gods and communes with them; you speak, or just rest in their presence.

In fact, it's virtually impossible to pray with words alone. After all, your body has to be in *some* position when words are spoken or thought. This position is an integral part of your prayer. The gods reveal themselves to us in bodies, and it is with our bodies that we pray to them. We both come before the gods in bodies, and we use our bodies to pray to them. The position you take "prays" as much as the words you say.

Just like with words, the nonword elements of prayer can be marked. Let's look at some of them.

## *Music*

First, prayer is often sung or accompanied by music, even if only by a drum. You can use the musical style to create a mood and to conform to the culture of the deity addressed—Irish music for a prayer to an Irish deity, Vedic chanting for Vedic ones. I myself would like to see fewer pseudo-Celtic songs and minor keys in modern Paganism. Experiment with country and western, blues, rock, rap. Pagans are supposed to be creative. Create.

In many traditions, prayers are sung or chanted. Vedic mantras, for instance, are always sung. American Indian prayers are often chanted. And some of the greatest music of the Western world is no more than musical prayer—Mozart's Requiem, for example. Different cultures and traditions have given different reasons for why music can enhance or empower prayer. In some Greek mystery religions, certain notes were thought to correspond to different aspects of the universe, or even to an Ultimate Reality. But there are practical reasons for the linkages between music and prayer as well. It's easier, for instance, to remember a song than a paragraph. Moreover, music cuts deeper than simple words. It has a power to move that's entirely separate from the words set to it. How much better, then, if words and music convey the same message?

Most of us, however, aren't Mozart and aren't apt to produce a Requiem. (Budding Mozarts out there, please get to work.) In the meantime, what's a poor Pagan to do?

If you worship in a tradition that has its own style of music, you already have the answer. For those of us who are following a European path, I recommend Gregorian chant. Yes, this is traditionally a Christian form of music, but it may have Pagan roots. I've heard Sanskrit chanting and very old Irish a capella music. They both sound remarkably like Gregorian chant. I have it on pretty good authority that both reconstructed Old English music and ancient Greek music do, too. I'm no musicologist, but if this is true, then Gregorian chant draws on an ancient European musical tradition. As such, it can serve as a powerful tool for Pagan prayer. Go ahead and use it. There are plenty of recordings; get some and listen until you have a feel for it.

In Western music, major keys are often (although incorrectly) thought of as brighter, lighter, happier. They would be more appropriate for the brighter deities, such as sky gods, or happy occasions, such as weddings or the spring.

Don't abandon minor keys completely, though. These can be great for meditation, calming the mind. They are also appropriate for chthonic deities or for the dead.

Time signatures are the musical equivalent of meters. In fact, it's difficult to write music for a prayer that doesn't have a meter, or at least a syllabic structure. One way to fill out the lines of a non-syllabic prayer so that it can be sung is with grace notes; a single syllable gets more than one note. This is very common in Gregorian chants and Irish sean-nós songs, among other styles.

Each time signature has its own effects: 4/4 is the easiest to sing, 2/2 drives on, 3/4 is a waltz and therefore easily associated with elegance, and so on. Unusual meters such as 6/8 are difficult to sing, so they are best kept to solitary rituals, but they have their own uses.

These are Western rhythms, of course. If you are worshiping deities from non-Western cultures, you might want to look at their rhythms—the pulsing beat of many American Indian songs, polyrhythms from Africa, rhythms in seven time for the Balkans. Or you might just want to stick with ones you can do easily; better a non-culturally specific rhythm done well than a poor performance of a culturally specific one.

Your choice of instruments may have meaning. We all connect bagpipes with Celtic music—especially Scottish, for instance—but they're found in other regions, too, and their mournful wail is worth experimenting with. Flutes are found in both Roman and American Indian rituals; again, they have a cross-cultural character. This is true of many instruments.

The simplest and most common type of instrument is percussion. Specific types of these are also associated with certain cultures: bodhrans with Ireland, slit drums with Polynesia.

Partway between poetry and music is chanting, which uses a small number of notes, sometimes as few as two. An effective chant requires or creates a strong rhythm. Chants are usually short. Chanting is very useful in groups, where the rhythm makes it easy to pray in unison. Chants are often repeated a number of times, which makes them great for guests to your group, since they can pick up a chant as it goes along.

# *Body Positions*

Other characteristics of all forms of communication include tone of voice, facial expressions, and body positions, especially of the hands. I won't go into all of them deeply here; I would just like to give an overview of body positions and encourage you to experiment with all ways to express an idea.

Think of it in everyday terms. When you're called into your boss's office, do you slouch or stand respectfully? When you're at a presentation, what message do you convey when you lounge in your chair? How different is the message if you lean forward and fix your eyes on the presenter? Since you communicate in many ways, it's a good idea to make sure all the messages you send say the same thing.

It's easy to think of the body positions traditionally associated with praying. Standing, kneeling, prostration, and the many positions of yoga are among those that have been used by Pagans.

In Western culture, the body position most identified with praying is kneeling. Many Pagans hesitate to adopt this posture because it seems to subordinate us, to make us slaves to the gods. There are, however, many ways in which the gods are indeed superior to us (why would we want to worship beings who weren't?). To acknowledge that superiority is, therefore, appropriate. Perhaps as more children are raised as Pagans, they won't resist kneeling, and the position will make its way back into our prayers.

A position that may seem even more demeaning, but is still appropriate for Pagan prayer, is prostration. To some, lying flat on the floor, face down, may seem a little like groveling. There are times, however, when the presence of the deity so overpowers you that there is no response more appropriate than prostration. At such moments, you only want to sink into their presence, and prostration is the way your body does this.

One famous prayer posture is the lotus position, in which you intertwine your legs like a pretzel (literally), prop yourself up so that both knees touch the floor, straighten your spine, and put your hands in your lap. Although this is a position traditionally more common for meditation than for prayer, it also makes a great posture for praying. It's stable and, with much practice, can even become comfortable. Moreover, it is conducive to waiting; in fact, it conveys nothing better than expectant but patient waiting. It says, "Come when you will, and you will find me here." It allows you to express respect without abasing yourself.

A prayer posture that was very common in ancient times is the *orans* ("praying") position. You stand with your upper arms parallel to the ground, your elbows bent upward, and your hands open with palms forward. In this position, you're expectant, on your feet, and waiting for the deity to come. You are ready to meet them, approaching as a subordinate without abasing yourself. You both give respect and expect to receive it, holding up your hands in respectful greeting. You're clearly unarmed; you don't presume to threaten the deity (as if you could). You stand ready to give or to receive. This position is acceptable for most deities; some, such as many of the Indo-European gods, consider it the best position for prayer.

As well as body positions, there are hand and arm positions. The Hindu mudras are fairly well known; less familiar are those of Thai dancing, which can tell a story just as words do. It would be interesting to compose a prayer in sign language, performing it either on its own or accompanied by spoken words. Sign language has its own rules of poetry that could be played with.

Whether you pray to a High God, an Ancestor, or a Spirit can determine which position is best. Attitudes of prostration are appropriate only for the High Gods. When calling an Ancestor, a position of respectful waiting is good. It's like waiting for a beloved grandparent—you have the right, by long association and familiarity, to take almost any attitude, but you choose to take a respectful one—not out of fear or awe but out of love and honor. You do it because it's right to do so. As you work with Ancestors, you may find yourself on more familiar terms and relax with them. Still, it never hurts to be polite. Remember, these beings were once like us. You know how you would be like to be treated; show them at least as much respect.

The Spirits are an odd case. Their influence is limited to an area, an object, an event, but within that context, they are very powerful. When in their area of action, therefore, treat them as if they were deities. They are, in fact, just that within their respective realms.

## *Motion*

Changes of position and gestures are a form of motion, which can be a prayer in itself, even without words. The gods understand the language of motion just as well as that of words. Moreover, words and motion can express the same thought. It is common practice in rituals to have this sort of redundancy, in which one meaning is embedded in more than one symbol. The meaning is thus strengthened, and all of you becomes involved in the prayer.

I have already shown how more than one posture can be appropriate during a prayer. Consider, then, the possibility that moving from one position to another may have meaning—the motion itself can convey a message. At the most basic level, the fact that you make a change from one posture to another indicates that the change matters enough to justify making extra effort. It shows that you care enough to know which posture is appropriate for which portion of your prayer.

Positions can be varied within a prayer. You may call the deity standing in the orans position, drop to a lotus position, and then prostrate yourself. You send out the call in a posture of respectful address, await the response in a posture of attentive waiting, and take an attitude of amazement at the wonder of the deity's presence. Note how, at each step, you are communicating with your body. You come before the deity united in mind, body, and soul: as an integrated human being. All of your being is directed toward communication with the deity.

One common motion is circumambulation, which means "walking around something." To circumambulate is to honor that which is circumambulated—an image, a sacred spot, a fire. This is a very common way of honoring the Spirit associated with the place.

The proper direction to walk in many traditions is clockwise. (If you work within a different tradition, study it closely enough to be certain whether the direction matters.)

There are, I think, two reasons for this. First, the Sun travels clockwise in the northern hemisphere. Thus, to move about something in this direction is to invoke the power of nature. You become the Sun, and the object or place circumambulated becomes that which the Sun orbits. Second—and I think that this is more important—moving around something clockwise means that your right side is always toward it. With apologies to the left-handed, in many traditions the right is the favored side. To put one's right side toward something is to honor it; to put one's left side toward it is to dishonor it.

There are times when it is appropriate to circumambulate counterclockwise, however. First is in the southern hemisphere, where directions are reversed. Second, counterclockwise circumambulation isn't just dishonoring, it's also disestablishing. Counterclockwise motion breaks things up and opens them. It can thus be used to open a doorway into the other realm through which prayers may pass. One warning, though: once this doorway is open and something comes through, you must reverse direction and honor the deity or Spirit thus summoned.

## Gestures

Somewhere between postures and motions fall gestures. Things done with the hands and arms have their own meaning. These gestures can be passive or active. For instance, there is the classic Christian posture of folded hands. This communicates a pleading attitude, but it can also convey a certain defenselessness, so it may not be a gesture you want to use.

Forms of gestures are mostly arbitrary. There are more natural ones, such as holding out cupped hands as a sign of giving. In between are ones that have been absorbed so strongly from culture that they are automatic and comfortable; something like, in a non-prayer context, shaking hands (which might be interesting to use in a prayer of coming together).

The orans position described earlier is a good replacement for the folded hands gesture. In this position, you come before the gods unarmed and open but not abased. You do not plead; you approach with respect and ask for a certain amount of respect yourself.

The very fact that your hands are still, whether in the orans position or resting in your lap if you are sitting, conveys a message. You are not attempting to do something but rather are waiting for the deities to perform some act. You have stilled your hands, and now you wait.

Moving hands, however, are sometimes more appropriate. For instance, you can start with your hands clasped together chest-high—you begin your prayer at rest. Then throw your arms wide—send your words out. Then bring them back into the orans position—you wait, ready to greet the Spirit you called when it arrives.

Giving offerings always involves hand movements. You may place something in or on the earth; you may pour it out; you may throw it into a fire or body of water. Think about what each of these gestures means to you, and you will understand your offering better.

## Dance

Pressed further, changing gestures becomes dance. Dance can be a prayer all on its own, an expression of emotions, an offering of beauty, a form of nonverbal communication. Dance does not lend itself well to spoken prayers, but ones recited silently while dancing can be effective. In group prayers, one or more people can dance with prayers that are spoken or sung by others, or one person can say a prayer while everyone else dances. Simple dances can work with simple chants.

Dance is the ultimate form of praying with motion. It has traditionally been used in many ways in many cultures. Each position may be intended to communicate something; the individual motions work together to make up a complete message, in much the same way that words combine to make a sentence. Or the message may, as in the more stationary kind of motion I mentioned above, be expressed by the dance as a whole.

Dance, when used in prayer, is most often meant to express emotion. Any emotion can be expressed through movement—from joy, to grief, to awe. The emotion you feel will usually tell you the right way to move if you listen to it.

Dance can also express an attribute of the deity invoked, or be a way of calling, in itself. For instance, deities of war are, oddly enough, often associated with dance—dance of a martial character, to be sure, but dance nonetheless. In Rome, in March and October, priests of Mars, the Salii, went about Rome performing a dance (in a 3/4—i.e., waltz—rhythm), in full armor no less. This dance honored Mars and served to invoke his blessing on Rome.

Dance can also serve as an offering, since it involves an expenditure of time and energy and is a form of art. Any honor or recognition you may receive from others when you dance (if it's a public prayer) can be dedicated to the deity to whom you pray. When you dance to the point of exhaustion, the dance not only serves as an offering, but can also open you up to the deity. Through the dance, you give all of yourself, creating a space for the deity to fill.

By now I might have given you the impression that every single thing about a prayer makes a difference. Good; that is the impression I *meant* to give. Prose or poem, meter, word choice, structure, gestures, movements, music, types of offerings—these all matter. Different choices will give different results.

Your choices reverberate on several levels. They will affect you psychologically, putting you into a certain frame of mind to receive the presence of the deities. Also, a prayer in an ancient and appropriate style will evoke thought categories associated with a certain culture.

On the theological level, certain styles may appeal to certain deities. Norse deities were used to being addressed with alliterative verse, Semitic with parallel imagery, etc. Praying in these forms might be expected to strike them as pretty and please them, something desirable in praises but also when asking for a favor.

Philosophically, doing the thing appropriate for a given situation is an act of beauty. Joining the right words with the right gesture with the right music creates an even higher form of beauty. If you give the gods nothing else, give them beauty.

# PART TWO

# RITUAL PRAYERS

*Chapter 5*

# PREPARING FOR PRAYER

Purification, the creation of sacred space, lighting a fire, and introductory prayers are all good ways to prepare for major prayers. They make the prayers themselves into little rituals, placing them in the context of your entire religious system. They are a very good way to begin scheduled rituals, such as morning or evening prayers.

I can hear you saying, "But what if I just need to pray at a moment's notice?" Don't worry. These preparations are not absolutely necessary. There will be times when you simply won't have the time or the means to prepare for prayer. As an extreme example, when your car is sliding into another on an icy road, there isn't exactly time to do a purification ritual. "Isis, help," may be all you can get out. And since that is perfectly in tune with what is happening, it is a perfect prayer.

If you have the time and the means, though, something more becomes appropriate. Part of living a Pagan life is doing that which is just right for the moment. Doing a more complete ritual when you can is just right for *that* moment.

The gods appreciate effort. They like to see that we are willing to take the time to do everything possible. You may find that your prayers yield more blessings if you perform the preparatory rituals whenever you can—not because the gods can't give you what you want without them, but because there is little motivation for them to do so if you can't even make the effort to prepare yourself to contact them. And don't you want to make an effort? Aren't they worth it?

Even if your prayer isn't a request for anything, you will be given benefits—an increased sense of knowing your place in the universe, a stronger awareness of the presence of the gods, a development of your spiritual discipline. When praying, try to make a full-fledged ritual out of your prayer whenever possible. The benefits are real and well worth the trouble.

*Chapter 6*

# PURIFICATION

When you pray, you come before the gods. You enter into their presence so that you can give them a message or offering. It is common to perform some act or preliminary ritual to prepare yourself for this encounter. The ancient Pagans certainly understood the value of preparation. For instance, in Iceland, it was forbidden to look on the holy spot of assembly unwashed. In Rome, priests placed a fold of their clothing over their heads before prayers. (This was primarily to prevent ill omens from being heard or seen during the prayer, but such a practical act had a psychological and spiritual effect as well; it cut the worshiper off from everyday distractions.) And in Greece, a ribbon was frequently put around the forehead before sacrifices.

In many religions, preparation is done by washing or donning special clothes. Frequently, this is prompted by a belief that dirt or ordinary clothing can pollute and must, therefore, be removed before the sacred can be contacted—either because the pollution will prevent the contact, or because the deities, once contacted, will be offended. These preparatory steps are often taken as much for the sake of the worshipers as for the worshiped. The cares of everyday life can intrude on your relationship with the sacred. A ritual act such as washing or putting on clean clothes can help you to free your thoughts from everyday obsessions and set them toward the gods. Ritual words of preparation can help you concentrate your mind in the right direction, so that the intent of your prayer is clear, both to you and to the gods. The gods know this and might quite justifiably be insulted if you can't be bothered to take the time to get ready for prayer.

The most common form of preparation is purification. This is done most easily by washing. Some Indian tribes purified with smoke, often from burning sage. This form of purification is also used in Catholic High Masses, where a censer is taken around the altar and swung toward the congregation.

Pagans who work with the four elements of air, fire, water, and earth can use both methods, one after the other. When you dissolve salt in water, it becomes a mixture of earth and water; when you burn incense, you combine fire and air. To use these mixtures to purify yourself, anoint your body (traditionally your forehead, lips, and heart) with the salt water while saying:

With the power of the sea,
that washes the shores,
I am purified.

In many traditions, however, water alone is considered sufficient. Roman and Greek temples often had bowls of water placed outside them for this purpose. They also often had signs that listed other requirements. In one case, for instance, those who had had sexual intercourse within the last twenty-four hours were forbidden to enter. The moral here is not that sex is necessarily impure, but that, if these signs were necessary, we can be sure that different deities had different requirements for prayer. Some deities might, by their very nature, be repelled by some things. A deity of lust might be repelled by someone who is celibate, for instance.

The best advice is to research the deities you want to pray to, and find out what form of purification they prefer. If there is no way to find this out, you can fall back on using water. You can wash your hands or anoint yourself while saying something like:

May I be pure,
fit to approach the gods.
May I be pure,
may all my impurities be burned away,
carried away on the incense smoke.

A variation on the Greek practice of donning a ribbon is to wear special garments or jewelry. These can be as elaborate as the robes used by ceremonial magicians, or as simple as the traditional Greek headband. With repeated use, these items become a signal that prayer time has arrived. Whatever accessories are used, their donning should be accompanied with a ritual utterance. A simple example for donning a headband might be:

I am encircled with the sacred,
girded about, encompassed,
that my actions here today
might be within the sacred way.

An example for putting on ceremonial robes might be:

The sacred covers me,
I am surrounded by the pure.

Ceremonial jewelry can include images of deities, items associated with deities (a Thor's hammer, for instance, or a feather for the Egyptian Ma'at), and general symbols of life, power, or spirituality (such as a pentagram or a triskele). You can wear this jewelry only for prayers, to put yourself in an instant prayer mode, or you can wear it all the time, making your whole life a time of prayer. Either way, it is a good idea to don these items in a prayerful manner. For instance, when I put on my Cernunnos image each morning,

I say:

> My lord Cernunnos, I offer you my worship.
> Watch over me today as I go about my affairs:
> keep me safe, keep me happy, keep me healthy.

Someone putting on a Ma'at feather might pray:

> Lady of Truth, be with me today.
> As I wear your feather, guard my words and deeds.
> May what I say and what I do
> be in accord with your sacred law.

You might use these words while putting on a pentagram:

> The elements are joined with the power of spirit.
> May I be blessed by the four.
> May I be blessed by spirit.
> May I be blessed by the five.

Purification and the use of sacred jewelry or dress are not mutually exclusive. They both encourage detaching from the distractions of everyday life and coming into the presence of the divine. Indo-European cultures, though, make a distinction between the sacred and the holy. They define the sacred as the dangerous power of the divine, which must be dealt with first. Only then can the holy, the blessing power of the divine, be acquired. Purification enables us to cross over into the sacred. Putting on special jewelry or clothing puts you in touch with the holy. If you do both, you acknowledge both aspects of the divine.

> I am encircled with the sacred,
> girded about, encompassed,
> that my actions here today
> might be within the sacred way.

# Purification by the Four Elements

*[Anoint your forehead, lips, and heart with salt water.]*

With the power of the sea,
that washes the shores,
I am purified.

*[Pass incense over your body.]*

May I be pure,
may all my impurities be burned away,
carried away on the incense smoke.

May I be pure that I might cross through
the sacred.
May I cross through the sacred that I might
attain the holy.
May I attain the holy that I might be
blessed in all things.

The impure is that which doesn't fit a time,
a place, an intent.
May this water wash the impure away,
and leave behind the fit.

Through pure water I am pure.
Through pure fire I am pure.
By the pure I am pure
to come before the gods of
incomprehensible purity.

I make myself pure to receive the pure as
guests.

Everything that is not proper to my
purpose today,
everything that would offend [deity],
everything that would interfere with your
worship:

May it all drain away,
removed by the purifying water,
replaced totally by that water's purity.

From all that I have done that I should not
have done,
may I be purified.
From all that has come to me that
should not have come,
may I be purified.
From all that is not in the right place.
or has happened at the wrong time,
may I be purified,
that I may put these things behind me and
step again onto the path of the Holy
Ones.
May I be pure, may I be pure, may I be pure.

That we aren't impure by nature, and only
made so by error, is made clear to us in this
ritual. Water washes away only what's on
the outside, removes that which does not
belong.

I purify you with water, then,
Making you what you truly are,
Making you what you already are,
Making you what you have always been:
pure to be in the presence of the gods.

May this water wash away everything
that keeps me from seeing the sacred
through which I walk, the Ocean of
Spirits through which I walk.

May the water with which I anoint my
forehead be a stream to wash away the
impurities of my everyday life.

May I be pure,
fit to approach the gods.

May I be pure,
may all my impurities be burned away,
carried away on the incense smoke.

Water on my forehead, to purify my
    thoughts.
Water on my lips, to purify my words.
Water on my hands, to purify my deeds.
Water, pure water, to purify my whole self.

I wash my hands:
may they be clean,
may they be pure,
to perform today sacred acts.

May I be pure
so that I will be fit
in order to make all I do today holy,
tributes to the gods whom I worship.

With this water from the sky [rain] I purify
    myself.
With this water from the earth [dew, frost]
    I purify myself.
With this water from the sea I purify
    myself.
So that I might be fit to worship the
    numina above.
So that I might be fit to worship the
    numina about.
So that I might be fit to worship the
    numina below.
So that I might be fit to worship the
    numina, pure themselves.

Pure water, wash from me everything not
    pure, that I might come before the gods
    prepared as is right.

Once I rinse this cup/bowl,
and a second time I rinse it,

and a third time again.
So it will be pure to contain the water
with which I now fill it at last.

*[For putting on ritual garments]*

The sacred covers me,
I am surrounded by the pure.

Clothes that are clean and fresh
I don to worship the gods,
to come before them without impurities.

## ANAHITA

Anahita, purest of all,
through your help may I be worthy
to come into the presence of the Holy
    Ones.

## APĄM NAPĀT

High Lord, bless this water,
so that it, properly purified,
may purify us, and, by its touch,
all the articles we will use in this rite.
Apąm Napāt, it is you of great power
that we ask to do this.

## APĀM NAPĀT

Apāṃ Napāt and the Waters
Apāṃ Napāt and the Waters,
provide me with clean water
with which to purify myself for this rite
and I will offer you ghee on the sacrificial
    fire.

Waters, I offer this prayer:
give in return pure water.
Apāṃ Napāt, I offer these words:
bless in return this water.
Together provide pure, blessed water,
that I may be pure,
that I may be blessed,

that I may be well and rightly prepared for
   my ritual.
Apāṃ Napāt and the Waters
removing the impurities my presence has
   imposed.

## ARIOMANUS

Lion-headed god, of fiery breath,
burn away from me all that separates
   myself from the divine.
Fear-inspiring entity,
do your worst,
do your best.

## THE ELEMENTS

*[while putting on a pentagram]*

The elements are joined with the power of
   spirit.
May I be blessed by the four.
May I be blessed by spirit.
May I be blessed by the five.

## HEARTH GODDESS

Purest of the pure, goddess of the hearth,
through gazing at you I am made pure,
qualified to perform this day's rites.
In return, I offer this milk.

## MA'AT

Lady of Truth, be with me today.
As I wear your feather, guard my words
   and deeds.
May what I say and what I do
be in accord with your sacred law.

*Chapter 7*

# BEGINNINGS

## *Group Openings*

Come today to worship the Kindreds.
Come today,
always come.

Come we together on this holy day,
across the distances that lay between us,
to this time,
to this place,
for one strong purpose:
to worship the Holy Ones in the proper
   manner.

Come, O come,
ever come,
ever and always come,
come to worship,
come to the sacred place:
Come, O come,
ever come,
ever and always come.

Stand tall, waiting,
for the coming of the sacred before you,
no fear, no concern,
with welcoming hearts.
Do not worry, they will come,
with flower-scented steps,
scattering blessings.

We are here:
we were always here.
We are here now:
we were always here now.
We are here together now:
we were always here together now.
We have always been here like this:
and we are always like this again.

Come and make offerings:
poems or prayers, well said,
songs or steps well prepared.
The deities see,
The Ancestors watch,
The Land Spirits look on,
And they will hear you.
Come, make offerings.

The Gods wait well,
those patient ones,
and will be here when you arrive,
ready to spend time together.

May the beating of the drum be the beating
   of your heart.
When you follow the beating drum may
   your heart follow.
May you come wholeheartedly to the
   ritual.

A family scattered is a family still.
Today is a family reunion in the home of
    our Mother and Father.

Individual in existence,
One in purpose,
Neither denying nor losing who each of
    us is,
we are one, gathered together.

With hands open in giving and receiving
we come to you confidently,
All-Gods.

When the rituals are performed rightly,
all of the ways of the soul are well:
May this ritual be performed rightly.
When the rituals are performed rightly,
all of the relationships in society are well:
May this ritual be performed rightly.
When the rituals are performed rightly,
all of the ways of the state are well:
May this ritual be performed rightly.
When the rituals are performed rightly,
all of the things of Heaven and Earth are
    well:
May this ritual be performed rightly.
When the rituals are performed rightly,
all things that are or may be are well:
May this ritual be performed rightly.

We come together today as a community to
    worship the Undying Ones.
This is as it should be; it is not good for
    people to be alone.
When we evolved from the species that
    came before us it wasn't just our larger
    brains that gave us an edge,
it wasn't just the tools that our larger brains
    inspired us to make that did this,

it wasn't just the upright stance that
    allowed us to use those tools easily that
    improved our ability to survive.
Most of all it was community.
It was our love of having other humans
    around us,
to help us when we were weak, to be
    helped when *they* were weak,
to be protected and to protect,
to be loved by and to love,
to gather together to reassure ourselves, to
    know that things will be okay.
That is one of the great strengths of our
    species.
It is part of us, not decided on, but written
    into our bodies, encoded in our DNA.
We may need guidance and explanations to
    live well in communities, but we do not
    need outside information to know that
    we must live together as communities. It
    is who we are.
So when we come together as a community
    to worship today, we are doing
    something that is precisely a human
    thing to do.
When we worship as a community, we are
    worshiping as fully human beings.
Let us join now in worship.

A school of fish, responding to currents,
A meadow of grass, responding to wind:
each individual, each in the same pattern.
That is us, as we come together for
    worship.

Still your fears,
replace them with awe;
Prepare for the Holy
with a single mind.

Come to where the people are,
Come to where the Gods are,
Come to the drums, Come to the bells,
Come dancing to the sacred place,
Come dancing, Come singing, Come.

I call, I call, I call you here,
to worship, to worship, the Ancient Ones.
Listen and come to the one who calls,
who calls, who calls, who calls to you.
Gather by the tree that rises,
and rise with it to celestial realms,
where Shining Ones gather
to hear our prayers:
make prayers to them here.

## THE ALL-GODS

I call you before the Holy Ones,
into the halls of the All-Gods gathered in
    council.
Here we will put our petitions to them for
    the consideration of the Wise,
and for the granting of the True, the Right,
    the Just,
as those who are True, and Right, and Just
    decide.

## XÁRYOMĒN

Xáryomēn, lord of the law of the people,
giver of well-disposed friends:
be our good herdsmen.
Bring us together.
Make us one.
May we come before the gods speaking
    with one voice:

## *Individual Openings*

Surrounded by all the numinous beings
    of earth and sky and water, I pray with
    confidence, for I know their help is
    certain.

I place myself at your service,
    gods of my people.
Open me to your wishes,
    make me a conduit for your will,
    bringing forth your desires in the human
        world.

This offering goes before me, opening the
    door.
Key to the gods, be my way-shower.

Living so long in the polluted world of
    man
I turn at last to the sacred land,
the pure land of the gods,
the holy land of the goddesses,
which is my true home.

*[Before a tale is told]*

It was a long time ago—
no one knows when, or even if (still the
    story is true)—that which happened,
    happened.
It is still happening, of course, and always
    will—
that's the way it is with true stories.
Listen carefully, then, because this story is
    about where you come from,
or maybe where you are.
Maybe you haven't found it yet.
Maybe it is something that's already
    happened,
so it will explain where you are,

or maybe it's going on right now,
so it will help you decide what to do,
or maybe it hasn't happened yet—
   forewarned is forearmed.
Listen carefully, then:
this story is true.

## CERNUNNOS

Half-stag, half-man, sitting between,
between this and that,
between this and the other,
god of the gates, open the gates,
Cernunnos who guides my steps.

## HERMES

God of the herm constructed on the
   borders:
you pass through as well as keep out.
Pass through my prayers, my offerings, to
   those I worship;
Pass through as well their presence, their
   blessings, to me.
The cattle of Apollo seemed to go one way
   when they had gone the other:
may our prayers go both ways,
may the Immortals go both ways.

## MANANNÁN MAC LIR

By hanging this triskele around my neck
I am placing myself under the care of
   Manannán,
God of Mystery.

## THOR

I draw a hammer on my forehead with my
   thumb,
dipped in mead,
to mark me as Thor's.

*Chapter 8*

# SACRED SPACE

## *Human-Created Sacred Space*

Another type of preparation for prayer is the creation of sacred space. A sacred space is one cut off from normal space in some way. You can create this by putting yourself in the center of the universe, then organizing it around you in the way envisioned by your tradition. This has nothing to do with the actual physical layout of the universe, but instead expresses a tradition's symbolic system. For instance, Wiccans associate the four directions with elements, colors, Spirits, tools, etc. A preparatory prayer for a Wiccan might involve becoming aware of these symbols and putting them, either mentally or physically, in their proper places.

Beginning by putting yourself at the center of the universe tells you who and where you are. Any relationship, including those with the divine, must start from that place. By expressing this awareness in a prayer, you establish it ritually, and you can then slide right into the rest of your prayers. Another advantage of centering yourself in this way is that it can be very calming. It can remove distractions, allowing you to concentrate on what you are about to do.

Finally, the sacred center is the place at which the divine power enters the universe. It is the hub about which all the rest turns. It is where the gods can be approached. By locating yourself there, you increase your chances of being able to commune with them. Perhaps they can talk to you wherever you are, but can you talk to them?

This is an example of a centering prayer:

> I place myself in the center of the world,
> where pillar and cauldron are joined, overflowing,
> continually pouring over, and sending waves of existence out into the world.
> Before I perform my acts of worship, I take you into myself,
> that what I do might be equally productive
> that out of me might wonders flow.

This prayer includes a description of a mythical conception of the universe. Here, existence is born of the joining of a pillar and a cauldron. In Wicca, these represent the God (pillar) and Goddess (cauldron). These images are found in other traditions, so this prayer may be appropriate for them as well. The pillar might be the Norse World Tree, the cauldron the well of Mimir at its base. Or the pillar might be the tent pole up which a shaman flies on his spirit journey. The cauldron might be the cup or bowl from which inspiring drink is consumed. Here is another prayer, appropriate for both Wicca and shamanic traditions:

To the east, to the south,
to the west, to the north,
to above and below,
I send my words flying.
From the east, from the south,
from the west, from the north,
from above and below,
may blessings come flying.

Those of the Celtic or other Indo-European traditions might use:

The waters support and surround me.
The land extends about me.
The sky reaches out above me.
At the center burns a living flame.

Centering prayers can also be used to place the universe in relation to a social structure. For instance:

World below, watery world, with chaos and
    order overflowing,
bring true creation into my life, with order
    and beauty,
with power and grace.
World above, far-flung heavens, ordering
    the world
with might and law,
bring true stability into my life, with law
    and structure,
with clarity and reason.
World about me, far extending, with land
    well set,

bring true being into my life, with help and
    love,
with health and prosperity.

I place myself in the center of the world,
where pillar and cauldron are joined,
    overflowing,
continually pouring over, and sending
    waves of existence out into the world.
Before I perform my acts of worship, I take
    you into myself,
that what I do might be equally productive
and out of me might flow wonders.

Above and below,
and me between.
Around and about,
and me in the midst.
Before and after,
and me here now.

Balanced on the earth,
I sit, in the center,
axis-mundi-spine reaches up.

This goes before me, opening the door.
Key to the gods, be my way-shower.

Open your eyes and look around
and see the sacred in our midst
and see us in the midst of the sacred.

If you truly know that you're truly here
then you'll truly know that the holy is here
and always was.

The Sacred Space is here.
The Sacred Time is now.
Nowhere to travel,
nothing to wait for.
Just know it to be true,
and you are there
and you are then.

It is by standing here that we know this
    place to be sacred.
It is by doing holy things that we know this
    day to be sacred.
It is by worshiping the Holy Ones with all
    that we are
that we will know that we are sacred,
and will carry the sacred into all places,
on all days.

I am here
and I belong here.
How could I not when every deed and
    decision I have made in my life has
    brought me here?
Whether arriving here has brought me
    good or ill,
or brought good or ill to others,
here is where I belong.
And it is from that I must pray.

We have come to worship today,
making this time sacred by worshiping
and this space sacred by worshiping
    together.

We are standing here.
You are standing here.
I am standing here.
We are standing here.
And today we will raise open hands
and pray to those who are holy
with sweet words of welcome.

With the tracing of this circle's edge I
    separate my space;
I separate the sacred from all that is
    profane,
from all that would profane my rites,
from all that would make this place unfit
for the entrance of the Sacred Ones to
    whom I will call.

Space about me,
be pure,
be sacred,
for my worship.

From the home to the wild,
I walk a sacred path.
From the wild to the home,
I walk a sacred path.
The wild is sacred.
The home is sacred.
The wild and the home, both sacred.
Most sacred of all, the Path between.

We are here.
We are here.
We are here.
And here is where we will worship the
    Holy Ones.
The time is now.
The time is now.
The time is now.
And now is when we will worship the Holy
    ones.
Never denying the holiness of Here.
Never denying the holiness of Now.
Never denying the presence of the Holy
    Ones in all Heres and Nows.

That side, mundane,
this side, divine.
We draw the line

for our ritual,
for this time.

With my knife I cut off a space—
separate, sacred, set apart—
for the practice of wonders.

The sky a tent above me:
it is good.
The earth a floor beneath me:
it is good.
The Gods supporting me:
it is good.
The Ancestors preceding me:
it is good.
The Spirits surrounding me:
it is good.
Each bit of the cosmos in its proper place:
it is good,
it is good.
It is good.

The sea surrounds my place of ritual:
I cast into it all that is chaos.
I leave behind all order in this place in which
    I stand.
I create here a cosmos,
a beautiful land in which to worship the
    beautiful gods.

## INDRA

I build a temple here for the time of my
    ritual,
placing it under the protection of Indra,
and of the vajra, the strongly thrown
    weapon.
May I, through its strength,
through his blessing,
worship well in sacred space and achieve
    my aims.

## RHIANNON

May this be the mound of Arbeth, where
    wonders are seen,
or blows received.
May I know wonders.
May I see a woman on a white horse,
    slowly riding,
swiftly riding,
waiting for me to ask her to stay.
May I see Rhiannon.
May she lead me to the Otherworld,
to share the feast of the Shining Ones,
to sing their praises, and drink of their cup.

## Natural Sacred Space

It is a little presumptuous, of course, to create your own sacred space at a place that is already holy in some way. Since Pagans revere many natural holy sites, this is an important point for them to remember. You may find yourself in front of a magnificent tree or at the edge of a deep lake, recognize that it is holy, and want to pray. It would be a bit rude to ask that the site conform to your own way of organizing sacred space. The right thing would be to conform yourself to the place, rather than trying to make the place conform to your needs.

To honor such a space, first calm yourself. Sit comfortably and quietly. Keep your body still. Then listen—not only with your ears, but also with your whole body and your soul. A wind blowing over a stone may sound like something speaking to you. The Sun striking a tree may raise a scent from the bark. The light on moving water may form a pattern. You may not understand the language in which the message is expressed, but something may indeed speak to you. Listen to it and appreciate the beauty of the expression, even if you don't know its meaning.

After you have listened, it is time for you to give back. You can start with a short prayer of praise, or one of calling. For example, you can say something as simple as:

> You who live in the depths of this lake,
> I sit and think of you
> and honor you as you deserve to be honored.

It is always good to follow this prayer with an offering. You are offering to the local Spirits, so your offering should be appropriate to the place. In the United States, corn (maize) is right, as is tobacco. In Europe, try wheat or oats. Bread is good anywhere, and coins also seem to be universally appreciated.

If you decide to mark out an outside space for ritual, either as a permanent place of worship or for a specific ritual more complex than a single prayer, you should make offerings to the Land Spirits. Otherwise, you are essentially stealing the land. To use the space for worshiping the gods without making offerings to the Land Spirits would be a little like going over the head of your boss to speak to the president of the company. Your boss wouldn't like it; the president wouldn't like it; and, in the end, you wouldn't like it. Always make offerings to the local Spirits. It's the polite thing to do.

Large bodies of water are traditional places for offering. Offerings in rivers or the ocean may be given as prayers or as thanks for successful crossings, or they may be given to the Spirit of the river as an apology for building a bridge.

Hidden in the folds of the land you dwell
and have dwelt since the world began.
I am one of the world's younger children
come to honor you with these offerings.

Whether god or goddess who rules this
    place,
to you I offer my friendship
and with it this gift.

Gateway of the gods, receive my offering.
As it sinks deep with you, let it open the
    door,
and let it be carried to them whom I praise
    in this way.

This time in which I find myself is no less
    sacred
than the times of the Ancestors when the
    laws were laid down.
This place in which I find myself is no less
    sacred
than the circles of stone beneath faraway
    skies.
I pray to all the beings that dwell in this
    world;
to stone and tree, to waves and breezes,
to person and beast, to deities and dust
    motes:
do not let me forget.
Keep my eyes open
to the sacred that surrounds me
and in which I live.

Gods who watch over this place,
whom I don't know.
Ancestors who watch over this place,
whom I don't know.
Land Spirits who dwell in this place,
whom I don't know:

I'm leaving this offering to you,
    unknowing,
out of my ignorance, to the unknown.

This space, this sacred space,
is guarded by the sacred beings of
    protection,
who answer those who call to them.
With confidence in their continued
    presence I begin my rites.

## The Directions and Elements

Each direction sacred,
Each direction perfect,
and I stand in the center,
the most sacred of all,
the most powerful place of all,
from which I will approach the gods,
and ask them to approach me.

I crack this egg, a foundation sacrifice,
at this sacred direction of my sacred space:
may the Spirits that receive it make it strong
    and holy,
fit for our ritual today/tonight.

Stepping from the center to the east,
three steps,
I mark my space out in that direction as holy.
Stepping from the center to the south,
three steps,
I mark my space out in that direction as
    holy.
Stepping from the center to the west,
three steps,
I mark my space out in that direction as
    holy.
Stepping from the center to the north,
three steps,

I mark my space out in that direction as
    holy.
Standing again in the center, I dwell in a
    space that is holy.


*[In the following prayer, mead is poured into
a bowl and then cast as offerings in the directions as noted. The prayer is complemented by
a closing prayer found in chapter 21.]*

We stand, pillars, in the center of the
    world,
while all else turns about us.
In the center, Chaos enters Cosmos.
It endangers and enlightens it,
gifting it with power:
Power to the south [offer]
Power to the west [offer]
Power to the north [offer]
Power to the east, [offer]
the place of prayer, the place of light,
the place of the Holy Ones.
And power to the center, [offer]
where we stand, pillars,
while all else turns about us.


East, where light rises
Are you there?
You are.
South, where light stands high
Are you there?
You are.
West, where light descends
Are you there?
You are.
North, where light is hidden
Are you there?
You are.
Center, where I am
Are you there?
I am.

We speak our prayers in the proper way,
to the proper directions
to those who dwell there.
Toward the east we pray,
to the Spirits of thought,
the Spirits of the words we use.

Toward the south we pray, to the Spirits of
    deeds,
the Spirits of our ritual acts.
Toward the west we pray,
to the Spirits of emotion,
the Spirits of the feelings we give.
Toward the north we pray,
to the Spirits of being,
to the Spirits of the bodies that turn.
We speak in the center,
where the directions join,
and bring us to life that we might pray:
from the center may we always speak.

To the east we cry!
To the south we cry!
To the west we cry!
To the north we cry!
To the World we cry!
This is the place where we will cry
to the Gods and Goddesses!

There is the east,
that I praise.
There is the south,
that I praise.
There is the west,
that I praise.
There is the north,
that I praise.
And there is the Center,
in which I stand,
and that I praise,
where I stand surrounded by the four,

each of them worthy of praise,
each worthy of equal praise,
each worthy of their due praise.

I place myself in Air, in the east I place
   myself,
under the protection of Raphael I place
   myself.
I place myself in Fire, in the south I place
   myself,
under the protection of Michael I place
   myself.
I place myself in Water, in the west I place
   myself,
under the protection of Gabriel I place
   myself.
I place myself in Earth, in the north I place
   myself,
under the protection of Uriel I place
   myself.
I place myself in the Above, in the Sky I
   place myself,
under the protection of the Father I place
   myself.
I place myself in the Below, in the Earth I
   place myself,
under the protection of the Mother I place
   myself.
I place myself in Spirit, in the Center I
   place myself,
under the protection of all the Holy Ones I
   place myself.

In this moment
In this place
In the midst of the elements
In the midst of the Two
In the midst of the center
In the midst of all the divine ones
I place myself under their protection.

I make this sign in the east,
the sign of Air,
to the beings of Air,
to call to them, to call them here,
to come to those who worship here.
Come, you are welcome, Spirits of Air.

I make this sign in the south,
the sign of Fire,
to the beings of Fire,
to call to them, to call them here,
to come to those who worship here.
Come, you are welcome, Spirits of Fire.

I make this sign in the west,
the sign of Water,
to the beings of Water,
to call to them, to call them here,
to come to those who worship here.
Come, you are welcome, Spirits of Water.

I make this sign in the north,
the sign of Earth,
to the beings of Earth,
to call to them, to call them here,
to come to those who worship here.
Come, you are welcome, Spirits of Earth.

THE BIG BOOK OF PAGAN PRAYER AND RITUAL

May blow from the east the wind of air, hot
    and moist, to form its part of this circle's
    balance.
May blow from the south the wind of
    fire, hot and dry, to form its part of this
    circle's balance.
May blow from the west the wind of water,
    cold and moist, to form its part of this
    circle's balance.
May blow from the north the wind of earth,
    cold and dry, to form its part of this
    circle's balance.
May the four winds join in the center in
    balance.

As we begin to celebrate our sacred rites,
we invite you, Lord of Air, to come,
rejoicing in your presence.

As we begin to celebrate our sacred rites,
we invite you, Lord of Fire, to come,
rejoicing in your presence.

As we begin to celebrate our sacred rites,
we invite you, Lady of Water, to come,
rejoicing in your presence.

As we begin to celebrate our sacred rites,
we invite you, Lady of Earth, to come,
rejoicing in your presence.

As we begin to celebrate our sacred rites,
we invite you, Lords of the Elements, to
    come,
we invite you, Ladies of the Elements, to
    come.
rejoicing in your presence.

To all of you we say that we invite you to
    come,
so we might rejoice in each other's
    presence.

I place air in the east,
its proper place:
may I be in mine.
I place fire in the south,
its proper place:
may I be in mine.
I place water in the west,
its proper place:
may I be in mine.
I place earth in the north,
its proper place:
may I be in mine.
I place spirit in the center,
its proper place,
where I am.
I am in mine.

Candle flame, burn for me,
and direct here pure [element]
to bless my circle with its power.

## TERMINUS

Terminus, stand at the corners of my space,
protecting and blessing.
Terminus, stand at this corner of my space,
protecting and blessing.
Be strengthened to do that through this
    offering.

*[At each corner, give an offering of an egg,
wine, and spelt.]*

# The Sacred Flame

Fire plays a very important role in many religions, and Paganism is no exception. Light, in general, is associated with the gods, and the presence of light with the presence of the gods. Fire is warmth, and warmth is life. In the presence of the gods, we feel alive. Fire is also a means of giving offerings. Our words go through the flames to the gods; through the fire, they are transformed into spiritual offerings. Sometimes, the offering is to the fire itself, either as an element or as deity. Thus, an offering in fire feeds the fire, the deities to whom it is offered through the fire, or both.

The lighting of a sacred flame often plays a part in the creation of a sacred space. The flame may rise from a candle, or an oil lamp, or an actual fire, either on a hearth or as an outdoor campfire.

Obviously, any offering given through fire must be flammable. Sometimes such offerings are fuels, such as vegetable or olive oil, or clarified butter. Nondairy creamer, surprisingly, makes an excellent offering, feeding the fire very nicely. Incense, paintings, grains, and prayers written on paper or wood also make excellent offerings.

Here are some prayers to go with fire offerings:

Fire of offering, you burn the sacrifice,
making it fit for the gods.
Burn away all my weaknesses,
making me fit for the gods.

I feed you with oil, fire of oblation,
that you might grow strong,
that you might grow bright,
that you might carry my prayers to the gods.

Take this, fire;
eat it and do not forget my generosity,
but carry my wishes to the gods
and say to them that I am your friend,
a giver of gifts,
who deserves their kind consideration.

It burns, it burns, it burns,
the fire about which we gather.
It burns, it burns, it burns,
the fire that is in our hearts.
In one we will burn butter.
In the other we will burn with prayer.

With both we will burn what the gods desire.
So they burn, they burn, they burn.

Speak with your many tongues,
carrying my prayers to the gods.
Take your share of my offering,
conveying the rest faithfully
to those to whom I offer it.
Fire of offering,
perform these deeds truly
as you have always done.

*[The individual flames are imagined to be
tongues, each of which can carry the offerer's
message; the fire joins you in praying.]*

## AGNI

Whether hidden in reed or wood or cloud
you are here in my ritual fire, Agni,
into which I will pour my offerings.
Bless me, bless my ritual today.
Open the way to the golden-eyed with your
    golden flames.
Agni, bless my ritual.

## PERKŪNAS

I light this fire of oaken branches,
of oaken logs,
with stone-struck sparks,
to honor Perkūnas.
On it I will make offerings.
Through it I will make offerings.
I will make offerings to the great hero.

With sparks from heaven, I light this fire,
these oaken flames.

With sparks from the earth, I light this fire,
these oaken flames.
And although I must eventually extinguish
    them, Perkūnas,
although they cannot be eternal, Perkūnas,
they will ever burn in my heart,
a continual sacred fire into which I can cast
    these words.

*Chapter 9*

# THE HOME

D omestic prayer is the most important kind. The great festivals come and go, the Moon circles the Earth, the Sun rises and sets, but their celebrations are done against the background of home worship.

There are divine beings of various sorts who watch over a family and its home, and they like to be recognized. Domestic worship is made up of those practices through which the deities, Ancestors, and Spirits who preside over the family and protect the home are worshiped, honored, and propitiated. We do this, as usual, through prayers and offerings.

A householder is responsible for all who dwell in the home, but especially for guests. Even if they are unwelcome, treat them with kindness until you have escorted them off your property. It is then your responsibility to patch things up with whatever Spirits have been offended. This obligation holds for the uninvited as well as the invited guest—the neighborhood children, the salesman, the evangelist at your door. Greet them pleasantly. Offer them hospitality. If you invite them in, offer them something to eat or drink. Your home will develop a reputation for hospitality, which will please the household Spirits no end.

## *Spirits of Place*

The most important sacred places of a household where worship is performed are the hearth and the threshold. If the home stands on its own property, the yard and the property's border are also sacred. Each of these places has its own Spirits and traditional ways to honor them.

The hearth was originally the multipurpose fireplace—it cooked our meals, warmed our homes, and boiled water for washing. Although today these functions have been split up between the stove, the furnace, and the water heater, they're no less sacred, and no less worthy of honor. There is a Spirit living in the hearth of each home; in fact, often that Spirit is a great goddess, perhaps the most important of the goddesses, since she is the heart of the home and the home is the heart of our lives.

You should honor this goddess primarily at the stove, since that is where our nourishment—that which fuels our own inner fires—is prepared. Keep a candle or oil lamp next to the stove, and light it when you pray to her. Don't forget to honor her at the furnace or water heater, though.

At least once a year, on a day appropriate to your deity, make special offerings at each of them. For instance, honor Brigid on February 2 (Brigid's Day) or Vesta on June 9 (Vestalia). Alternatively, you could choose the anniversary of the day you moved in.

The threshold is also a place particularly appropriate for worship, marking a point of transition between one place and another. In-between places throb with power; they're like circuits formed through the flow between positive and negative forces. Like electricity, their power can help or harm. The purpose of threshold devotions is to make sure that the positive forces are directed to family and friends, and the harmful ones to intruders.

The yard is a place where wild things can roam in safety and do you no harm. By letting them move about on your "turf," but outside, you give them a secure haven, while ensuring your own safety. Through them you can approach the outside world and introduce yourself to it, while still keeping one foot securely inside your home. Many Spirits roam this outdoor space, and all are worthy of prayer and praise.

The boundary line of your property is the threshold of your household world, and has the same meanings your house's threshold has. It is where what's yours finally ends, and the common area begins. It is where you must say goodbye to the familiar. There you can ask that border Spirit to prevent anything harmful from entering your property while you are away.

## Patron Deities and Ancestors

Besides the Spirits of place, there are deities who watch over individual members of your household, their patron deities. Worshiping them should be part of your home practice. There are too many deities, each with their own worship requirements, to cover them all here. Suffice it to say that the usual rules for prayer and offering given in part 1 apply for these deities as well—purification is good, fire is great, prayers have a traditional structure, and everybody likes presents.

Just as a house has its protective Spirits, and individual members of the family have their patron deities, so, too, the family as a whole has its protectors. These are often the Ancestors. In the case of family worship, they are primarily the genetic ancestors, those who founded the family and those who kept it going. Of course, families can grow by adoption as well as reproduction, so those who are adopted into a family are also adopted into the line of its Ancestors.

Many of our ancestors would be appalled to learn that we are praying to them. At least, that's how they would probably have felt when they were alive. But they're dead now, and we can hope that their perspective has changed, that they have acquired the wisdom granted by distance. Even if they don't want worship, technically we are honoring them rather than worshiping them, and they can't mind that much.

Samhain is the day on which the ancient Celts honored their ancestors, and many neo-Pagans have adopted it for this purpose. Most cultures have such a day, and you should use whatever one is right for your ancestry. If you are, like so many of us, of mixed ancestry, Memorial Day makes a nice compromise.

Somewhere in your home—by the hearth, or in the entranceway, or on a kitchen shelf—erect a shrine. In it, put images of the patron deities of the members of your household, images of the Ancestors, and a source of fire (a candle or oil lamp). Images can be statues or more abstract. My wife's patron is Venus, and for a long time, I used a star-shaped stone (making it also roughly the shape of a person) that I had found on the seashore as her image. An antler can serve as an image of Cernunnos, a mirror as one of Amaterasu. Ancestors can be represented by generic statues of a man and a woman. This shrine provides the divine beings most closely associated with your home with their own place in it. The fire, which represents divinity, both honors them and is a means to contact them. It is here that you should pray and make offerings to these protective beings.

## Water and Fire

Before beginning your household rituals, it's good to call on those most holy of things, water and fire. In many other cases, you may have to pray without them, but in your own home, you have them ready at hand. Purify yourself with the water, then light the fire. A short prayer, such as "I light the fire of offering," would be nice. If you are honoring your hearth deity, you will want to light her flame with a short prayer, such as "I light the fire of [her name]." There is no need to establish sacred space. A home is by definition a sacred space.

If you are praying to the threshold, yard, or border Spirits, go to where they dwell. Leave the fire burning in your shrine during the ritual, though. It's your anchor.

When you make offerings indoors, such as to the hearth, make them into a bowl. If you can, leave them there for twenty-four hours, then take them outside for the Land Spirits to eat. Offerings to land and border Spirits can usually be made right on the spot. In the case of a threshold, if your door opens to the inside, liquid offerings can be made right on it. If your door opens out, put your offerings in a bowl right inside the door and dispose of them as usual.

Remember that you pray with deeds as well as words. Not stepping on your threshold as you come in or go out can be a prayer. With time, it will become a habit; your conscious mind will not notice, but with your unconscious mind, you will be praying.

## Traditional Roles

Household prayers may be said by any member of the family (and if you live alone, you will, of course, be doing all of it by yourself). Traditionally, however, certain people had certain responsibilities. Maintaining these traditions will put you more strongly in tune with your Ancestors.

The worship of the hearth goddess was the responsibility of the wife and mother in ancient times. The father was responsible for performing the rest of the family worship on his family's behalf. He was, in other words, the priest of the family.

You don't have to stick to these roles. The Spirits like to be remembered, no matter who is doing the remembering. As the main cook in my house, I've been the one to maintain the hearth-goddess worship. You can share these responsibilities in whatever way seems fit for your family. Assign some duties to your children as they grow. Learning not to step on the threshold is something that can be done as soon as a child can walk. Honoring their own patrons is something that should be taught to children early as well.

A distinction can be made between the prayers of family members to the household Spirits and prayers to the Spirits on the family's behalf. Someone should be doing the latter. This is enough, but it is very basic. It's good if all members of the family, as individuals, are in a right relationship with the household Spirits. This relationship exists alongside the one each person has with a personal patron deity. Through the worship of a patron deity, each person is established as an individual; through the worship of the household Spirits, each person is established as a member of a family.

# The Borders

About my house, establish your place of
    warding.
Stand watchfully at the corners.
Be a shield between our house and all that
    would work evil.
Guard our land and all who claim its
    protection.

Here on the border, you stand your watch.
I have come out here
to assure you that your attention
    to duty is appreciated,
bringing not only words,
but gifts to place before your marker.
Watcher on the Borders, the steward of this
    land offers to you.
This grain is for you, and this beer is for
    you.

## TERMINUS

He who sits at the edge of my land
sits at the edge of all I own.
Watchful Terminus guards my space.

Stand firm, stand unmoving, stand strong,
at the edge of our land,
border-stone, Terminus:
protect and defend all my family
and all I own
from all that would harm.
Ward my property well.

I place this stone on the edge of my land,
over which I will pour oil and sweet wine:
be watchful, Terminus!
I place this stone on the edge of my land,
onto which I will sprinkle spelt and white
    barley:
be watchful, Terminus!

I place this stone on the edge of my land,
at which I will speak words of praise:
be watchful, Terminus!
Be watchful over my land, my home, my
    possessions, my family, and me.
Ever awake Terminus, be watchful!

## TERMINUS, HERMES

Pillar on the border, whether Terminus or
    Hermes,
mark my passage
and welcome me home safely.
Receive as offering this garland.

# The Spirits of the Yard

The yard Spirits are half wild, and their actions are not always what we would wish.
This is especially true when they are ig-
nored. Give the leavings of your offerings
to the inside Spirits to the yard Spirits—
as well as, from time to time, an offering
of their own, such as a piece of buttered
bread. And remember, no matter how reas-
suring order may be, it can be a bit oppres-
sive. Try to keep part of your yard, even a
back corner, as a haven for the wild. Leave
it alone, let weeds grow there, and don't
mow it. Give the Spirits who live there oc-
casional offerings, too. Leave the offerings
in place until they're gone.

Was the milk eaten by the Spirits,
washed away by rain, or lapped up by a
wandering cat? Who knows? Who cares?
Perhaps the Spirits have come in the form
of rain or a cat. It doesn't matter. What matters is that you do the right thing. In this
case, having a piece of the wild in the midst
of your tame yard will bring you a bit of the
wildness and peace that true wild can bring.

Roam about our land at will, Spirits,
keeping it holy by your presence.

Guardians of rocks and trees,
of grass and garden,
of wild places and tame,
of outbuildings and outside:
be benevolent to us,
to those who tend your realm,
and we will be benevolent to you.

A piece of wild on the edge of the tame,
you are home to wild Spirits who live with
    us.
You who live here, be pleased with this
    offering.
Give us a piece of the wild to keep us alive
    and fresh.

## HOUSE SNAKE

Snake, little snake, that lives under my
    house,
I leave you this bowl of milk:
you, my friend.

## SILVANUS

Silvanus of the wild,
be Silvanus of my land,
and I will pour wine to you as a libation.

## TERMINUS

Lord who protects borders,
protect me, my household, my land,
and all who enter here as guests.
In return for which, in promise of future
    offerings,
to establish, maintain, and strengthen
    friendship between us,
this wine, this spelt, this egg,
willingly given.

## LAND SPIRITS

Those who dwelt in this land before it was
    ours, and was still wild,
we offer you our apologies for displacing
    you,
with this offering of [scattered grain/corn/
    wheat/etc.; poured-out milk/beer/wine/
    etc.; strewn tobacco] we complete the
    cycle of gifts:
our offering for your land.
By the exchange may we be friends,
by friendship may there be peace,
and by peace may we live lives together in
    happiness.

## The Door

Door Warden,
living in lintel, in threshold,
above and below;
in posts rising up on either side,
strong supporters:
with reverent touch I worship you,
with stepping over the threshold right foot
    first,
I offer my respect.

Protector of the Door, be:
closed against enemies
open to friends
welcoming to guests who approach you.

Before opening you for the first time, Door,
let me introduce myself with this gift.
We'll be working together closely from
    now on,
so let's get off on the right foot.

## BES

A little dwarf sits beside my door
and wards away all danger
while welcoming the stranger.
Bes, to you this beer I pour.

## CARDEA

Cardea, goddess of hinges,
uphold this door in its protecting role.

## JANUS

Janus, god of doorways,
bless my goings out,
bless my comings in.

Guard my door, Janus,
keeper of the keys.
Watch it with care,
keep my home safe.

*[For when you are locking up for the night]*

May the blessings of Janus guard this door.
Janus it is who guards our doors.

## PERKŪNAS

Perkūnas protects the world from the
    forces of disaster,
his might opposing with victory that which
    would overwhelm.
I inscribe this cross over my door that
    he might know this house is under his
    protection,
that he might keep from harm all who
    dwell within,
and all guests we might honor through
    hospitality.

# The Threshold

I'm stepping with my right foot,
over, not on you:
see my respect.

Rise as a wall against danger,
lie still, a gentle pathway,
for blessings.

Lying flat,
we walk over.
Spirit of the threshold,
watch over us.
We go out,
We come in,
Watch over us.

Threshold Spirit, guardian and protector
    of my
house's entrance,
I honor you as I pass through the door.

## JANUS

Lord of the threshold,
of doors and gates lord,
place where inside and outside meet:
Janus is my threshold.

# The Doorposts

Upright standers,
we walk between.
Spirits of the doorposts,
watch over us.
We go out,
We come in,
Watch over us.

*[Touch the doorpost reverently as you say this.
You can say it each time you leave your house
or when you leave it for the first time each day.]*

# The Hearth

## PRAYERS TO THE HEARTH GODDESS

The following prayers can be addressed to the goddess of your own hearth. Where appropriate, you can substitute the name of your own hearth deity, of course.

Fire softly glowing in the heart of my
    home,
Goddess of the hearth, life of my dwelling,
keep my family free from discord,
free from want, free from fear,
free from all that would disturb us
and that would disturb your perfect peace.

The fire from the waters is here.
The fire from the land is here.
The fire from the sky is here.
From below, from about, from above,
Fire has come here to my hearth:
Burn there, Lady of Clear Sight.

*[Water (below), land (about), and sky (above)
are the traditional realms of many cultures,
especially the Indo-European. This is a
prayer for lighting your hearth flame.]*

A burning point are you, Lady.
A center point are you, Lady.
A place of light are you, Lady.
A place of warmth are you, Lady.
The heart of our home are you, Lady.

To you, Fiery One, I give this milk;
I pour it out in your honor.

*[Offerings to a hearth deity should be homey
consumables, such as milk, bread, or butter.
Wine is too fancy, mead a bit affected. Beer
isn't bad, though.]*

She burns in the center of the Hall of the
    Gods,
and around her they gather in
    contemplation,
in council.
She makes them one family of comrades.
When they gather where she is those who
    contend are at peace,
those whose nature is constant motion,
rest.
Burner and Warmer,
Dweller on the Hearth,
even the gods continually praise you.
So one would expect me to feel awe when
    I see you,
but I feel friendship and love coming
    from you,
and I can only return it in kind.

This fire I sit by is the Goddess of the
    Hearth.
Not a sign, or a symbol, or an image, or
    a representation, or a manifestation of
    a goddess who lives on some celestial,
    spiritual, unobserved place:
Here in front of me is this goddess herself.
Warmed and lit by her, and eating food
    cooked through her,
I will sit, and know her here, and thank her
    for this wonder.

We gather at the fire and the fire draws
    us in
and holds us in her arms.
She speaks the words our hearts, our hearts
    must hear.
that ever where she is, we are safe,
safe from fear.

*[With an offering of food]*

We eat together, home's center,
with the same food on our tables.
It's nice to eat with a friend.

Lady who sits on the throne of the hearth,
who appears to us in scarlet robes,
with golden fringe:
increase our family's peace with your
  welcome love.

A stove is a hearth,
and the goddess who watches over hearths,
watches over this stove that cooks the food
  of our family
and is the hearth of hospitality:
with the lighting of this oil lamp I bring
  you honor.
I bring you into my heart, a heart that loves
  you.

You are in the shining fire
here in the home's heart.
Stay with me
Stay in our home
And each day I will honor you.

Little fire, I will tend and feed you,
and you will bless me from your vast store.
Red-robed Lady, who is covered most
  gently to preserve your spark,
I, the lady of this house, in the presence of
  my family,
strike this match, this small flame
to cause you to grow on the hearth,
and place this bread, this salt, upon the logs
  that you will also eat,
to warm, to give light, to this home of
  yours.

Purest one,
the season of fires is past,
the warm time is come.
And so I clear your hearth,
and wash it clean,
preparing it to serve as a pure place
when I shall again lay a fire here.

## BRIGID

The home's central point is a glowing fire,
the heart of our home shining brightly.
Brigid, Queen of Fire, bless all of your
  people,
all who dwell in this house.

A new land
A new house:
the same hearth goddess.
Welcome, Brigid;
with you on the hearth, I'm home again.

## DOMOVOI

Old man behind the stove,
here is some bread:
take as much as you want.

Domovoi, you don't have to be content
  with the crumbs that fall when I bake,
because I am giving you this piece of
  bread,
torn from a home-baked loaf,
out of friendship, grandfather.

I place this bread for you, Domovoi, next
  to the stove:
may this home be prosperous,
this family happy,
through your help.

## GABIJA

Dear fire, beloved Gabija, stay with us
here,
in the home where you are loved.
You have everything you could need here:
this food, this milk, this bowl of water to
keep dirt away,
the pleasant conversation of your family to
listen to.
Rest comfortably here in your bed, and
share your blessings around.


I light this fire.
I call you, Gabija, to send our offerings to
the gods,
to the goddesses.
We promise you we are pure,
fit to come before you, purest one.
Here is today's first offering
of food that will be part of your feast to
come.
Bless us, then, as we begin our rites.


So pure, so clean, so powerful,
Gabija sits in our house's center.
In token of her purity, greatest of what is,
I place this bowl of water for her to wash
with,
although that is unnecessary.
Salt and food to you, as is right,
Holy Gabija, whom it is right to praise.

## VESTA

Vesta, eat what is offered to you and
transform it, as food is transformed,
into blessings for me, and for all my
household.

## WESTYĀ

Your moving flames are my home's still
center,
the many tongues, your tongue, speaking
silence.
I will sit here and listen.
Lukipotyā. [Shining Lady]


The next four prayers can be said each
time you light a fire in a fireplace, but they
are just as good for lighting a pilot light
when you move into a new home. With
"wood" changed to "oil," the first prayer
is equally good for an oil lamp.


The fire that burns on my hearth is the very
heart of my home.
By feeding the fire with wood and with
air, I am feeding my home with what it
needs most.
I give you these things, fire on my hearth
and more gifts will follow as we live our
lives together.


I light a fire on my family's hearth and
praise the gods of our home.
I burn incense to the High Ones and pour
out libations to the Ancestors.
Hear my words, see me as I perform the
rites, receive the gifts I offer to you.


See, here I stand,
with flame in my hand.
The fire is laid before me.
Everything is prepared.
The house stands about me.
Everything is prepared.

See, here I stand,
with flame in my hand.
The heart of the home
is about to be lit.
The house is about to live.
Bright Goddess,
Queen of the Hearth,
The fire that will warm us,
The fire that will cook our food,
The fire that will light our homes.
You are the Queen of the Home
and I am your priestess/priest.
I light the heart of the home.
I awaken the house to life.

I place you here in the center of my house:
be the navel about which all turns;
be my home the world you support.
With your warmth enliven the house.
With your warmth enliven those who live
    in the house.
With your warmth enliven those to whom
    hospitality is given in the house.
Be, then, the very power by which
    hospitality is given,
linking those who live here with the greater
    community.
Be, then, not only the center of the house
but its connection with that which is
    outside the house.

Be the one we face and the one who faces
    others.
I place you here in the center of my house,
and I will worship you here.

## *The House*

Enter [my/our] home, and find your own,
for the old ways are kept here
and hospitality is a law all are proud to
    honor.[1]

Goddess of the hearth, beat strong and pure
    in the heart of my home.
Lord of the threshold, keep vigilant guard
    over the entrance to my home.
Spirits of the land, keep watch throughout
    the yard of my home.
God of the borders, stand ready to repulse
    all disorder from my home.

---

1    In saying this blessing, a person is taking on the role
of the gods themselves and honoring them with right actions. It is a good blessing to inscribe on a plaque and hang
by your door. Of course, you must live up to it.

# The God and the Goddess

Wicca is the most popular form of neo-Paganism. In its most basic form, Wicca has two deities—the God and the Goddess—all of the other deities being considered manifestations of them. In some versions of Wicca, the other deities are believed to have their own existence, but the God and Goddess are still seen as having the qualities of all the deities. The Wiccan God is associated with the Sun and sky, thought of as dying and reborn with the year, and often called "All Father." The Goddess is the "All Mother" and is linked with both the Earth and the Moon.

## THE GOD AND THE GODDESS

May the pillars of this home stand as erect
    and faithful as the phallus of the God.
May its floors support it as faithfully as the
    wide-extending body of the Goddess.
May we, those who dwell in this house,
continually receive blessings from the
    presence of the God and Goddess.

## BAST

Come out of your desert, perfumed Bast,
and into my home, where you will be
    honored,
here receive offerings of beer and of milk,
you who watch over many children.

## CLOACINA

Cloacina, who has received the leavings of
    my offerings,
here is your own offering of sweet red
    wine
to thank you for keeping our pipes clear to
    carry away our sewage,
and bring us fresh water
for cooking, for cleaning, for drinking.
Cloacina, without you this would be a sad
    house indeed.

Keep my home healthy, Cloacina;
dispose of waste and dirt through your
    pipes.

For now, though, what will flow through
    you is this poured wine.

Cloacina, to you these leavings,
and to you this fresh wine:
your share and your due.

## HERMES

Closely have I read,
and often,
of how you stole Apollo's cattle,
and by clever stratagem sought to hide the
    deed
and avoid your guilt,
becoming thereby the god of thieves.
Trickster, I ask you to turn your trickery
    against those selfsame thieves,
and defeat the aims of those who would
    despoil this house.
Hermes, I praise your intelligence, that will
    ever find a way in,
and ask that it be just as effective in
    keeping burglars out.

Hermes Kleptōn, who protects thieves,
instead guard my property from thieves.
Even as you support the Cosmic Order,
you, herald of Zeus who enforces divine
    law,
you, god closest to men,
enforce the little order of human law,

the way of mortals,
and the order smaller yet of this home,
my little cosmos,
and preserve it inviolate from intruders
    with burglary on their minds.
Hermes, god of thieves, this time protect
    against thieves,
and send them on their way with no gain.

## Lug

May those who come to my home leave
    with knives well greased,
their breath smelling of beer.
May I be openhanded and generous, a good
    host,
Lug, true king who restores and maintains
    society's order.

## Ancestors at the Shrine

Ancestors,
be present in our shrine.
Watch over us, your children,
giving wisdom and guidance when needed,
and linking us together.

Here in this home, the Ancestors are thick
    about us,
the Dead are thick about us,
but we who live in their midst are
    ourselves living,
and when we think of them, remembering
    them with a child's fondness,
they live, too, and we live together happily.

I have chanted your names each Samhain
    as is my duty.
I have offered thanksgiving gifts for the
    births of my children, as is only right.
I have not forgotten where I came from,
    and have kept the old ways, as is only
    proper.
I therefore turn in confidence to you, spirits
    of my Ancestors,
and ask your protection for my family and
    all its property.

Old Ones who grace our shrine,
who grace our line,
who grace our lives:
we honor you with right living,
making you proud of us;
the best offering you could receive.
But today a small offering, a token.

## House Spirits

Be under the protection of the Hearth,
House Spirits:
We will offer to you at times.

May the Spirits of the wood and minerals
    that make up this house
live well, live honored lives.
Aware of your presence, we place
    ourselves under your protection with
    this offering,
and promise more in the future.

*Chapter 10*

# CALLINGS

Callings serve two purposes. First, they do just what the name implies: they call deities, letting them know we have need of them. Pagan deities aren't omnipresent; they take part in the world, rather than stand outside it. They are, thus, subject to limitations. If we want their presence, we have to call them, like children calling for their parents in the night. The demand is based on love, and parents respond to it.

There is also an element of responsibility at work here. Parents are responsible for their children, and so will respond to their calls. The gods know that they have more power than we do, and this gives them a certain responsibility. They'll help us, because they know it's right for them to do so.

Second, callings prepare us to receive the deities. They set up a relationship through which the gods may come to us. And they prepare us so that, when the gods come, we will know them.

Callings do not, however, force the deities to come. Prayers do not invoke with all-powerful names. They reach out and ask the gods to reach back.

Sometimes, the best way to call a deity is simply to keep silent and let the deity arrive. And if prayer is a conversation with divine beings, it is only right that we should occasionally let them speak, too.

We lift our hands.
We lift our voices.
With words and gifts, we offer to the gods,
calling them here.

Come share some time with me,
be my companion, my guest, my welcome
    visitor,
and I will play the gracious host to you, my
    friend.

Scary, huh, their presence?
Be brave
Hold fast
And face them proudly on your feet when
    they come
And come they will
when we call.

Gathered here, with the gods all around, we have to ask ourselves what they want. The old stories, and the rituals handed down in old books, say clearly that they want gifts. The question is, what gifts? The gods and goddesses are individuals, so they have differing preferences. Some like libations, some like things burnt in fire. What to pour out, what to burn varies as well, so to please them, we will have to learn what each most desires.

With all those differing desires, though, there is one thing they all want: open hands bringing gifts, not begrudgingly but willingly, even eagerly, glad to see them.

May that be what we offer them today.

If I have a patron deity, may I know who
  they are.
If I do not, may one come and make
  themselves known to me.
That is why I'm saying this prayer and
  making these offerings,
as if scattering them for the winds to blow
  to the proper place,
or casting them into the waves to follow
  the currents to where they belong,
into the ears and possession of my patron.
My prayer is to an unknown deity,
but is no less sincere for that.

I who stand before you,
I who come into your presence,
I who am your worshiper,
call out to you,
[Name].

I sit still, that my motion may not hide your
  presence.
I do not speak, that my words may not hide
  your voice.
I will still my thoughts, that my thinking
  might not block your arrival.

Gods of old, long have you waited,
seemingly forgotten and outgrown,
waiting with the patience born of wisdom,
for your children to remember you

and to come to you with open hearts.
Awake, come, that day is here.
Once more we pour libations,
once more the old songs rise,
once more the dance steps are traced,
once more your names are spoken.
Never more will the altars be unattended.
Never again the time of waiting.
Your children look to you once again
and pledge to you their faith.

Hail to you, Mighty Ones of old,
from ancient times till now your splendor
  endures.
We, your children, call out to you again;
as in the childhood of our race, we
  acknowledge our debts.
Deities of light and deities of darkness,
both gods and goddesses: we praise you.
Not forgetting one, not leaving any out,
we send our prayers to all of you.
Listen to our words; you will find them
  sweet.
Your children pray to you here.

*[By "race" I do not mean black or white,
but "species." I use the word simply because
"race" scans better than "species," and
sounds less scientific and more emotional.]*

THE BIG BOOK OF PAGAN PRAYER AND RITUAL

Sitting in anticipation of their coming,
  I open my mind to make their way
  smooth.
May the gods hear what I say and answer
  me, blessing me with their presence.

Accept my hospitality, Holy Ones;
be my guests at this feast.
Renew the ancient bonds,
continually recreated.
As I give, so will you,
for that is how true friends act.
Great company of gods,
I welcome you.

I call to the Holy Ones with open hands
asking that they come, that they grant me
  their presence.
Mighty and Shining Ones, worthy of
  worship,
I stand before you with welcoming words.
Come to me that we might feast together
  again.

With this small flame I send a message—it
  is my burning beacon fire.
May you see it, Shining Ones,
and draw near to me.
Filled with the holy power the gods send to
  those they love
I rise up in ecstasy, taken by them to the
  Land of Blessings.
Fill me, carry me, lift me in glory;
welcome me to your home.

Do you smell this?
Do you smell my incense as the smoke
  goes up in your honor?
I am the one who waits for you,
praising you, even in your absence.
Do not withhold yourself from me,

from one who brings you gifts,
from one who awaits you patiently.

I pour out this libation to you, as has been
  done since ancient times.
Come and accept your due.

May we sing with beauty
that they may hear beauty
and hearing beauty they will come:
they will come in beauty.

Each one we name will hear his name,
each one we name will hear hers.
May each, hearing their name, come.
We call them by their names:
[name deities].

With soundless chant, send your non-voice
  to those
who listen well when we are silent.

I sit in anticipation for those whom I have
  called,
who come to those who call and who wait.

When the drum beats, the gods answer.
When they hear its call, the goddesses
  come.

May all the mysteries that surround me be
  known to me:
I open myself up to them.

A door is opening, there in the air above
  the fire that is burning our offerings.
A gateway is forming, through which
  passes the road of life,
that makes its way for our world to that
  other,
where the gods dwell.

Look, they come; the Spirits are coming,
through the door, the gate, on the road.
Dancing, walking, beautifully moving they
    come,
to fill this sacred space:
everywhere you look, there are Spirits,
everywhere shining.

The dry sound of my rattle cries out my thirst.
I long for the presence of the Ones Who Bless.
What I cannot say with my parched soul,
my rattle speaks for me.
May Those Who Hear, hear this,
my prayer spoken in a rattle's voice,
and may they, hearing, come to quench my
    thirst for them.

I pour this cup:
come to me, [God's name], from your holy
    place.
I place this bread:
come to me, [God's name], from your holy
    place.
Come to the one who offers so faithfully,
and bless me, bless the one who offers
    faithfully,
bless me continually throughout my life.

Listen, I am calling to you,
all of you Holy Ones, calling to you,
all those I worship, calling to you,
sacred, divine, I'm calling to you:
Come to the one who is calling to you.

May this incense rise to the sky
and call the celestial ones here to my rite.

I pick up my drum:
it will be my voice calling to you,
Holy Ones,
a steady beat of praise.

## THE GOD AND THE GODDESS

Shining Goddess, love and support,
Shining God, support and love,
with horns of the crescent appear in the
    sky,
with horns of the stag appear in the field.
Appear in my presence,
before my eyes, in my heart:
God and Goddess, may I know you are
    here.

Come, Horned God, to the sacred space.
Come, Mother Goddess, to the prepared
    circle.
Come among us, we who belong to you,
just as we belong to you.
With joy, welcome!

## THE GOD

We call upon the All-Father:
Come to us!
By the raging wind:
Come to us!
By the blazing fire:
Come to us!
By the surging water:
Come to us!
By the cold, still earth:
Come to us!
By the Spirit of All:
Come to us!
Come to your people:
Come to us!

He it is who appears suddenly; he does not
    give me time to prepare.
And how would I prepare, anyway, against
    one such as him?
Nothing can withstand him, if that be his
    wish:
the victor, inexorably advancing.

Lord of Radiance, I wait for you.
I will not resist.
Come like a blasting wind;
even then I will be here with mind open
   before you,
even then I will be here with heart open
   before you,
even then I will be here with hands open
   before you,
awaiting your coming.

I am here, Lord, beneath your overreaching dome,
calling to you from the world so far below
   you.
I send my words up to you, building a road
   on which you might descend.
See them there, glowing in the air, the
   straight road leading to me.
Come to me, I ask, guiding yourself by my
   prayer,
come without error, and without delay, to
   me.
Between us there is a bond, strengthened
   by the thread of my prayer.
Come to me, who worships you.
Come, answer my prayer.

Tell me, Lord, what your message is for
   me. I have tried to decide for some time
   just what it is that you have to teach
   me. Now, at the end of my resources, I
   finally do what I should have done first:
   ask you yourself. Speak to me, Lord,
   and I will listen.

The Serpent King is stirring within me,
awakening, his fire and force growing.
The raving one awakes, who is spendthrift
   with his power,

breaking through, breaking down, breaking
   apart what is outworn.
Do what you must, thunder and lightning,
but leave behind a newly ordered creation,
an oak growing from the wet ground.

God in the forest, in the branching trees,
God in the city, in the moving crowds,
God within me, in my heart's drumming,
about and inside:
He is there, Hornéd Lord.

From out of deepest forest,
Come, Lord, I call.
Feet not denting the moss,
not cracking sticks,
not rustling leaves.
With silent power come, Horned One,
feet not pierced by jagged rocks,
not slipping crossing smooth stone,
sure-footed come, most-loved king.

Like wildfire consuming brush and trees,
roar into my life, Wild God;
like storm wind between rocks on
   mountain cliffs,
roar into my life, Wild God.
Like waves eroding sand and shingle,
roar into my life, Wild God.
Like lightning bolts striking the high-raised
   oak,
roar into my life, Wild God.
Like blizzard covering the frozen land,
roar into my life, Wild God.
Burn, and storm, and crash, and strike, and
   blow,
roar into my life, Wild God.

From the forests in which you roam:
come, great one, come, Great God.
From the fields in which you dwell,

come, great one, come, Great Lord.
From the mystery in which you dwell,
come, great one, come, Great King.
Great and wonderful,
with overpowering force,
come, Great King, Great Lord, Great God.

## THE GOD AS DEATH

Come, Stern Lord:
Come to us!
Out of the darkness:
Come to us!
By the tempest wind:
Come to us!
By the devouring fire:
Come to us!
By the overwhelming sea:
Come to us!
By the opening earth:
Come to us!
By the Spirit that waits:
Come to us!
Come to your people:
Come to us!

## THE GODDESS

We call on the Great Mother:
Come to us!
By the singing air:
Come to us!
By the dancing fire:
Come to us!
By the ocean water:
Come to us!
By the silent earth:
Come to us!
By the Spirit of All:
Come to us!
Come to your people:
Come to us!

When the Priestess stands in the circle,
filled with the divine Female Power,
she is not the symbol of the Goddess,
she is not wearing the Goddess:
she is the Goddess Herself,
here among us,
here, blessing us with what is only Hers to
    give.
That is why the Priestess is standing here
    in this circle.
It is why she stands in the center and waits
    for the Goddess to come.
Let us wait for her.
Let us sing for her.
Let us sing for the Goddess,
so that seeing us ready she might come.
[singing]
Come to us, Mother,
Oh, come to us here;
Come to us, Goddess,
Oh, come to us here.
[repeat as desired]

I pray to her who is the Mother of All
and ask her presence today.

Mari, Mater, Anna:
I call to you by these ancient names.
I call to you by these names you are known
    by
and ask you to come to me.

Great Mother, help me. I have studied
    your ways for many years now, and
    still you hide yourself from me. I can
    call to you under a multitude of names,
    but still you do not come. I can tell a
    large number of your stories, but still I
    do not know who you are. I have many
    pictures of you, but still I have not seen
    your face. Though I throw out titles and

powers and associations in mad armfuls,
still there is nothing there when the
whirlwind I create has become still. In
that nothing, then, in the quiet after my
storm, I will await you. Come to me,
if such is your will, or do not come to
me, if such is your will. Still I will wait.
What else can I do?

Enter into the body of the priestess, Goddess,
in manifest form, be in our presence.
Display your wisdom in her words;
may what she says be your very speech.
Show your actions in her deeds;
may what she does be your ways.
Through her eyes, gaze on us here;
through her vision, see us before you.
Through our prayers, descend on her here;
through our prayers, descend on her,
    Moon.
Lovely and Mighty, be with us, Goddess.
Be with us, Goddess, in our priestess's
    body.
Fill her here with your very self.

Whether as Isis, Goddess, come to us,
    come to us.
Whether as Demeter, Goddess, come to us,
    come to us.
Whether as Pṛthivi, Goddess, come to us,
    come to us.
Whether as Gaea, Goddess, come to us,
    come to us.
Whether as Ishtar, Goddess, come to us,
    come to us.
Whether as Athena, Goddess, come to us,
    come to us.
Whether as Hera, Goddess, come to us,
    come to us.
Whether as Diana, Goddess, come to us,
    come to us.

Whether as Freyja, Goddess, come to us,
    come to us.
Whether as Epona, Goddess, come to us,
    come to us.
As the Goddess of many names, Goddess,
    come to us, come to us.
By whatever name, Goddess, come to us,
    come to us.
As our Goddess of All, Goddess, come to
    us, come to us.
Come to us, come to us, come to us here.

## THE GODDESS AS DEATH

Come, Dark Mother,
Come to us!
Out of the night, on owl's wings:
Come to us!
By the screeching wind:
Come to us!
By the cleansing fire:
Come to us!
By the absorbing water:
Come to us!
By the covering earth:
Come to us!
By the Spirit that waits:
Come to us!
Come to your people:
Come to us!

## THE ALL-GODS

Hear, All-Gods, these words of ours.
Come, all of you:
there is always room for you,
here and in our hearts.

My words drop into a bottomless well
and reach you,
All-Gods.

My words are nothing with so many given
   you in all time and space.
And so I say them,
speaking myself into that never-ending river:
All-Gods.

All the Gods, we pray to you.
All the Goddesses, we pray to you.
With sweet words,
with ready hearts,
we call you with praise.
Be with us in our rite.
Be with us here today.
Come to us, Holy Ones!
Come to us and give us your blessings.

## AGNI

Do not hide from us, in water or reed,
fire of offering, High Priest Agni.
Be strong on our altar, raised to the gods,
you who are first to receive our offerings.
Lap with your many tongues this butter
   poured into you,
this golden gift, clarified, pure,
into your flames, clear and pure.
Grow strong, grow high, fed by word and
   butter,
increase in strength through our prayers
   today,
words poured out like sweetest butter
in your praises.

## AMATERASU

To my dancing mirror,
reflecting early dawn's glimmers,
come, Amaterasu-ōmikami,
and dance yourself before this worshiper
who comes to you with purified hands,
who prays to you with purified mouth,
to the purest of all,
the Sun who carries all before her.

Come out of your cave, Amaterasu-
   ōmikami,
and see the dance,
and dance yourself, before your mirror.

Don't hide in your cave of clouds,
   Amaterasu,
and deprive our world of your splendor.
Come to the mirror we have prepared,
washing it with clear water.
See, we are clean, too;
nothing is here that would defile.
We are worthy of your presence and eager
   to see you.
Leave your cloud cave and shine for us.

*[There is a little ritual prescribed in this
prayer. The person praying washes themselves. (Japanese deities are real sticklers
for purity and cleanliness.) A mirror is also
washed and set up in a shrine. The worshiper then bows and claps their hands before
praying.]*

## APĄM NAPĀT

High Lord, Apąm Napāt,
come among us.
You who bring peace,
ending strife,
be in our midst.
End all disagreement between us
that we might worship you together,
that we might worship all the Holy Ones
   properly,
in Good Order.

## APOLLO

Apollo of the shining bow,
with hair of flame, with beauty shining,
truth's bright friend and falsehood's foe,
master of both lyre and singing:
Be with me, bring art and grace,

Be with me, bring light and song,
Be with me, bring all that is beautiful,
bring all that is beautiful when you come
    to me.

## Aśvins

Come, Aśvins, in your golden chariot,
to all who require saving
from all dangers around them.
Come to this offering of honey,
most beloved of you.
Come to those who call to you,
most beloved of the gods.

## Brigid

Come to us in the fire on our hearth;
consume the logs gladly.
Come to our home, Brigid of Protection;
consume the logs gladly.

Triple fire shining in the hearth of our home,
Brigid, Healer Brigid, to you our worship,
to you our hearts calling.
Triple flame burning in the hearth of our
    strength,
Brigid, Mighty Brigid, to you our worship,
to you our hearts calling.
Triple blaze leaping in the hearth of our souls,
Brigid, Poet Brigid, to you our worship,
to you our hearts calling
Triple tongue speaking, to you we listen.

## Cernunnos

Be with me, Cernunnos,
whether I am moving or standing still,
whether at home or abroad,
whether at work or at rest.
Be my strength and my counselor,
providing both the judgment to choose the
    right path
and the courage to walk it boldly.

## Cybele

Come, Cybele, come.
Come, Cybele, come.
Come, Cybele; come Cybele,
Come, Cybele, Come.
Hear the tambourine.
Hear the sounding drum.
Hear us as we call you,
come, Cybele, come.
[repeat as desired]

## The Dagda

Dagda Mor, I speak your name,
Emptier of cauldrons, your child calls you:
into the past
through the mists
over the border between our worlds
my words go flying straight to you.
Eochu Ollathair, I speak your name,
Marker of borders, your child calls you:
out of the past
through the mists
over the border between our worlds
travel the trackway, straight to me.
Morrígain mate, hear my words.
Champion eater, receive my gift.

## Dawn

Dawn in my heart,
Maiden who brings hope to those who
    despair;
light to those wrapped in darkness.

## Dievas

Ride from your high-lying land, Dievas,
to we who wait for you,
who wait for your freely giving hands,
who wait for the establishment of justice
    and order that you bring,
who wait eagerly for you to be in our midst

with your all-illumining power.
Come, Dievas, lord of sky;
come, we pray.

## DIONYSOS

Dionysos, Lord of the Vine,
inhabiting spirit of the wine-filled cup,
bring joy to those who come together here.
Bind us together in the brotherhood of the
cup.

Come roaring, with bellows of bulls,
come tearing apart, with blood-bearing
hands,
Dionysos, come, with maenads in your
train,
leopard-riding, come, with claws and teeth.

You who fill your devotees with ecstasy
pouring yourself unreservedly through
their lips,
I ask you for your presence here today
that our gathering might be properly
blessed.

## DIOSKOUROI

Into our presence ride, Dioskouroi,
on white steeds, golden-maned,
sparks from hooves as they strike.
Ride together, side by side,
equal but different,
to those who worship you,
those who pray to you, savior gods,
who watch those who find themselves in
strife.
We have need of you, Zeus's boys:
wherever you are, hear and come.

## DYÉUS PTÉR

May my prayer be the road on which you
come

from your celestial home, Dyéus Ptér.
May my words be food for your shining
horses
as they carry you to me, Dyéus Ptér.
Enter this space, guided by what I speak:
Come to one who is faithful to you,
Come to one who does not neglect his
duties to you,
Come to one who is not stingy with
offerings.
Dyéus Ptér, come to me.

## EARTH MOTHER

Broad-pastured one,
who spreads beneath us,
on whom we walk,
in whom we plant,
from whom grows grass
that feeds our herds.
Mother Earth, to you we call,
to bless our rite with your holy presence.
You who give birth and receive the dead,
The beginning and the end of all.

I called you to this place where you already
are.
Foolish me, to call Earth to earth.
Instead, then, I will turn my mind to you
and remember to see you all around me.

A creature of earth, I call to you, Earth
Mother.
Yet you are here already,
surrounding, supporting,
holding me gently,
so my call is rather to myself,
that I might see you as you really are:
Blesséd, blesséd, most blesséd one,
Holy Mother Earth.

## FREYJA

Come, cat-drawn, Freyja, to me.
Come, word-drawn, Freyja, to me.

## THE GREEN MAN

Through encircling leaves I see your face;
you smile, and hoot, and roar,
as outstretched branches and rising trunk,
and dance along the forest floor.
I hear you, Green Man:
swiftly come.

## GʷOUWINDĀ

Your outstretched enfolding arms offer
    cattle,
pour out rich milk,
that we might, like children, grow in
    prosperity.
Leading cows you come to your
    worshipers,
who, pouring golden butter, come to you.

## HEKATE

You whom even Zeus reveres,
who standing at the crossroads,
where magic dwells,
watch all ways:
be at the center of my life;
may I see through your eyes.

## HEPHAESTUS

Though the gods thought you ugly,
I do not, Hephaestus,
For how can ugliness create such beauty?
Though cast out from heaven
you are welcome in my tools.
Then come, Hephaestus, then come,
and together we will create wonders.

## HORUS

Come, Horus, among us,
striding powerfully,
one foot forward,
ever-arriving:
be here today in our presence,
clearly existent in our midst.

Hawk-headed, come, Horus,
sweeping all that could harm before you,
burning it away with your solar-blessed
    eyes,
that I might worship you in the right way,
as you deserve.

## IRIS

The rainbow is a mystery of fire in water,
Sun through clouds;
since ancient times the bridge between the
    everyday and the divine.
You who proclaim the messages of Zeus,
who proclaim the will of Fate,
fly to us swiftly along the colored ribbon
that reaches from sky to earth.
Iris, come gently that we might gladly hear
    your words.

## ISIS

Come, Winged One, come.
Come, High Throne, come.
Come, Keening Wife, come.
Come, Loving Queen, come.
Come, Isis, come,
Come, Isis, come.

Listen to the sound of the sistrum's call,
calling you to me, Lady of the Throne,
calling to Isis, the World's Loving Queen,
O Mother of Horus, it is you I call,
with rattling music of the sistrum I call.

## KAMI

Kami of this place and this time,
I respect you, so I have come to see and
   praise you,
but not before I have purified myself,
becoming fit to stand in your august
   presence.

## LUG

As lightning strikes down from grey skies,
come among us,
your spear flashing,
Treasure of the north flashing.
True king, Lug,
we call you to be here,
promising to follow your just laws,
as is right.

## MANANNÁN MAC LIR

As I'm sitting on the sand between high
   tide and low tide,
with the cold passing almost unhindered
   through my now wet clothes,
part of me is saying, "What, are you nuts?"
But there's the other part,
the one that's reaching out eagerly,
desperately even,
wanting to see and know you,
to join hands together as friends meeting
   after too long apart.
That's the part that is taking the cold and
   wet and lighting a fire in my soul with it,
warming my freezing body.
You won't come to me unless I set out for
   you.
And we will meet in the middle.
That's why I'm sitting *here*, in the space
   between the land and the sea.
That's the middle, isn't it?
My prayer goes out on the ebbing tide.

May you come to meet me on the return,
riding on the crest of the waves,
crashing into my heart's shores.

May your horses, their manes foam-
   flecked,
their hooves forever crashing onto shore,
carry you constantly into my life,
Manannán mac Lir, wave-rider.

From tearing ocean into welcoming bay,
Come homeward, Sailor, on silver keel.
Cross beacon-guided the shattering shoal,
and gently come, and joyful stay.

From tearing ocean into welcoming bay,
past guardian jetty, guide your boat,
and tie its rope to pillared pier,
and gently come, and joyful stay.

From tearing ocean into welcoming bay,
set foot on land with blessing touch,
and enter home, and sit at hearth.
Come homeward, Sailor; come, Son of Sea:
O gently come, o joyful stay.

As the mist on your ocean, Mac Lir,
dissolves with the touch of the Sun as it
   rises toward its height,
so may all that separates me from the
   presence of the Gods melt away.

I see a man coming toward me,
in a brazen chariot;
the horses that pull it are snorting sea fog.
The green sea to me is a grassy field to
   him,
over which he rides;
the scattered sea foams are flowers about
   his wheels.
Who is this man who rides this way?

Not hard:
It is Manannán, son of Sea,
whose chariot approaches,
the god closest to man.
Clear away the sea's mists, Son of Sea,
that bar the way to the sacred land.
Guide me safely, belled-branch led,
along the sacred path;
guide them, the Holy Ones, with the sound
   of the ringing, to me.

## MARS

I hear you in the shaking of the shields,
in the clatter of the spears,
in the stomping of your priests on the
   ground,
Father Mars.
We call to you who are already here.
May we be aware of your presence.
Awaken this in us who speak your name in
   reverence.

## NUIT

You come in the silence, Nuit,
when space is left open for your infinite
   emptiness.
And so it is that speech, and deeds, and any
   searching won't find you.
Only waiting.
I sit here and wait with openness, with
   longing but no expectation.
Though all else is empty, the longing
   remains.
I hope you will not begrudge me that, and
   will still bring me to you.

Goddess of Infinite Stars,
and of the Infinite Space between them;
of Everything, of Nothing,
of the Nothing that is All.
I call to You from below,

to You above,
and beyond,
and between.
Take me into Your darkness,
bring me to shine as one of Your
   numberless stars.

Long is the hair of the Star Goddess
and long is the night in which I wait for her.
Lost in the expanse of limitless space
containing infinite numbers of stars but
   filled with emptiness.
I cast myself into her measureless
   darkness,
confident that she will come if only I wait.
Though the night may be long, I will still
   wait for her,
offering my patience in sacrifice to win her
   presence.

*[This would work for the Egyptian goddess
Nut, as well. Since the Wiccan Goddess is
sometimes called "Star Goddess," it can even
be used for her.]*

## ODIN

Odin, come, as wanderer come,
to bring wisdom, to bring teaching.
Or, if not, send Hugin and Munin,
to give, through them, swift thought and
   accurate memory.

## PATHWAY GOD

Lord of the Pathway, to you I call;
Lord of the Pathway, I lift my voice to you.
Gate Keeper, Waiting One,
Open the door,
that I might pass through to the land of the
   Gods,
there to be refreshed by the power of the
   Great Ones.

## RHIANNON

On the edge of sight, I can see a wonder:
a woman on a horse walking slowly away,
her Moon-pale steed taking even strides.
If I send swift thoughts racing after her
I cannot overtake her;
her careful steps keep ahead of my
    impetuous racing.
I call out to her:
"Lady, for the sake of the one who loves
    you,
I beg of you, stop."
She comes to a halt and I can approach.
She says, "It would have been better if you
    had done that first."
I remember, and call to her in love,
and wait for her to stop for me.[2]

## SELENE

With your outpouring light do not just
    bathe my outside, Selene;
I offer you the hospitality of myself.
May you find a well-appointed home there.

## SOMA

May he who, pressed out, is life, is power,
May he whose roaring calls us to the ritual,
    to drink,

---

2    This prayer recalls the story of Pwyll, King of Dy-
fed, from the *Mabinogion.* Pwyll sees a wonder: a woman
on a pale horse, riding slowly. He sends messengers on
swift horses to overtake her, but no matter how quickly
they go, she keeps ahead of them, all the while continuing
to move slowly. Finally, Pwyll himself tries to overtake
her, without success. In desperation, he eventually cries
out, "Lady, for the sake of the one you love best, I beg of
you, stop." She stops, stating, "It would have been better
for your horse if you had said that first." The woman is
Rhiannon. In the story, she is a woman, but there is enough
magic about her to make it safe to assume that she was
originally a goddess. There are, in fact, enough parallels to
other stories to suggest strongly that she is a Welsh version
of the Indo-European goddess of sovereignty, the one who
allows kings to rule. (Her name means "Great Queen.")
This makes her one of the most powerful of all goddesses.
I have changed the wording slightly to make the scene
more appropriate for a prayer.

May he, granting gifts, filling us with
    immortality,
May he, king Soma, be praised in this
    prayer.
May he, hearing me, come to join me in
    this rite.
May my words draw him hither.

## SRAOŠA

Sraoša, come, first of the gods,
to me today,
so that, as I sit before the fire of offering
my words may be well formed,
may be beautiful and dear,
may be true,
so that they will greatly please the Shining
    Ones.
You whose body is the speech of prayers
come to me and bind me to proper
    language.

## TELEPINU

If we have angered you in any way,
    Telepinu, we are sorry.
If anything we have done has caused you
    to withdraw, we ask forgiveness.
Without you the land is dry,
without you the grain does not grow,
without you the animals do not multiply,
without you we do not prosper.
Return, we ask, and revivify the land,
make it and all of us and all we own
    fruitful.
Come and smell the cedar oil we pour out!
Come and taste the sesame seed we lay
    out!
Come and anoint yourself with the pure
    olive oil we set up!
Come to us, be happy.
Come to us, calm your anger.
Come to us, still your soul.

Come and remain with us throughout our
days.
Telepinu, do you hear?
Wherever you are, listen to our prayer and
come.

## THOR

Wielder of Mjǫlnir, Mighty Protector,
Enemy of the Midgard Serpent;
Killer of Giants, Crusher of Foes,
Strider across valleys and mountains:
Thor I praise, friend of people,
and call him to my feast.

Enemy of the Midgard Serpent,
who is fated to bring us doom,
come to us with crashing Mjǫlnir,
to protect us from all that would beset us,
from all that would oppose our rites.

## THUNDERBIRD

Come, with thunder flapping in your wings.
Come, with lightning flashing from your
eyes.
Come, with rain clouds carried in your
claws.
Come, greater than falcon.
Come, greater than red-tailed hawk.
Come, greater than buzzard.
Come, greater than eagle.
Come, greater than all that flies.
Come, bright Thunderbird,
Come into our lives.

## UNKNOWN DEITIES

There are gods of all and gods of each.
At this moment, when I don't know whom
to turn to,
gods or men,
I know at least that there is one deity,
or many,

who will hear my prayer and see my need,
and will answer me with blessings.
Though I don't know who receives this
prayer
and this offering,
I know you are mighty and worthy of
worship.
Accept my gifts and overlook my
ignorance.

## VĀC

Each word, you.
Each syllable, you.
Each sound, you.
Each thought of utterance,
you, O Vāc.
May all my spoken words
and even all my unspoken
be you, O Vāc.

## VELNIAS

Velnias, though lord of the dead whom we
separate from,
you are yet a helper to all.
Velnias, although ruler of the dark beneath,
you are yet beautiful to behold.
Velnias, although king of the world
beneath,
you walk freely under Saulė's light.
Velnias, you appear in manifold forms,
as any of the living things that draw their
sustenance in that which grows from
your soil:
appear to us and bless us as we offer freely
and gladly to you.

## VENUS

Venus, rising from the sea,
manifest yourself before me
that I might worship you
that I might praise you

that I might pray to you for love
that will fill my life with happiness.

## ZEUS

I do not ask, as rash Semele did,
to see your true form.
But come in whatever form you wish
to this altar, smoking with incense,
Zeus who hears the suppliant's prayer.

## THE ANCESTORS

From the first self-replicating molecule to
    we who stand here today
has been a long, precarious journey,
the bush of life branching and branching
    again,
with most twigs ending in brittle death, in
    brutal extinction.
Even with all its dead branches lying
    broken on the ground beneath it,
the bush still lives,
connecting our own small twig to all the
    rest.
We are related to all life, with many shared
    ancestors,
going back to that first self-replicating
    molecule,
each with their own wisdom to give us if
    we ask pleasantly.
That's why we are here on this occasion.
We have spoken sweet and kind respectful
    words to you,
the way you deserve.
Come together and join your family
    gathered here.

Ancient Ones, whose realm is the night:
We call to you, we call you here,
and when you come, may we face without
    fright,

the Dead, and death, from whose deep
    land,
we call to you, we call you here,
we call to you here, to come to us.

## EAGLE SPIRIT

Come, Eagle, carrying in your feathers the
    Heavenly Ones, riding to us.

## FOREST SPIRITS

Hidden from me in the forest around me
within each tree, behind each rock,
the Spirits of the wild are gathered,
unseen by people who walk, heavy-footed,
    through their world.
I will sit quietly and wait for you,
leaving you these gifts.

Surrounded by the forest's trees, I am
    surrounded by the Spirits of the forest. I
    sit here, on the needles and leaves, and
    spread my arms in greeting. Come to
    me, if you wish; I hope for your coming.
    I wait here for you, hoping to see you.
    And if you do not come, I will still leave
    these gifts for you, for my hands are not
    closed. My hands are open in generosity
    toward you, they are extended in
    friendship toward you.

## LAND SPIRITS

I see trees, I hear birds, I feel stones and
    dirt against my walking feet;
insects crawl on me or buzz around me,
    trees stand solid, and smaller plants
    bend as I push through.
The earth smells of rotting leaves, and of
    life.
I see and hear and feel and smell so much
    in this forest.

But with my greatest attention I will miss
    you, Spirits, unless you make yourself
    known.
Come to me; if you don't want to be seen
    with my eyes, come in other forms,
or even come in ways I will find hard to
    perceive.
I promise to wait for you with careful
    attention.
Only come.


From the branches of the trees they are
    peering.
From the faces of the stones they are
    looking.
From the surface of the waters they are
    rising.
They are coming here to drink this milk I
    have poured out for them.


On the trail of cornmeal the Spirits come,
    dancing,
their feet not smudging its golden road;
along it they come to those who have
    made it.

Do you hear me, Land Spirits?
I am calling to you.
Here I am, Land Spirits:
Come to me.
Here are gifts for you:
Come and I will give them.
I am calling you, Land Spirits.
Come and talk to me.

Riding the sound of the deep drumming
come to me as I call to you.
Come to the rhythm of the heartfelt
    pounding,
come to me as I call you here.
All of you who inhabit this place
Come to me as I call you here.

*Chapter 11*

# PRAISE

Once you've called the divine beings to you it's time to praise them. Of course, you don't have to wait for them to come. Praising is good any time.

Prayers of praise do just what the name implies: they praise the divine being.

Praise prayers can serve other purposes. First, they can call a deity to us. Praise forms an image in a worshiper's mind through which contact can easily be made and sends out a clear signal to the gods that their presence is desired. Second, they can serve to make us more aware of a deity's presence. The difference here is one of perspective: in the first case, the deity is thought of as not being present, and in the second the deity is already there. That is to say, in the first case, it is the deity who must be reminded, and, in the second, it is the worshiper. A third reason for prayers of praise is that the gods deserve them. It is one of the characteristics of divinity that deities are worthy of praise. It is only fitting that we should offer it. No one who has ever had firsthand experience of a deity will have any trouble understanding what I mean.

The appropriateness of prayers of praise may vary with the deity. For instance, when I am in the presence of Cernunnos, I find that my reaction is one of silent awe, rather than of speech. Nonetheless, I frequently say prayers of praise to him when I wish his presence, falling silent when that is achieved. On the other hand, I find it easy to speak to Brigid; in fact, speaking to her is the easiest way to ensure her presence. Experience and study will teach you what is appropriate for each deity.

Prayers of praise customarily take two forms, both of which may be combined in one prayer. First, they may consist of titles and descriptions strung together. These are particularly difficult to write, because they tend to degenerate into laundry lists. At their best, however, they can lead to ecstasy—for instance, when the person praying is so attached to the deity that the joy of contact comes with each title and accumulates. A list can be carefully constructed so that each title builds on the preceding one, raising awareness a step higher as each name is spoken.

Prayers of praise can also relate the deeds of a deity. I have already mentioned the Homeric Hymns. What we know of the early stories of the Vedic gods comes from the hymns of the Rig Veda. This technique is similar to the listing of titles, which are often simply short references to myths. Indra slew Vṛtra with his vajra, and Thor is "Fenrir's Bane." Myths can also be more clearly related.

From all directions about me, the Spirits
   are praying.
The Spirits of east and south are praying.
The Spirits of west and north are praying.
The Spirits of below and above are
   praying.
The Spirits are praying with me.
We all together are praying to the ancient
   ones.

Looking out at my yard, I see a leaf falling
   from a tree
and I raise a prayer of awe for the gods
who caused such a marvel to be.

How shall I find words that can capture the
   truth?
I am far too bold even to try.
For how many before me have dared this,
   to praise you,
searching themselves for new ways of
   speaking?
If I could find only one phrase that
   expressed a sunset,
or a word for birds' wings, or a sound for
   clouds,
I would be content.
But so many are your wonders and so
   inadequate my small attempts
that I can only hope to have reflected some
   of what you are.
Or perhaps I serve you best when I fall
   silent in your presence.

What is done in the night,
you see it.
What is done in the day,
you see it.
Who can hide from you,
who are found in all things?
Where would we hide from you,

who are found in all things?
Why would we hide from you,
whose love pours out on all things?

I think now of the ancient times, when
   your worship first was established. It
   has been a long time now since your
   worship was celebrated as it should be,
   with processions in the marketplaces,
   with games to unite the scattered tribes,
   with hospitality granted to strangers
   in your name. Throughout the lonely
   times, you have waited patiently, in the
   sure foreknowledge that the night would
   end. See now, on the horizon; the light
   of dawn begins to creep over the edge
   of the world! We need not wait much
   longer before the Sun will rise again
   and shine down once more on a world
   in which your worship is no longer
   neglected.
Through the long night, we have kept your
   faith; in secret or in disguise we have
   performed the sacred acts. Sometimes,
   even unbeknownst to us, we have
   kept ancient lore alive. Now we hope
   to return to the light, to practice your
   ways openly and without fear, drawing
   the thoughts of others to you. In the
   backs of our people's minds, they have
   remembered you, too.

Holy Ones of old, we pray to you!
We who have been faithful pray to you!
Repository of all wisdom,
out of which all others have only a share:
it is to you we look when in need of advice.
The words you speak drop like late
   summer rains,
refreshing after a drought,
awakening the dormant grass.

Again and again I call to you,
again and again you answer me.
Old and Wise Ones, it is you whom I
worship.

This drink pours out, even as your bounty
pours out.
What I do here is only an image of your
greater generosity.

I pour out libations to the ancient High
Ones,
I make my offerings to those who should
be worshiped.

All gods,
all goddesses,
all who are worthy of worship:
hear me.
I remember you in the pouring of this wine.

I face east and I pray,
the Holy Ones I praise:
To the Shining Gods and Goddesses, praise.
To the Wise Ancestors, praise.
To the secretive Nature Spirits, praise.
To the Sacred Ones,
To the Holy Ones,
To the Numinous Ones:
Praise, praise, always praise.

I meditate on your name, chewing it over
and over,
[God's name], [God's name], [God's
name];
with each saying it digs deeper into me,
burrowing a path into my soul,
where it may build a home to dwell
within me,
where you will live,
hearing me when I seek you out,

with no real seeking needed, you already
there.
[God's name], [God's name], [God's
name].

Words fail me in your presence
and at your coming all that is left to me
is wow!

Any or all of the gods
Words fail—I pray,
you come:
Words fail.
Your presence shatters them,
and pushes the pieces away,
too far from me to ever find again.
I don't care.
They have served their purpose:
they were meant to fall before you.
So small a gift for something so great.

## THE GOD AND THE GODDESS

When God and Goddess unite in love,
mystery is born,
and from mystery all things.
Mystery born from mystery born from
mystery:
the Great Mystery:
this is their gift.

Glorious the Sun,
and glorious the day in which it shines.
Glory to the Horned God!
Glorious the Moon,
and glorious the night it brightens.
Glory to the Mother Goddess!
Glory to the Begetter!
Glory to She Who Gives Birth!
Glory to the Great God!
Glory to the Great Goddess!
From all that is, glory!

## THE GOD

God of the In-between,
you I praise,
you who sit at ease in the midst of chaos,
you who sit at ease on the edge of a sword.
Can anyone attain the mastery you show
as you hold your place between life and
    death?
Can anyone rival the poise your presence
    radiates
as you sit in the gateway between past and
    future?
Can anyone sit so still, but be so ready to
    move
at the exact time the moment requires?
Lord who holds death and life equally in
    your hands,
I stand in your presence today and give you
    my praise.

You are a bull, and greatly to be praised,
worthy of sacrifice, Lord of life and death.
You are a ram, and greatly to be praised,
worthy of sacrifice, Lord of life and death.
You are a stallion, and greatly to be praised,
worthy of sacrifice, Lord of life and death.
You are a boar, and greatly to be praised,
worthy of sacrifice, Lord of life and death.
You who are the sacrifice,
You who are the sacrificer,
You who are the Lord of life and death:
Worthy are you, greatly to be praised.[3]

---

3    Although Wicca does not practice literal sacrifice, it
does have a sacrificial theology. The God is not only the lord
of all life; he is also the one who dies with the year, who is cut
down in the fall, to reign in the Otherworld as Lord of Death.
As such, he is the first sacrifice. The line "worthy of sacrifice"
is thus, as I said earlier, ambiguous, meaning both "worthy to
receive sacrifice" and "worthy to be offered in sacrifice." The
animals with which he is identified in this prayer are the four
animals assigned by the Indo-Europeans to the four directions, starting in the east with the bull and moving clockwise.
They were also the animals most desirous as sacrificial offerings. This prayer may also be used as a litany.

You are the hunter.
You are the hunted.
You are the killer.
You are the killed.
Forever going away,
forever coming back,
completing the circle
of life and death.

He is a bull in the field of the gods,
ruling the herd:
worthy of worship, worthy of praise.
He is a stag in the forest of the Spirits,
ruling the wilds:
worthy of worship, worthy of praise.
He is a king in the city of the Ancestors,
ruling the world:
worthy of worship, worthy of praise.
The Lord of forests is the Lord of the city,
king of gods, Spirits, and Ancestors,
king of people in this world and the next:
worthy of worship, worthy of praise.

Hoof and horn and antler tine
Roaring bull and stag divine
Spreading oak and towering pine
Filling bread, inspiring wine:
Praise, and praise, and praise be thine!

Wonder and awe, as I sit in your presence,
you who sit in the gateway,
in this world and in the other,
mediating the power that shines through,
letting pass what I need, and what I can
    use,
holding back in mercy what I cannot.

Seen against the brightness, your dark
  silhouette
is still and sharp and clear.
Sitting fiercely, with perfect intent,
pure in your purpose, source of terror and
  comfort.

A roaring fire, you sit in my heart's center.
A rampaging bull, you tear through my
  soul.
A searing bolt, you cut through my life.
A skirring arrow, you slice me in two.
A standing stone, you are my anchor.

A tall-standing oak is our God,
supporting the worlds on his limbs,
each world ordered according to the
  spreading of his branches.
Into each world, his twigs extend,
bearing the leaves and acorns that are our
  lives.
From what source is this tree nourished?
Where do its roots extend?
Deep within the void they reach
and are fed there from the substance of the
  Goddess.
He makes known her will, giving it form,
from which we might know it and live
  according to its pattern.
Shaper and essence, open my eyes, open
  my ears, open my heart,
that I might perceive the sacred pattern and
  conform my life to it.[4]

---

4    The cosmos envisioned in this prayer is similar to
that of Norse tradition, with the cosmic tree at the center
of the universe fed from the well of Mimir at its feet. I
have changed the Norse ash to an oak because I prefer oak,
but the other differences are a result of the duotheism of
Wicca. The well becomes the Goddess herself, but its role,
both as the source of the tree's nourishment and the pattern
it gives to existence (its wyrd), has not been changed. This
prayer could equally well have been placed in the chapter
on petitionary prayers, but the majority of it is praise, so I
have included it here.

You who wear the antlers:
both beast and man.
You accompanied by stag and dog:
both wild and tame.
You who sit upon the threshold:
both in and out.
You who are the Lord of the in-between:
to you I pray.

Lord of the Shining Sky
who sees all we do.
We praise you.
We sing to you.
We offer to you.
The one who stands high
is worthy of praise.
The one who stands straight
is worthy of praise.
The one who stands stiffly
is worthy of praise.
Mystic Phallus, the Moving One
Mystic Phallus, the Shining One
Mystic Phallus, the Shattering One
Who opens all doors
Who breaks all locks.

## THE GODDESS

Wheels turn
and the seasons turn
and the earth turns
and the stars turn.
The universe turns
and I turn with it.
Queen of the turning,
my face turns toward you in wonder.

She is great and not to be held
because it is her arms that hold.
She is ever-present and not to be seen
because there is nothing to compare her to.
Ride across the plains

and you are on her body.
Climb the mountains
and you climb her breasts.
Go into the ocean
and you are in her very womb.
Mystic Yoni, not to be held.
Mystic Yoni, not to be seen.
Mystic Yoni, only to be loved.
Mystic Yoni, Gift-Giver.
Mystic Yoni, Birth-Giver.

I can't really forget you because my life is
    your living.
If I seem to not remember,
know that that's just my mind and not my
    heart.

You are She, the One without beginning.
You are the Mother of All, Who gives birth
    to the world.
You are the Essence, from Whom all things
    are formed:
Wherever we may look, You will be there.
You are She of many names:
When Your true face is known, all naming
    ceases.
In Your presence all stop in wonder:
All life is a prayer to you.

Are you not in this day, in the light and the
    dark?
Are you not in this month, in the growing
    and the decrease?
Are you not in this year, in the warmth and
    the cold?
Are you not in all these things to which
    you have given birth?
Are you not in all your children, one of
    whom stands here speaking words of
    praise?

Too much everything,
too much owned and done,
too much required of me, owed by me,
has driven me to the presence of the
    Goddess,
where there is never too much.

She is the one who is Lady of all,
and she is the one of whom I would speak,
the one who gives birth and the one who
    brings death,
beginning and end of the course of our
    lives.

You are the cauldron of wisdom,
from which inspiration flows.
You are the broad Earth,
that gives birth to all life.
You are the circling Moon,
ruling the tides of oceans and women.
You are the endless night sky,
filled with numberless stars.
You are a grove of birch trees,
shining in the forest deeps.
You are the Mother of us all,
and we look to you in wonder and awe.

In the dark night sky,
the stars are shining
jewels on the body
of the goddess of night.

She walked the path that descends to death;
herself still living, she braved the journey
and brought rebirth to those beyond hope
dwelling in the coldest regions,
living in the halls of Earth.
Facing Death boldly, she led him to love
and taught him the secrets that only she
    knew.

It was her great courage that taught us to
    dare
and her example that we should follow
in the heart of trouble that may beset us.[5]

I speak of she who is beyond comparison,
the greatest of mothers
who gave birth to all wonders.
To us, you are Mother,
and to everything else.
The Mother of friends and the Mother of
    foes,
you do not distinguish between your
    children,
but spread your love freely
without judgment or preference.

Here in the center of the turmoil of the city,
I turn my thoughts to her.
Beneath the buildings, deep beneath them,
lies the Earth that is our Mother,
the very body of the Goddess.
She cannot be hidden;
wherever life is found, there she is.
Great Lady, keep me mindful of you
as I walk through the city.

I raise my voice in praise of the Goddess,
remembering the great things she has done:
they are worth reciting.
She is the one from whose fertile womb
    everything we see was born.
They came out from her, ready to be
    ordered.

Not only in the old time did she do this
    wonder, though:
every day is born from between those
    miraculous thighs.
Each moment, each event, is continually
    born from her.
Is this not a miracle?
Is this not worthy of praise?
As continually as you give rise to the
    world,
just as continually will I praise you.

Space was born from you in the time
    before time,
and time itself, and death.
The Dying One was born,
leaping fully armed from your womb,
rising up to order the world.
The waters poured out, to be placed in their
    proper locations,
and solid ground was born, to support their
    weight,
to be the cup of their encircling border.
The directions were placed, each where it
    belonged.
And life itself was born, the unpredictable,
always yet going where it belongs.
Last of all, and most unpredictable,
your youngest children, we were born,
not always knowing where we belong.
And now I wish to praise the Mother,
who made these things to be,
the source of existence, granter of life.
You to whom we all belong,
you who know the way we should go,
I praise you with my words,
I hold you in my heart.

She it is who puts the prayers in my mouth,
and she to whom I speak them.
They come from her, arise in me,

---

5    This prayer refers to the legend of the descent of
the Goddess in Gardnerian Wicca, in which the Goddess
goes to the land of the dead and confronts the god of the
dead. She then becomes queen of that land and brings rebirth to its inhabitants. This prayer is especially appropriate for times of despair. It could, for instance, be recited
at a funeral. The Goddess brought rebirth to the spirits in
the Otherworld; she will bring it to us. She, herself, went
through darkness; she will bring us through it as well.

and return again to her,
so that my praying is a part of her eternal
    cycle;
and when I pray, I take the part she has laid
    out for me.
When I pray, it is her words I pray;
when I sing, it is her song;
when I act, it is her deeds I do.
I cannot step outside the way she has laid
    out,
for there is nowhere outside to step.
Ground of being, you contain all within
    you,
both that which acts and that which is acted
    upon.
Nowhere is there anything that does not
    arise in you.
Nothing is there that does not praise you by
    its existence.

I send out words in praise of the Goddess,
from whom all worlds flow.
Mystery of mysteries, this continual
    creation,
like a fountain forever bubbling up from
    the Earth's darkness,
she is a cup that is never empty.
Generous One, eternally giving gifts,
I pray to you, I praise you,
I remember you throughout my day.


Goddess of growing things,
of warm and moist earth,
of soil-piercing shoots:
praised in all lands,
praised through all ages,
praised by all peoples,
praised with rites of life.
Mother of All Tribes,
of men and women both,
of beasts and plants and people:

praised in all lands,
praised through all ages,
praised by all peoples,
praised with rites of life.
Queen of all countries,
of crafts and industry,
of poets and of priests:
praised in all lands,
praised through all ages,
praised by all peoples,
praised with rites of life.

A lioness protecting her young,
you rage when aroused.
Nothing stands before you,
no troubles can resist you,
no enemies defeat you.
A roaring in the distance announces your
    arrival,
scattering the dealers of cares.
You shake the Earth beneath their feet,
upsetting all their plans.

Wheat for you, Mother of Grain.
Barley for you, Mother of Grain.
Maize for you, Mother of Grain.
I scatter them for you, Mother of Grain:
a tribute to your well-famed generosity.

## THE ALL-GODS

I praise every god in my daily prayers,
leaving not a single one out.
The universe does not exclude any of them,
    so how can I?
Praise, praise, to the infinite number of
    Blessed Ones.
Praise, praise, let there be praise of them
    all.

[This makes a good prayer for the beginning
or the end of the day.]

If I try, All-Gods, can I understand *one* of
   you?
No chance.
Understand *two* of you?
Calculations can't even begin.
Understand *all* of you?
A better chance, since my understanding
   collapses in the effort, and you pour into
   the gaps,
filling me with you, who understand
   yourself completely.
Maybe even then I can't say that I
   understand you,
but at least I'm where the understanding is
   going on.

Beyond all imagining is the glory of the
   gods.
Beyond all imagining is the power of the
   gods.
Beyond all imagining is the being of the
   gods.
So I stand here and imagine the best I can.

If at any time in my prayers I have omitted
   any of you,
I pour out these words,
All the gods who are.

Fill it as I might with statues, All-Gods,
my shrine could never contain images of
   every one of you.
That would take a shrine the size of a
   universe.
But isn't that what this universe is?

I'd planned to ask you something,
but now that you're here—

When I try to understand you, I have
   to wonder if it is even possible; the

mortal knowing the immortal, the small
containing the large. I know, though,
that that's not actually your wish. I
don't think you completely understand
*me* either, and want only to stand in
relationship to me. I'll try to please you,
and seek uncomprehending friendship,
All-Gods.

Infinite in number,
Mind-boggling to conceive:
Only a few of you enter my life
and for that I am glad.
As each comes to me I will do them honor
as the Order impels.

## AGNI

Here in this world
There in the air
There above the sky
Agni burns as priest.

Fire is born from waters,
who lovingly enclose him,
feeding him like butter.

*[With an offering of ghee]*

The shining rivers flow for Agni.
Three streams of gold feed him.
Fed, he bears on his back our words
and, rising, brings them to the gods.
First of the gods, rightly given the first,
he carries them into the highest of heavens.

## AIRYAMAN

If man and woman come together in
   marriage,
be pleased, Airyaman.
If those who suffer are brought to healing,
be pleased, Airyaman.

If people live in peace,
be pleased, Airyaman.
By rightful order,
be pleased, Airyaman.

## AMATERASU

Amaterasu-ōmikami, through purifying
  myself
I am polishing your mirror.
Amaterasu-ōmikami, through praying to
  you
I am polishing your mirror.
Amaterasu-ōmikami, through dancing
  gracefully before you
I am polishing your mirror.
Amaterasu-ōmikami, through acting with
  beauty
I am polishing your mirror.
For you are the beautiful maiden who
  shines, pure,
in the day sky,
in which your mirror shines.

## APĀM NAPĀT

Apām Napāt, shining like gold in the
  depths of the sea,
like your maidens I would protect you,
keeping clear your light.
And so I pour out water before you,
I pour out ghee on your fire,
to enliven and brighten you,
to quench your thirst and your hunger.
And for those who surround you with their
  dancing, power these
balls of rice,
that they might better mother you.
Child of the Waters,
with these gifts to you and yours I come
  before you.
Hear my praise, worthy one!

## APHRODITE

See her, rising from the foam,
stepping onto land at the ocean's edge,
most beautiful of all that live in both,
and more beautiful than all in the land
  above:
Aphrodite, goddess of beauty and love.

## APOLLO

I pray to the one whose arrows bring health
  and illness,
to Apollo the beautiful one.
From your lyre come tunes of harmonious
  enchantment,
and I listen enraptured,
sweet-singing Apollo.

When your arrows pierce my soul, Straight
  Shooter,
may it be only to kill any falsehoods there.
Your music is true, Apollo.

## ARTIO

Artio, lady of bears,
you dwell not in the wild but in the city,
protecting it from outside dangers,
from those who would come as ravening
  beasts.
You both love and ward off the great
  animals who
might come to us as bears,
strong and dangerous.
But you are the strongest of all,
and ready to aid.

## BRIGID

Brigid who burns on my hearth:
Brigid who burns in my head,
you bring me inspiration,
Brigid who burns on my hearth.

Brigid who burns in my heart,
you bring me healing,
Brigid who burns on my hearth.
Brigid who burns in my hands,
you bring me talent,
Brigid who burns on my hearth.
You bring the burning that gives life.

## CERES

With one hand she blesses, with the other
 she proffers grain,
feeding spirit and body of those who pray
 to her,
Need-provider, Ceres the Grower.

## CERNUNNOS

You sit between, Wearer of Antlers,
between the shining one
and the one who leads us into the dark;
between the one that hunts, friend of men,
and the one who is hunted, the best of prey;
even you are between animal and man.
I praise the great between, where power
 is found,
I praise you, Cernunnos, liminal lord,

Your patience is infinite as you sit in calm:
you don't move, though everyone else does—
It is through your stillness that you are
 everywhere.

Both beast and god,
and neither,
you sit, Cernunnos,
stately,
the door to the Otherworld,
opening,
to those who pray here.

He's laughing at me.

No sound escapes from his mouth,
his eyes don't dance,
and his body is still
(so still).
But have no doubt—he is laughing.
I'm sorry I'm not as perfect as you,
 Cernunnos,
moving without action or changing,
being, in fact, the fate that allows or denies
 all change.
But I promise I'll sit with you,
until someday we will laugh together.
Although still at me.

## THE DAGDA

Prodigious, pot-bellied, pot-emptying god,
Good god, thunder-club armed,
bumptious, bumbling, bumpkin god,
most noble of gods, most noble and best.

## DIANA OF EPHESUS

Mighty in fertilities,
Mighty in cities:
Great is Diana of Ephesus!
She who stands strong,
She who is the Crowned One:
Great is Diana of Ephesus!
Great is she,
worthy of my praises:
Great is she, Diana of Ephesus!
Great is Diana of Ephesus!

## DIEVAS

Dievas has come down from his mountain-
 top home.
Have you seen him?
Keep your eyes open—the next traveler
 you meet might be him,
hiding his royal garb beneath an everyday
 coat.

The next stranger you meet might be him,
hiding his divinity beneath a human ·
    appearance.
The god of fate, establishing order, may be
    right in front of you,
hidden from those who look only at the
    surface.
Pay attention!
The divine is all around.


You are the keeper and establisher of law,
    Dievas,
of order in the cosmos and among your
    people,
ordering the world as Fate requires.
Though some say you are old,
and, indeed, you are the first among the gods,
it is with the power of youth that you draw
    your great sword
to enforce your will,
which is just.

## DYÊUS PTÉR

I stand under the bright sky, shining, clear,
blue, and empty of all except itself,
and praise the Sky Father,
the Shining Sky Father,
Lord of Cosmic Law, enforcer of justice:
you see all that is done;
may my deeds be true.

## EARTH

I will stand only a moment before my
    shrine to bow to your image,
and then I will go outside and place my
    hands on your very self,
a loving caress.


Each step a child's caress.

## FREYR

A friend who is filled with the force of life.
A god who is great with the sweetest grace.
A lord who is laughing with love's strong
    might.
A Healer is Freyr who makes things whole.
And he is the one with wonderful gifts
holding my health with a hand that is
    strong.

## GᵂOUWINDĀ

Your outstretched enfolding arms offer
    cattle,
pour out rich milk,
that we might, like children, grow in
    prosperity.
Leading cows you come to your
    worshipers,
who, pouring golden butter, come to you.

## HEIMDALL

Not content, Son of Nine Mothers,
with standing as warder for the land of the
    gods,
you stand in opposition to the father of the
    Wolf,
the engenderer of the Midgard Serpent,
whom you will slay at Ragnarok, though
    falling yourself.
A son of a giantess, you opposed, and will
    oppose,
that friend of giants who comes sailing
    against the world.
Sprung from the Vanir, you live on the
    edge of the world of the Aesir,
your ears, ever sharp, are constantly on
    guard, pure god, white god, protector of
    the divine,
ever-awake watchful one.

You, like Odin, Father of Men, and your
　　father, too, who possesses the wisdom
　　of runes,
give birth to the races of your children,
　　mankind,
and taught them the runes, that we might
　　be wise,
while seeing yourself that which will
　　come.
Even Thor, the greatest of champions, is
　　awoken to war by your warning.
Truly you are a great divine one,
truly a god high and wise,
who well deserves these words of praise,
and this golden mead, like your golden
　　horse.

## HERMES

Herald of the gods, with herald's staff
　　proceeding,
you who are trusted with the messages of
　　the wisest of immortals,
you are a teacher of those who seek the
　　mysteries,
setting their feet on the way.
In worship I speak these words.

You devised the lyre,
then lightly gave it up,
a peace offering to the god you had
　　wronged.
A little thing for you,
a moment's work,
but the perfect gift for the music god
who sets each in its place,
in proper order,
so that he might restore the order you had
　　violated with your thieving raid.
You created the occasion, and the means
　　for overcoming it:

a wonderful god who can conceive his own
　　overcoming
and then overcome that!
Clever god, with clever mind and hands,
I praise your insight and creativity:
the right thing for the moment is what you
　　bring,
a surprising talent in a god of thieves.

## HERNE

Herne, your antlers fill the sky,
shading out the stars that shine there,
bringing in the darkness your own kind of
　　light,
the light of mysteries, the light that only
　　you can bring,
in your night.

## HESTIA

Though no widow, I praise you, Hestia,
with the pure scent of this incense
I'm burning for you.

## HORUS

The desert burns with heat:
it is *your* heat, Horus.
The wind that blows through it is your
　　breath,
carrying the voice that makes your will
　　known.
Piercing rays falling from the Sun,
from your eye, Horus.
You destroy Set, destroy Apophis,
destroy the enemies of all that love life.
We pray to you not just for doing this,
　　however,
but in honor of your presence,
brightest of the gods.

## INANNA

It is she, Inanna;
she is the great Inanna.
The victor over enemies in war,
It is she, Inanna;
she is the great Inanna.
The victor over barriers to love,
It is she, Inanna;
she is the great Inanna.
The victor over all that opposes us,
It is she, Inanna;
she is the great Inanna.

## INDRA

With a cast of the vajra you killed the
    serpent Vṛtra and the waters erupted,
    lowing with pleasure.

The six-eyed armless one lay prostrate
    after you did this, O Indra.
A soma draught intoxicates you,
you burn with divine flame when you ride
    forth, O Indra,
when you ride against demons,
and all your enemies tremble.

When Indra, mad with soma,
hunted Vṛtra,
his weapon, many-pointed, copper-red,
    flashing,
pierced the limbless one,
set free the cows;
the water gushed out,
the earth grew green.
To Indra these words, Mighty Lord,
of praise.

## IRIS

Seeing her bow across the sky after the rain,
I praise lovely Iris.

## ISIS

Mother, Wife, Mourner, Magician;
Sistrum-Rattler, Revenge-Director,
Ecstasy-Inducer, Love-Inspirer:
Isis.

## LUG

With flashing spear,
which travels with eye-blink speed from
    clouds above,
you strike the earth, Lug,
showing your great power.
With well-cast stone, hurled from your sling,
you put out the baleful eye,
that destroyed all on which it looked.
Gathering gods together,
and goddesses, too,
you formed them together into a
    formidable army
to set against the enemy.
Long-armed one of many skills,
Great are you, to whom I speak these
    words.

## MANANNÁN MAC LIR

Who is it whom we see?
We see a man with silver hair, with silver
    beard, flecked
with salt foam.
We see a man in a cloak of no colors, or is
    it of every color?
When it moves, it hides and reveals;
    sometimes things show through it,
sometimes they ripple as if on their
    surface,
sometimes they fade softly at their edges,
    as if imprinted on fog.
We see a man holding an apple branch:
its fruit is golden, and rings like bells when
    he shakes it.

And its golden-toned music soothes us,
would sing us to sleep if we
listened to it for long.
But he shakes the branch and the apples
sound just until we hear it,
and leaves an ache in our hearts when its
echoes fade.
We see a man who drives a chariot without
reins.
His horses ride sure-footed, wave-maned
across the sea,
which seems a flowered plain beneath the
turning, diamond-flashing wheels.
We see a man who is alternately too bright
for our eyes to bear,
and then compassionate in his gaze.
We see this man. Whom is it we see? That's
easy—we see Manannán, a guide to
those on journeys,
who shows the way where there are no
tracks;
We see a comforter who smooths away
memories that rot the heart.
We see Manannán mac Lir,
Comforter and Guide,
Son of the Sea.

You, coming across the waters with unwet
chariot,
are right to be praised, Manannán mac Lir.
You, casting a spell of forgetful news with
your fog-cloak,
are right to be praised, Manannán mac Lir.
You, grasping a cup of truth, detector of lies,
are right to be praised, Manannán mac Lir.
For all these things,
for all you have done,
for all that you will do to those who look
to you,
it is right to praise you, Manannán mac Lir.
and that is what I do with this prayer.

## MARDUK

Smasher of cities, who slew Kingu and
Tiamat
with his mighty club, with his storm mace,
Marduk I praise.
Overcomer of chaos, Ordainer of cosmos,
Marduk I praise.
Blessed by those who live in the city when
they expect protection,
and by those on the farms when they ask
that the crops prosper,
Marduk I praise.
You who were raised to the kingship by the
gods by right of
your power,
who rule over gods and men,
who bring blessings to those who worship
you,
and withhold them from those who do not
acknowledge you:
Marduk, you I praise.

Marduk is the one who rules the earth;
Marduk is the one who rules the land.
With strong legs he strides across,
with great arms he wields his mace,
with clear mind he rules in wisdom,
with farsighted eyes he sees all things,
with golden mouth he speaks the truth,
with perfect justice he declares the right.
Marduk is the one who is the greatest of
lords,
Marduk is he of whom I speak,
Marduk is he who receives my praise.

## MĒNŌT

Measuring and measuring again,
checking your math over and over,
your reckoning always right,
but you faithfully measuring out the next.
When I doubt,

and hesitate,
and check my calculations for precision,
I am worshiping you, who expect no more
    from me
and no less.

Straight
True
Right
Well-formed and measured.
Clear
Pure
are you, Mḗnōt.

## MERCURY

Clever Mercurius:
God of commerce, God of prosperity,
God of wisdom, god of travel,
Guide of souls:
I offer you my worship.

With quickest feet you make your way,
Mercury, herald of the gods,
bringing their wisdom to the mortal realm.
From an inexhaustible purse you pour out
    wealth
on those in need when they turn to you.
Over those on journeys you watch, a
    protector,
bringing them safely home.
Mercury, holy one, who makes distances
    small,
I send these words across the gulf between
    my world and yours.

## MERCURY AND ROSMERTA

Mercury and Rosmerta,
you both provide;
one through trade,
one through growth;

both bring prosperity
to those who worship them.
Praise to you, with open hands!
Praise to you, with open hands!

## MITRAVARUṆA

Mitravaruṇa,
without you how would we know the Law?
How would we know the Truth?
How would we know the Right?
Without you there would be no way to live
    in the world,
or for each to live with all.
For you are the ruler of Law
without which nothing can be true.
It is through you that everything is joined
    together
to form this beautiful world.

## MOON

It's sweet to rest in the night under the
    Moon,
a queen surrounded by her handmaiden
    stars,
who empties her store of love over my
    head,
white light, silver light, warm light:
this is her gift to me and to all who look
    toward her.
You are in the sky above me, and you are
    in my heart.

Each day of your cycle you rise at a
    different time,
with a different appearance, Moon,
yet each time at just the right moment
and in the right shape.
You are faithful in changing circumstances
and so I know I can depend on you.

## NIGHT

Exactly how many eyes do you have,
    Night?
I keep counting them,
and each time I come up with a different
    number.
However many there are,
when they look down may they find me
    acting virtuously.
Or if they don't, I hope that, seeing what
    *other* people do,
you'll understand.
I lose myself in the wonder of your infinite
    blackness,
and, pierced by the light of your
    unnumbered stars,
rest in the confidence of your mercy.

## NUIT

It is only in the Void that you are found,
manifest in the Nothingness,
the blackness between the stars:
You are seen in their sparkles.
I look up into your star-bedecked darkness,
    Nuit,
and am enfolded by Nothing.
I would ask you for gifts,
but what would you send then?
I ask for Nothing,
the greatest gift of all.

## OGMA

If I wanted to do something really stupid,
would you stop me, Ogma?
Of course not;
your job is to advise and inspire, not
    control.
Thanks.

## PAN

Io Pan, the shout in the hills,
Io Pan, the hooves on the rocks,
Io Pan, the song in the wild:
Io Pan, Io Pan.
Io Pan, the scattering of the flocks,
Io Pan, the singing of the pipes,
Io Pan, the roaring in the fields:
Io Pan, Io Pan.
Io Pan, the goat,
Io Pan, the man,
Io Pan, the god:
Io Pan, Io Pan.

Great Pan, you have not died,
but live always among those who call you,
with prayers, with songs,
with dance and the beaten drum,
we call you,
we worship you,
we celebrate you,
Great Pan, undying.

## THE PARCAE/FATES

Even Zeus the Father follows your
    decisions
when he nods his head "yes,"
or shakes it, disapproving
when he sits in judgment.
Parcae, Fates,
Spinner, Measurer, Cutter of the thread of
    life,
though your decisions may not please me
they are what is right,
allowed even by the King of the gods,
who knows them truly.

## PELE

An old woman or a young one,
but whenever I see you, you are burning as
    flowing magma.

Hair's tresses that when cool and hard still
    burn inside,
forming these islands,
are yours, Pele, clearly so.
Whether I see you sitting on the edge of
    the road,
or in my room,
or even just in my imagination,
I will give you leis,
which aren't as beautiful as you.

Your hair, the twisting ropes of lava;
your eyes, its glow;
your body, the island cooled from the
    volcano's seething:
how could I not worship you, Pele,
how could I not see how you deserve praise?

The lava glow in the distance
tells me you are here, Pele,
mother of islands.
As I walk across the ground you form I
    think of you.

## PERKŪNAS

Far-famed defender of those who suffer,
archer, whose flaming arrows strike the
    ground in spring
and awaken it to life
impregnating it with your shining essence:
you defeat the evil ones
who threaten your worshipers.
You shine from the dark clouds when they
    cover the sky.
You come with rain.

## PERKᵂŪNOS

My voice might not be as loud as yours,
but it comes from my essential being, too.
May it rise through the crash of clouds and
    into your ears, Perkᵂū́nos,

you who obliterate all that stands in your
    way.
May I be filled with the booming
    brightness you hurl and not by my fears.
May my body tremble with the strength of
    your arms and not my weaknesses.
May all I do be with your unfailing
    accuracy and your power that cannot be
    withstood.

## RE-HORAKHTY

The desert burns with heat:
it is *your* heat, Re-Horakhty.
The wind that blows is your breath,
carrying the voice that makes your will
    known.
Piercing rays falling from the Sun,
from your eye, Re-Horakhty.
Destroy Set, destroy Apep,
destroy the enemies of all that love life.
We pray to you not just for doing this,
    however,
but in honor of your presence,
brightest of the gods.

## SARASVATI

Your sitar's tune carries me away,
flowing.
It weaves together the universe in beauty
that is yours.
Your fingers dancing on the strings
speak of truth.
Sarasvati, you enliven all with your song.

## SEA DEITY

In the space between high and low tide,
I build a shrine for you, deity of the sea,
from stone and shell, and seabird's feather,
a beautiful gift to your beautiful self.
Take it when you come,
when your waves rise upon the shore,

with the tide rushing in:
absorb my gift into my body,
and be praised and strengthened by what I
    have created.

## SILVANUS

Silvanus of the woods
is Silvanus of the fields,
protecting each one constantly,
guarding all our lands faithfully.

## STORM GOD

Ruling the storm, he comes in the night,
loosing his axe again and again.
The Bull of Storms comes bellowing,
scattering seed over the Earth.
A wild beast is he, spreading fire and water
    as he rampages.
In his wake he will leave fertile ground.[6]

After the destruction of your thunderbolt,
    the rains come, and the fields grow
    green.
Too often I pray for your demolition of
    obstacles,
and too rarely for a good to replace them.
Even as I pray to you for your raw power,
use it to remove, as well, this weakness of
    mine that separates:
the end from the beginning,
destruction from creation,

---

6    This prayer to the god of storms contains imagery from several traditions. There is Mjǫlnir, the axe of Thor ("thunder"), that returns to his hand when it is thrown so he can throw it again. I've included several aspects of the Vedic Indra: the bull scattering seed (rain), the combination of fire and water (lightning and rain), and the description of this god as a wild beast. The prayer may be used for any storm god, however, such as the Canaanite Ba'al ("Lord") or Gaulish Taranis ("Thunder"). The last line reflects the old belief that the spring's thunderstorms fertilize the fields. This prayer may, therefore, be used as a prayer for rain in spring.

your fire from the life-giving water that
    cools and feeds the earth as you pass by.

With a right arm strong enough to cleave
    universes,
he slew the serpent who thought he could
    destroy the cosmos.
And every day with steadfast dedication to
    the right cause
he renews the battle against disorder with
    his aim never swerving from true.
Axe-Wielder and Bright-Striker:
did you hear me telling your story?

## SUN

If I look too long with unshielded eyes,
they, cut right through by your penetrating
    spears,
will burn into blindness, will bring me to
    dark,
a fate undesired by me, and by *you*.
Your pride in your might deserves to be
    known,
which never with unseeing eyes would
    it be.
Even not looking, then, is worship of you.
Know this, then: averting my eyes, I still
    praise;
I honor with words, though perhaps not my
    gaze.

Now in the sky is the highest flying of
    eagles
He with the eye looks down on us.
See, there he is,
Giver of light.
See, there he is,
Giver of warmth.
Who can hide from his bright spear?
Who can hide from his sharp arrows?
They find prey

They find predator
They find both eater and eaten.
He sees the one who walks on the road
May it be his road we walk on.

Bright One
Blazing One
Flaming One
Shining One
Burning One
Hot One
Revealer of Truth
Shower of the Road
Nothing is seen without your light
but you cannot be seen.
Truth burns our eyes.
We are not strong enough to see it.
We walk it instead.
The straight road leads to you.

The eagle of the Sun rises high
with the burning ball in his claws.
He can see us here.
No one can hide.
When the Sun is high
dishonesty hides away.
No evil can stand the great light.
Secrets are done by the Moon
but the Sun makes everything clear.

Shine your rays, your beams, your light,
on all who need your light, your warmth,
    your presence.
All that lives requires your brightness,
and all that speak owe you their praises:
Sun, who looks on the world below, I
    honor you today.

The earth turns its circles with you as its
    midpoint,

you are at the center of our system of
    planets, moons, asteroids, comets;
your well of gravity holds each in its
    moving place:
you are the one who gives order to your
    dependents.
You do all these things, for you are great,
    Earth's star.
Whether god or nuclear furnace, you
    deserve these words of praise.

## TARANIS

Brightest bull, Taranis;
wheel wielder, Taranis;
soil soaker, Taranis;
serpent slayer, Taranis.

## THOR

With ruddy beard and unwithstandable
    crashing hammer,
you wage unceasing battle against giants
    and serpents,
all of whom fall before you, Thor; even the
    greatest snake of all,
the World-Encircling Serpent, your oldest
    enemy,
will know your hammer bringing it to
    death in the end.
Yet such immense and divine power,
which someone like you could easily wield
    against anyone
according to your whim,
which streams in you as if it were blood,
    suffusing every cell
of your divine body,
urging you on to battle,
that most, gods and men, giants and
    dwarves,
would be unable to rein in;
you can control it, Thunderer.

You take the side of the common folk
    against everyone who tries
to oppress them.
How easy it would be for you to be an
    oppressor yourself, Thor!
But your brusque facade hides a noble
    heart,
and so you know *true* nobility when you
    see it,
nobility not of blood, but of deeds and
    honor.
For fighting on the side of true order I
    praise Thor!

## TVAṢṬṚ

The irresistible weapon, the vajra,
you formed with your maya,
for the greatest of heroes, Indra.
Although it brought death to you at his
    hands,
still you live,
granting skill to all who pray to you,
which is what I do today.

## TÝR

Týr, I thank you for your sacrifice,
a hand given to sustain the world,
even though you knew it would only be for
    a while.
Help me to make sure I don't waste a
    single precious day
for which you gave such a precious gift:
not just your hand,
but the oath that you swore with it,
your honor, your truth.

Putting your head in the mouth of the wolf,
you swore a false oath, god of oaths.
And the jaws closed,
    and severed the hand with which you had
    sworn.

You offered falsehood to save the true,
forestalling the end of the world:
worth the cost.
I praise your sacrifice, just Týr,
and I praise you who made it.

## UṢAS

A maiden with spread-out fingers,
Uṣas rising,
her blessing fingers,
Uṣas smiling;
A maiden baring her breasts,
Uṣas rising,
her rosy breasts,
Uṣas dancing;
A maiden in the east,
Uṣas, praise!

## VELES

Though I live in the light, I praise you
    Veles,
you, in your dark cave.
Yet, from it you send cattle, children of
    earth,
and so even those who live apart from you
    praise you,
as I do today.

## VELNIAS

Velnias, how welcome you are when you
    walk among your people!
How great is your help and how thankful
    we are to you!
Builder of great works for us, we marvel at
    your power!
Even though we draw away from you in
    fear when darkness overwhelms you,
and threatens to encompass us,
yet we praise you whose power is as great
    to bless as it is to harm.

## VIṢṆU

With one step he measured out the earth:
He is Viṣṇu, great in creation.
With one step he measured out the air:
He is Viṣṇu, great in creation.
With one step he measured out the sky:
He is Viṣṇu, great in creation.
With three steps he measured out the three
worlds:
He is Viṣṇu, great in creation.

## WEYLAND

Greatest smith Weyland,
through your skill you, though imprisoned,
won freedom,
your hammer, your anvil victorious,
leaving destruction behind.
It is the power of your creativity I praise
today, not your revenge;
your power to bring into being,
not that to bring death,
for it is powerful and beautiful enough to
cause awe and deserve honor.
And it is for that that I speak, that you may
know of my respect
for your power,
and your ability to bring into being things
useful and lovely.

## WIND

As if shaken from the fingers of my
upraised hands my words scatter
on the wind blowing across oceans,
through the branches of trees,
across long extending steppes,
at last to me, who can feel their touch,
and who sends them on their way again,
more beautiful, I hope, for my song.

## XÁPŌM NÉPŌT

Unkindled water,
hot blood flowing,
twin horses, shining:
he rides within.

## LAND SPIRITS

Praise to the Land Spirits
who watch over these woods,
their beautiful home;
praise and these bright stones:
a beautiful gift for the beautiful ones.

## OCEAN SPIRITS

Each drop of wind-blown salt spray is a
Spirit of the ocean,
among whom I pray,
and to whom I pray.

## RIVER SPIRIT

Crossed by a bridge, your waters are still
as sacred
as when our ancestors slogged across them
at fords.
Perhaps *more* sacred, since they are
undefiled by our muddy stirrings.
Although held aloft, I am still connected,
and still honor you, River Spirit.

## ROCK SPIRIT

Hey, I recognize you, rock.
Do you know *me*?
I'm the one who says "Hi" to you when I
see you.
We can be good friends, you and I.
I'll say "Hi" next time I see you.

## SPIRIT OF A PLACE OR THING

This is small, but it has its Spirit, which I
honor.

## WATER SPIRITS

If I could slide between the raindrops, why
would I want to?
Why avoid the purifying water that runs
over me, carrying untruth away?
Do you know, Water Spirits, that you do
this?
Not just feeding the earth but supporting
truth?
I wouldn't avoid truth, so I don't avoid *you*.

*Chapter 12*

# LITANIES AND MANTRAS

## *Litanies*

There are two types of prayers that do not necessarily fit into the standard formats: litanies and mantras. A litany is a call and response. It is thus appropriate for group practice. One person calls out something, and the others respond. The most common responses are phrases like, "We praise you," "We pray to you," "Bless us." I give responses like these in these litanies, but it's easy enough to make up your own.

It's also pretty easy to make up a litany. Simply research the deity you wish to pray to and learn as much as you can about their attributes. Make a list, and bingo—a litany.

Although litanies are generally group prayers, they can also be used by individuals. The repetition can build to ecstasy. When I use one, I find myself rocking to the rhythm. My whole body prays.

Litanies can have a single leader for the whole prayer, or celebrants can sit in a circle and each person in turn can contribute a call. I don't recommend the latter because instead of concentrating on the litany, celebrants are trying to think of something to say when their turn comes. It's generally better if only one person is so distracted.

## The Goddess

Mother of all,
we praise you, we praise you.
Earth beneath us,
we praise you, we praise you.
Queen of queens,
we praise you, we praise you.
Love of our Lord,
we praise you, we praise you.
Shining lady,
we praise you, we praise you.
Giver of wisdom,
we praise you, we praise you.
Open-handed one,
we praise you, we praise you.

Shield of the people,
we honor you, we praise you, we worship
    you.
Divider of time,
we honor you, we praise you, we worship
    you.
Well of inspiration,
we honor you, we praise you, we worship
    you.
Mother of nations,
we honor you, we praise you, we worship
    you.
Granter of prophecy,
we honor you, we praise you, we worship
    you.
Seeker of lore,
we honor you, we praise you, we worship
    you.
Bestower of sovereignty,
we honor you, we praise you, we worship
    you.
Knower of secrets,
we honor you, we praise you, we worship
    you.
Encompasser of worlds,

we honor you, we praise you, we worship
    you.
Mystery of mysteries,
we honor you, we praise you, we worship
    you.
You who are worthy of honor,
we honor you, we praise you, we worship
    you.
You who are worthy of praise,
we honor you, we praise you, we worship
    you.
You who are worthy of worship,
we honor you, we praise you, we worship
    you.
You who are worthy of honor, praise, and
    worship,
we honor you, we praise you, we worship
    you.
You who are worthy of honor, worthy of
    praise, worthy of worship,
we honor you, we praise you, we worship
    you.

Earth's Queen
blessings to you, bless us.
Ocean mother
blessings to you, bless us.
Star's breath
blessings to you, bless us.
Heart's rest
blessings to you, bless us.
Life's lover
blessings to you, bless us.
Strong teacher
blessings to you, bless us
First wife
blessings to you, bless us
Love's source
blessings to you, bless us.

Who is the one who gives birth to the
  world?
The Goddess is she, the mother of all.
Who is the one who comforts the ailing?
The Goddess is she, the mother of all.
Who is the one who shines in the
  nighttime?
The Goddess is she, the mother of all.
Who is the one who changes yet remains
  the same?
The Goddess is she, the mother of all.
Who is she who extends beneath us?
The Goddess is she, the mother of all.
Who is she who rises above?
The Goddess is she, the mother of all.

## ANIMALS

Birds of the air,
blessings to you.
Fish of the sea,
blessings to you.
Snakes in your holes,
blessings to you.
Deer in the forest,
blessings to you.
Cattle in the fields,
blessings to you.

## NUIT

Queen of Stars
we pray to you.
Mother of All
we pray to you.
Presence of Emptiness
we pray to you.
Nowhere found
we pray to you.
Beautiful Nuit
we pray to you.

## ODIN

We pray to the one who knows the runes
Odin is he, Odin is wise.
We pray to the one who hears memory's
  tales
Odin is he, Odin is wise.
We pray to the one who rescued the mead
Odin is he, Odin is wise.
We pray to the one who hung on the Tree
Odin is he, Odin is wise.
We pray to the one who travels unknown
Odin is he, Odin is wise.
We pray to the one who inspires the poet
Odin is he, Odin is wise.

## THUNOR

Thunor of the heath,
praise to you, Thunderer.
Thunor of the hills,
praise to you, Thunderer.
Thunor of villages and towns,
praise to you, Thunderer.
Thunor of the welcome rain
that enlivens the fields
and causes our fields to grow.
Praise to you, Thunderer.
Praise to you, Thunderer.
Praise to you, Thunderer.
To you, Thunderer, this well-earned praise!

# Mantras

A mantra sums up the essence of a deity, and perhaps a desire of the person praying, in a few lines (four is about the maximum). They are repeated many times. In fact, they can be repeated so often that, after a while, they become automatic, forming a background to your life. It is important that they have a rhythm so that they can do this; an arrhythmic mantra is a distraction, requiring constant attention.

In some religions, such as Hinduism, there is a belief that certain sounds perfectly express certain truths. Repetition of these sounds, especially aloud, evokes their truths, which can be the nature of a divinity. If you accept the belief that sounds have this kind of power, I recommend you research the tradition you are drawn to and find out what mantras it uses. It is unlikely that you will stumble on your own onto one that expresses just what you want it to. In general, however, it is quite possible that the names or titles of deities, in their original language, will function in this way. Even if they don't, they will be effective in other ways.

Mantras serve to keep you constantly aware of the attributes of a deity. The more you repeat a mantra, the deeper an understanding you achieve of that deity's nature. This doesn't always happen in a conscious way. The awareness may percolate in your unconscious for some time; then, all of a sudden, you have an "aha!" experience, a flash of insight comes to you, seemingly from out of nowhere. Then you can return to your mantra with a new outlook.

Repeating a mantra can serve as constant praise. Over and over, you can send out words that recite your deity's deeds. In this way, the deity remains aware of your attention, which is, in itself, a form of praise.

Mantras are especially good for making certain contact with a deity. It can sometimes seem hard to reach the gods. They may be testing you, or you may not be in a state to receive or understand them. If the first is true, a mantra will show just how much you desire contact; if the second, repetition of the mantra will move you into a track along which you may approach the deity.

# Rosaries

A mantra can be used with a rosary. Rosaries are most closely associated with Christianity, but they've been used by a number of other religions as well. I myself have used one for many years as part of my devotions to Nuit, the Thelemic goddess of infinite space. A rosary is simply a number of beads strung together in a circle with some space between them. You keep track of the number of prayers you say by moving your fingers along the beads. There is a large bead or some other marker to tell you when you have gone once around. The exact number of beads (and thus of prayers) is up to you. You can make it appropriate in some way to the deity to whom you are praying or to some aspect of your religious tradition.

For instance, my Nuit rosary has five groups of eleven beads each, each group separated by two slightly larger beads. The numbers five and eleven are significant to Nuit. The total number of small beads is thus fifty-five. The large bead at the end (which has its own prayer) makes fifty-six beads—another significant number. The dividing beads, again with the large bead, number eleven. A Wiccan rosary might have thirteen beads, for the lunar months in a year, or twenty-eight, for the days in a lunar month. A Celtic rosary might be arranged in three groups of nine. And so on.

You don't have to have a physical rosary. I sometimes say my Nuit rosary lying in bed at night, my fingers counting the prayers under my pillow. By tightening one finger at a time, one hand counts out eleven prayers—one for each finger in one direction, one for each back, and a final tightening of the whole hand. My other hand keeps track of how many times I've gone through the cycle of eleven. With a system like this, you can count prayers almost anywhere.

> Watcher on the threshold, guide and guard me.
> [For any gatekeeper deity, such as Janus or Cernunnos.]

> Life's soft fluid, gently welling,
> source and gift to all who live.
> [For the Wiccan Goddess or a river goddess.]

## ANDRASTE

Run before me into battle,
Andraste, protect me in my fight.

## APOLLO

Shaft of reason, light within me.
Clear sight and reason,
open my eyes.

## BA'AL

Ba'al, ride the storm with me.

## BRIGID

The fire of Brigid is the flame in my heart.

## CERNUNNOS

Cernunnos, Lord, guide my way.

Open the way,
open the way,

Cernunnos, Lord,
open the way.

Disputer of passings, opener of gates,
Cernunnos, Lord, guide me through.

## GAṆEŚA

Open the way, Gaṇapati.

## GWYDION

With magic's might, may Gwydion come.

## INANNA

May I descend with Inanna, may I rise with
Inanna.

## ISIS

Isis whose wings support all beings,
be my help, be my supporter.

I call on you Mother, Isis, Queen.

Queen of heaven, bless my home.

## JUPITER
Jupiter, Best and Greatest,
Rule in splendor.

## LUG
Bright shield, bright spear, bright Lug,
   come.

## MA'AT
May no act of mine disturb your feather.

I ask to write truth on the tablet of life.

## MANANNÁN MAC LIR
Over the deeply sounding sea
carry me safely, son of Lir.

Part the mists and guide me through.

## MARDUK
End the chaos, mighty Marduk.

## MARS
Protect my people, ruddy Mars,
with sword upraised be at my side.

Force and fire, strength of arms.

## MIϑRA
Lord of oaths, Miϑra, friend,
keep my feet clearly on the path of the
   right.

Thousand-eyed Miϑra, may I be just.

## ODIN
Mead thief and rune snatcher,
with wisdom endow me.

## OSIRIS
Asar slain and Asar living,
Lord of death and of rebirth.

## PAN
Awaken me, Pan, walker on the edge,
Lord of mad music, god of wild longings.

## PERKŪNAS
My shield and protector, Perkūnas, be.

## QUETZALCOATL
Quetzalcoatl, rescue me.

## RHIANNON
Great Queen Rhiannon, guide and protect
   me.

My guide is Rhiannon as I ride through
   life.

## TARANIS
Taranis, Thunderer, be my protector.

Defeat my foes with flashing flame,
with thunder and lightning, Taranis, lord.

## THOR
Smasher of serpents, empower me, Thor.

## VENUS
Venus of beauty, grant my desire.

Love's dear patron, beauty's queen.

*Chapter 13*

# THANKSGIVINGS AND GRACES

Prayers over food and drink are a special type of thanksgiving prayer. The connection between them is shown quite strongly in the North American harvest festivals that have been given the name "Thanksgiving."

As Pagans, we believe that it's not only the gods we should thank for our food, but the food itself. Our eating is a constant reminder of one of the central mysteries of neo-Paganism, the connection between life and death. Our life depends on the death of our food, so it's only proper that we should thank that food.

Eating is, in fact, a sacrifice. In ancient times, this was made clear, because sacrificed animals were eaten. People shared their animals with the gods and with each other. Eating together draws people together, and eating with the gods brings us closer to them.

Even though we no longer conduct religious sacrifices, we take part in the give and take of life and death. Even today, we can think of the killing required for food (even vegetables die to feed us) as a kind of sacrifice, to be acknowledged to the deities, and to the animal and plant Spirits.

You might want to do this in reverse. Instead of a sacrifice being your food, let your food be a sacrifice. The Romans gave a bit of their food at each meal to the hearth goddess. It wouldn't be a bad idea to offer a bit of yours to her, or to the Ancestors, or to your family's patrons—if not at every meal, then at least regularly.

## Thanksgivings

Thank you, O Mighty Ones,
for all you have done for me.
May I not forget you, though the world
  turn against me.
Though I fall with my enemies rejoicing
  about me,
it will be your presence that will comfort
  me,
and I will still thank you for the
  incomparable rightness of every
  moment.

The gifts the gods give me are many and
  wonderful
and I am grateful to the gods for their
  generosity.
Knowing that it would be wrong to forget
  them,
I lift my voice in thankfulness.
Holy Ones, thank you, for all that you have
  done.

Standing in the presence of the mighty
  gods,
my mind is turned toward all I've been
  given.
I thank them, as is only their due,
for they pour out blessings on all their
  children.

It is only fair to thank you, blessed ones:
You have given me so much;
I give to you from my little.

Sitting in the presence of those who
  deserve praise,
I turn my thoughts to thankfulness,
thinking of the gifts they have granted to
  the world
they love so well.
Intertwined with the world's substance,
the gods have created and sustained,
brought forth and upheld,
wonders beyond humanity's lifetimes'
  imagining.
Out of the multitude of scattered gifts,
I have been witness to only a few.
Yet still I experience awe;
still I am moved to gratitude;
still I approach you with thanks.
Givers of gifts, accept my words as my
  own gift to you in return.

From you have come answers to my
  prayer.
From me come offerings in gratitude.
See what I give you:
a grateful offering with grateful words.

In payment of my vow, I offer [offering] to
  [name of god or Spirit].

Thanks to my patron for my continued
  prosperity,
for my continued health, for my continued
  life.
Continually I will pray to you,
always remembering you.

From you have flowed freely many gifts,
given with no conditions, offered with
  open hands.
Continually you have renewed the world
  with your largesse;

Continually you have brought new
   wonders into being.
I come before you, then, with unnecessary
   gratitude;
no matter what my actions are, yours will
   not change.
What you do is in perfect accord with your
   nature.
I wish to be more like you, to take you as
   my model,
And, though my gifts may be unnecessary
   for you,
they are all too vital for me.
I hold them out to you, then, generous
   ones.
See—I am generous, too.

The circle turns, it turns around,
carrying me with it, and I turn, too.
These wonderful things that came from the
   gods
are being returned to them, to keep the
   turning going.

The balance is kept:
I do not only take,
I also know how to give.

Even if "Thank you" would be enough, I
   offer you this in gratitude for answering
   my prayer.

If I have forgotten your presence today,
   [god's name],
thinking I faced troubles all alone,
forgive me this failing.
Knowing that now, when I had the time to
   stop and think,
I knew that you were there
and that your help made things easier,
made adversities gentler,

slowed my anger
cleared my thinking,
so that my judgments came, as much as is
   possible,
from a peaceful heart.
We can take it for certain, can't we,
   that your help will be needed again
   tomorrow
When I need your help then,
if I don't think of you then,
in the heat of the moment,
please don't hold it against me.
When time comes for reflection, I will
   think of you again with thanks.

## THE GOD AND THE GODDESS

From those into whose hands we place a
   gift we expect words of thanks,
from those to whom we mail one, a thank-
   you note.
Those who don't follow these rules of
   etiquette we call rude.
We don't want you to call us rude, Mother
   and Father,
or to be rude even if you are too polite not
   even to think it,
so we thank you for your many presents,
especially the ones you're giving us now.

## THE GODDESS

The Goddess has given birth to another
   wonder
in this marvelous life of mine.
I will thank her daily for the gift of life
and for all she distributes from her free and
   open hands.

I am burning incense to the Queen of
   Heaven,
a sweet smell on Earth to bring her to
   .mind,

to give her the best of what I have,
as is only her proper share.

## APĀM NAPĀT

For clean water, I am grateful, Apāṃ
　　Napāt,
so I pour out for you some of my own
　　drink.

## APOLLO

I asked to do well, and Apollo gave me
　　even more:
he gave me Excellence.
And with his *arête* I performed,
and all who heard and saw praised me for
　　my skill.
Now I thank you, Apollo, for your part in
　　this,
praise your *arête* so well known
and so welcomed to all who turn to you.
My performance was a hymn of praise
and this prayer one of thanks.

## MITRA

It is proper to set aside a portion of each
　　offering for Mitra,
who brings people together to eat in
　　groups.
So I place this food apart separately,
in its own dish,
to be offered later in my home shrine
for the friend of mankind,
who joins us all in friendship.

## PERKŪNAS

Arrows of flame flash from above,
cast by Perkūnas, champion against
　　enemies.
And I raise my hands in wonder of this
　　beauty,

and that such power can protect us as well
　　as destroy.
This is why I look on you with gratitude,
you who are our champion, our hero.

## SEQUANA

Far from where the river springs,
the ship parts the unstopped river,
at the heart of a city brightly lit,
renowned for art; for beauty and splendor;
your gift to the world, Sequana,
and for this my gift to you.

## TARANIS

Praise to you, Taranis, riding in your
　　wagon from beyond the mountains,
its wheels spraying rain with each turn,
over the waiting, parched land.
Such a gift inspires one in return.
Ours is so little compared to yours, but it's
　　our best, Thunderer,
and given in true gratitude.

## VELES

From your place beneath the bottom of the
　　hill
you send fertility to all the earth,
to crops and cattle,
bringing prosperity to all who rely on it,
and all who rely on them,
not only family but merchants,
and all who rely on *them*,
sending rings of wealth throughout our
　　land.
Though we may at times fear your
　　darkness,
we are wisest when we think on you with
　　respect
and thank you for all that you do.
We send our gratitude to you, then,
for the life and wealth you bring.

## ŽEMYNA

On this holy day I worship dear Žemynėlė,
with poured-out beer,
with the drinking of beer,
first for you, then for us.
Let us drink together:
a gift for you, and then an honoring,
in thanks for your continual giving.

## ANCIENT PLANTS AND ANIMALS SPIRITS

Though you can't really say it's alive,
my car drinks the blood of plants and
    animals that died long ago.
So I thank their spirits for making it
    possible for me to drive to where I will
    buy my own food,
whose spirits I will also thank.

## OCEAN SPIRITS

A perfect feather I found on the beach
I place on the sea's edge for the waves to
    take,
a gift for the Ocean Spirits,
completing the circle.

## WIND SPIRITS

The Spirits are riding on the wind.
Here is a gift for you:
flour, the raw stuff of food,
scattered in the air to be carried away with
    you.

# *Graces*

I am setting a place at my table for the
    High Gods.
Blessed ones, come and eat with me!
I am setting a place at my table for the
    gods of my household.
Blessed ones, come and eat with me!

I am setting a place at my table for the
    Ancestors.
Blessed ones, come and eat with me!
I am setting a place at my table for the
    Land Spirits.
Blessed ones, come and eat with me!
Numinous Ones of Earth and Sky,
eat with me, be my guests.

I invite the Holy Ones to my table.
Come; sit with me, eat and drink with me.
I offer you the hospitality of my home.
You are always welcome here.

We sit down to the table of the gods
where the company of heaven meet,
and we share with them our food.
Blessed ones, be our dining companions!

Upon this food, place your blessings,
Holy Ones.
Our eating of it is a ritual of praise for all
    you have done.

Come, holy gods, and bless this food that
    will feed
my body, through the actions of which you
    are
daily made manifest in the world.

This food is the work of many made
    palpable.
Before eating, it is right to acknowledge
    their labor.
We thank all of these people
and all their protective Spirits.

In the sacrificial fire, I place an offering of
    food:
I send my prayers to the god with my body.
Holy Ones, receive this offering.

Be honored by it, by my life's true
    sacrifice.
The food that I eat is offered to you.

*[Here, the sacrificial fire is the life within us.*
*We place our food on it, and bless the gods*
*with whom we have relationships.]*

I pour out this drink to you, Holy One:
share my good fortune.
I place this food out for you, Holy One:
share my friendship.


How wonderful!
How marvelous!
This food is the gift of the Earth from
    which it grew.
How wonderful!
How marvelous!
This food is the gift of those who drew it
    forth and those who prepared it.
How wonderful!
How marvelous!
This food is the gift of the gods and
    goddesses.
How wonderful!
How marvelous!
We give, in return, our thoughts and
    prayers,
our words and deeds.
A gift for a gift,
with thanks to the givers.
How wonderful!
How marvelous!


Gathered here with family and friends,
    we take time to consciously think of
    everything the Gods deserve to be
    thanked for. In fact, even if they had
    done nothing in this last year but gather
    us to be here with our loved ones, they
    would be deserving of gratitude. For
    this, and for so much else, thank you,

Holy Ones, who respond to our love
    and gifts with those of your own. Your
    people here today will always thank
    you, with sincerity, with mindfulness,
    with daily and true devotion, for all you
    give us.

Blessings and thanks to the earth from
    which this food comes.
Blessings and thanks to the plants and
    animals from which it is formed.
Blessings and thanks to the people who
    brought it forth and prepared it for us
    today.
And blessings and thanks to that One,
Infinite, Mysterious,
lying behind it all and giving it and us our
    being.

This drink, life's changing.
This food, life's form.

Seated across from us,
or to our right or left,
or in their own mysterious sacred way,
may the Gods come to eat with us.

## THE GOD AND THE GODDESS

Though my food may be fast,
may my life be long:
this is my prayer,
God and Goddess.

Models for our lives,
Lady and Lord,
when we eat this food, we are doing as
    you do,
taking part in the chain of life and death.
Bless this food, then,
that it might nourish both body and spirit.

Mother Earth, who gives life to all living
    things,
Lord of the Harvest, who turns them into
    food:
bless, together, this food I am about to eat.
Bless it, Mother; bless it, Lord:
may I eat holy food.

## THE GOD

The grain was thrust into the ground:
it became a baby.
It grew into a plant:
it became a child.
It produced seed:
it became a man.
It was cut down:
it became our bread.
Fertile God, who freely cast the gloried
    seed in the welcoming body of Earth,
we worship you when we eat this bread.

Mixing, joining together.
Slapping against the board, kicking in the
    womb.
Kneading, moving down the birth canal.
Rising, coming into the world.
Baking, passing through the flames.
Eating: he is in us.

The God goes into the grain: the God *is* the
    grain.
He grows as the grain grows, for he is the
    grain.
He is cut down, he is threshed, with the
    grain,
the God who is the grain.
He is ground into flour, which is the God.
Baked from the flour formed from the
    grain,
the bread both contains and is the God:
by eating it we draw the God in,

by consuming it the God becomes part of
    our bodies.
We re-form the threshed and ground God.

## THE ALL-GODS

For all we eat
For all we drink
For all you give:
Thank you, All-Gods.

Blesséd, blesséd, blesséd food,
blesséd may it be;
blesséd, blesséd, blesséd Gods,
may it be blessed in me.

## COW

Thank you, cow,
white, or red, or spotted—of whatever
    kind—for your white milk,
and cheese,
and golden butter,
which you give us for food.

## DIONYSOS [OVER ALCOHOL]

Within this water lurks fire
and so it is a dangerous thing,
where opposites dwell in balance.
But the dangerous spots of in-between
are also the places of power.
God of ecstasy, guide us in the proper use
of this thing of danger and power.
May we use it well for your purposes.

## EARTH MOTHER

Mother Earth, all of this set before us
    comes from you,
coming through the labor of women
    and men,
who planted and harvested,
who bred and butchered,
who preserved and transported,

who brought to market and cooked.
We have worked with you,
co-laborers in this employment.
And now we thank you for the opportunity
to share in love with you this meal.
Here is some of the food, so that we might
   eat together
as loving friends do.

## VEDIC DEITIES

You are fire in water, Agni, in the
   lightning-filled rain.
You are fire in water, Soma, in the
   inspiring plant.
You are fire in water, Apāṃ Napāt, in the
   gold palace.
Fire in water is the source of greatest
   power
and fire in water is what I drink here.

## VESTA

Vesta who cooks our food,
here is your share of the meal,
set aside, to be burned later,
to feed you.

## FOOD SPIRITS

Praise to you, souls of the plants and
   animals whose lives were spent to make
   this food:
May these words turn your deaths into a
   holy sacrifice.

Plants whose lives I take,
animals whose deaths I cause:
here you are remembered,
and your endings are not for nothing.
I tell you this:
your deaths will be transformed into life
and that life will be one of which the gods
   will approve,
one lived in honor of their sacred law.

Come, Spirits of my food,
and feed my life.
We will live our lives together from
   now on,
you living in me.

## GRAIN AND ANIMAL SPIRITS

Grown, gathered, and ground, this grain is
   Earth's gift.
Bred, born, and butchered, this beef is
   Earth's blood.
We who eat do not forget.
Our eating is worship of those whose gift
   and blood this is.

## WATER SPIRITS

Praise to all the Spirits, the gods and
   goddesses, of all the rivers of the world.
This drink is of their waters, filling me
   with them.
Praise and thanks.

# Chapter 14

# CONSECRATIONS AND BLESSINGS

## *Consecrations*

I will paint an eye on the prow of my boat:
may it see its way home to harbor each
  time
I set out on the waves.

See this bowl, you Holy Ones,
as I place it, filled with gifts, on my altar.
You will see it again,
see it, in fact, continually,
because I am dedicating it only for this use,
only as a place for offerings.
I make it holy, as you are holy.

### A DEITY OR DEITIES

When I bless this [tool], may it be with the
  power of [deity/deities].
When I hold it, may it be [him/her/them]
  holding it.
When I use it, may it be with [her/his/their]
  power.
May it be [his/hers/theirs].
May it be mine.

### THE ELEMENTS

I pass this [object] through smoke:
I pass this [object] through smoke:
may it be consecrated by air.

I hold this [object] in the flame:
may it be consecrated by fire.
I sprinkle this [object] with rain:
may it be consecrated by water.
I insert this [object] in the ground:
may it be consecrated by earth.
I blow on this [object] with my breath:
I consecrate it with my life.

Air, look at this carefully.
Remember it so that you'll recognize it
  again next time you see it,
next time you run across it in your sphere
  of influence
or if you have yourself wandered out of it.
You're responsible now.
If the past is a guide, I know you won't
  fail.

Fire, look at this carefully.
Remember it so that you'll recognize it
  again next time you see it,
next time you run across it in your sphere
  of influence
or if you have yourself wandered out of it.
You're responsible now.
If the past is a guide, I know you won't
  fail.

Water, look at this carefully.
Remember it so that you'll recognize it
    again next time you see it,
next time you run across it in your sphere
    of influence
or if you have yourself wandered out of it.
You're responsible now.
If the past is a guide, I know you won't
    fail.

Earth, look at this carefully.
Remember it so that you'll recognize it
    again next time you see it,
next time you run across it in your sphere
    of influence
or if you have yourself wandered out of it.
You're responsible now.
If the past is a guide, I know you won't
    fail.

Air, I place you on one side, where you can
    bless and protect this [object].
Fire, I place you on one side, where you
    can bless and protect this [object].
Water, I place you on one side, where you
    can bless and protect this [object].
Earth, I place you on one side, where you
    can bless and protect this [object].
Spirit, I place you around and in the center,
all through, where you can bless and
    protect this [object],
as if it were yourself.

[Hold object.] I bless you.
[Lift the object up and then back down.] Air
[Rub the object until there is a feeling of
    warmth.] Fire
[Softly stroke the object in a clockwise
    inward spiral.] Water
[Hit object with an open palm, not
    allowing it to bounce back.] Earth

[Hold object in cupped hands and blow on
    it.] Spirit
You are blessed with words and actions.

# Altars and Images

I set up this altar beneath the sky,
a high place on which to place my
    offerings to the High Ones.
I consecrate it with clouds of incense,
sweet smells beloved by the ones to whom
    I dedicate it.

One stone on another I pile,
building an altar on which to light my fire,
which will be for me a sign of the divine
    presence.
My altar rises from the ground,
reaching toward you.
My arms are uplifted,
reaching toward you.
My fire will leap upward,
reaching toward you.
When I pray at this altar,
may my words reach you.

## ASHERAH

I erected this pillar here on the high place.
I raised this altar of unhewn stone.
Now I pour out beer and offer bread
to Asherah, Heaven's Queen,
Queen of the World.

With these words I open the mouth of this
    image of [deity],
calling to [him/her] to enter it,
that I might be in [his/her] very presence.
That [he/she] might speak words of power
    to accomplish my will.

Holy Ones, having placed your images
    here in my shrine,
I purify them and it with cast water.
Holy Ones, having purified your images
    and this shrine,
I establish the invoking power of flame in it.
When it is lit,
when its dancing light illumines you
    and me,
I will know you are here with me.

I place this image in my shrine,
its presence there a sign of your presence
    in my life, [deity].

Washing this image, I am washing this
    deity,
removing the impurities my presence has
    imposed.

Pillar set up in the shrine of my home,
as I anoint you with this sweet-smelling
    oil,
I pray that Asherah enter you,
I pray that your eyes be open,
I pray that you be Asherah,
here in front of me.
Asherah in my shrine,
Asherah, in front of me here in my shrine:
smell this sweetly scented oil with which I
    anoint your body.
Be honored, be powerful, be present before
    me,
Asherah, yourself, in this pillar.

All I need is this pillar
over which to pour libations,
at the base of which to place cakes,
to serve as an image of you, Asherah,
and I will indeed do these things,
your faithful worshiper.

Asherah, I anoint you,
your devoted follower performs this act of
    worship.
Protect the one who does this
and make [his/her] actions prosper,
bringing to fruition all their affairs
under your caring hand.
I stand in your presence
and ask this;
I pray to you,
and it is done.

## Ba'al

Ba'al of the Mountain,
I stand here before you.
I light incense at this stone that I have set
    up for you,
an altar of offering,
this beer that pours over it.

## Bes

Bes, I put your image here,
here above my child's bed.
Here be a faithful protector.
Protect [her/him] as you have the power
    to do.
Though you are small, you are powerful,
powerful to protect.
From nightmares, protect.
From monsters under the bed, protect.
From mosquitoes that come to bite, protect.
I open your mouth:
may you speak protecting words.
Here, with your power, protect.

## Scythian Ares

May this upright sword be your image,
Protector of Soldiers,
when I look at it I know you.
May the offerings I burn in the high fire
    before you

pass through to you and be received well
and inspire protection.

## VENUS

I turn with love to the goddess of love;
I establish her in my home,
building this shrine,
installing this image,
in a place prepared and pure.
Venus, Savior and Victor,
I establish you in my heart,
building a shrine,
installing your image,
in a place prepared and pure.
In return for my love,
given gladly and freely,
bring love into my life
where you are ever praised,
lovely goddess,
goddess of love.

## ZEUS

May this image of Zeus Xenios adorn my
    porch
to welcome strangers to a hospitable home.

# Blessings

A blessing expresses a wish that a deity
look kindly on a person other than the one
praying. It differs from the usual prayer in
that the one praying offers themselves up
as a link between the deity and the person
to be blessed. They stand in, as it were, for
the deity, serving as a mediator.

May this [object] that I put around your
    neck be a sign of the protection and
    concern of [god's name], and as a

constant reminder to you and to others
    of [their/his/her] ever-watchful presence.
I anoint you with oil,
fuel of fire,
burning on your forehead,
to fill you with the fire of life
that will bless you at all times.

They work hard, starting early, these
    sanitation workers,
carting away the garbage,
making our homes and streets beautiful.
Bless them, then, all you gods of health
    and beauty,
and give them the strength to do their job.

## THE GOD AND THE GODDESS

With the love of the God,
be blessed, be blessed.
With the love of the Goddess,
be blessed, be blessed.
With the love of the God and of the
    Goddess,
be blessed, be blessed.
With Their love, may you be blessed,
be blessed, be blessed.

## THE GOD AND THE GODDESS (FOR A CHILD)

Just for a moment, it's not your father
    standing here, but the God.
Just for a moment, it's not your mother
    standing here, but the Goddess.
From past days,
through this day,
to all days:
they are here,
and they are blessing you with all they
    possess.

For all your life, it is your father standing
 here.
For all your life, it is your mother standing
 here.
From past days,
through this day,
to all days:
we are here,
and we are blessing you with all we
 possess.

## THE ELEMENTS

Not a whirlwind, but a cooling breeze.
Not an inferno, but a cheerful hearth.
Not a flood, but a quenching draught.
Not an avalanche, but a ground on which
 to stand.
No dangers from the elements, but
 blessings:
may my words bring this gift to you.

*Chapter 15*

# TIMES OF THE DAY

By praying at the special times of the day, we put ourselves in accord with the daily pattern of time. This assures that, in other ways, we will act in accord with nature. Just as important, it is only right to begin and end the day with thoughts of the gods. They deserve it.

Since, in most neo-Pagan traditions, the Sun is male and a symbol of the God, I have addressed most of the solar prayers to a god. In ancient Pagan religions, however, the Sun was frequently female, and the dawn as well, as shown by the Greek Eos, the Hindu Uṣas, the Roman Aurora, and the Germanic Eostre, all of whose names are related and mean "Rising."

> As comings in and goings out,
> my prayers bracket my day.

> As I walk out today, it is on the deep earth.
> As I go out today, it is under the high sky.
> Holy earth, holy sky, I honor you as I go.

## THE ALL-GODS

Today is not one of the great holy days
that are dedicated to one god or another.
Yet it is still sacred, as all days are,
so on it I praise all the gods,
who deserve honor for every new day.

## ŽEMYNA

I kiss you tenderly,
with love, with affection,
Žemynėlė, as I start my day.

## False Dawn

False dawn after darkness is comforting.
But soon;
Oh, the glory!

False Dawn is not a lie but a promise,
of light to come.
Dawn goddess, in anticipation of you,
    praise.
Sun goddess, in anticipation of you, praise.
Bright day, waiting and ready,
in anticipation of you, praise.

### PLANET VENUS

Morning Star, coming even before dawn,
announcing her coming:
how good to see you after the long night!

I'm up early today,
and wasn't happy about it
until I saw you shining,
Morning Star, Venus.

### UṢAS AND SŪRYA

The Earth rolls forward with silent thunder,
turning toward the Sun in the false dawn.
I stand on the wet grass, anticipating the
    sunrise.
While, far away, at the edge of vision,
the goddess Dawn opens her gates
and the Sun enters the day.
Open your gates wide, youthful one, do not
    hold back.
Open your gates, Uṣas, and let Sūrya stride
    forth,
so the morning prayers might start
and the day's business begin.

## Dawn

I awake with the Sun's light
and dance forth with Dawn.

Dawn, I have seen you come and been
    happy before:
receive this offering.
Sun, I have seen you come and been happy
    before:
receive this offering.
Night, I have seen you come and been
    happy before:
receive this offering from one who holds
    you in high esteem.
I will see you again, and see your
    daughters the stars.
Now is the time to turn toward your sisters,
    Dawn and the Sun,
welcoming them with this well-intentioned
    offering.

Dawn rises in the east
She pulls her cloak behind her
It covers the sky while she pushes away
    night.
Slowly grows in the east the golden flower
Slowly its bud opens
and then, suddenly, surprisingly,
with a flash of golden light,
He is there.
The Sun is born again.
She has raised him again
He is freed from the earth.
He spreads his wings
and climbs into the sky.
His eye looks down
and we look up.
People awake
Cattle awake

Singing birds awake.
Creatures of the night go to sleep
Secrets hide
Deeds are done in the open.
Day begins.

Scatter your welcome light, Dawn,
as freely as a hostess spreading a feast for
   guests.
Place before us the banquet of this day's
   deeds
and we will share it with you.

Sing into being over the horizon,
the rose, the many pinks of your coming,
and waken our minds from their dream-
   bestowed haze.
Open our eyes, ready our ears,
for the thundering flash,
for the sudden shout,
with which the Sun will bound over the
   horizon
through the gates opened by you,
who are welcome to my night-darkened
   soul.

When the sky is red with the
light of the morning,
I lift my hands in a cup to catch your gifts.
That is when the young dancer
goes through the sky
and covers it with her cloak.
The morning is a good time,
a time to think of the day to come.
I stand on the grass
wet with your tears
and think of you.

On the sky's dew rainbow
come swiftly, softly, into my heart, rosy
   maiden,

veiled in pinks,
Dawn.

Do not delay, Dawn, to rise from your rosy
   bed,
to speak the words the Sun wishes spread:
that you come, that he comes behind,
scattering before the sorrows dark has
   spread:
Do not delay, Dawn, do not delay.

The young maiden Dawn is the bringer of
   comfort,
deserving of praise.
To you, lovely one, these words.

Your singing brings the Sun that I need,
but in it I hear that this day you're
   announcing means one less in my life.
Your morning song is my mourning song.
Even though you herald the Sun I find it
   hard to feel affection toward you,
but a goddess who can bring both light and
   death deserves honor.
Take this prayer as such.

## The God

From Mother Night, the God is born,
returning to us, pouring out blessings.
I raise my hands to the newborn babe
Who, even so young, does not hesitate,
but rides forth manfully in his shining
   wheeled chariot.
Rise up on the right path, Lord;
rise up and distribute your light freely
as a king in his hall scatters gold.

## Aušrine

Riding the rainbow, rise in the east,
singing Aušrine.

## Eos

The goddess of dawn sends her maidens
    before her
as heralds to announce the coming of the
    light.
There, in the east, the light increases and
    she appears on the horizon.
Eos, bring the dawn.
Eos, bring the light.
Eos, bring the day.

## Helios

Your eye is creeping over the horizon,
Helios who sees all:
May you see in me only the good.

## Saulė

Standing in the darkness before sunrise we
    wait for you, Saulė;
we wait for your presence, there on the
    world's edge,
to see you dance among your maidens.
Look, we will dance for you,
on this day when your light begins again
    to grow.

## Sun

I set my face toward the eastern horizon
and wait, in the dark, for the coming of
    day.
See, there, he rises, the shining one rises,
and I stand here praising, revering the
    wonder.

On the rim of the world, she is dancing.
In her bright robe, she is dancing.
Young and lovely, she is dancing.
Bringer of vision, she is dancing.
Dance, Sun maiden, into the sky,
bringing the day to those who wait for you.

As the Sun rises, I face his glory,
grateful that the darkness has come to an
    end.
Though darkness is sacred, its soothing a
    gift,
I am a human, a creature of light.
So I face you in thankfulness
and greet your return with praises and
    prayer
and the honor that is due you.

I raise my hands in honor to the Lord of the
    morning,
who rises in glory in the east of the world.
Piercer of darkness, illumine my path as I
    go through my day.
Way-shower, illumine my path as I go
    through my life.

Rise up, rise up, Sun in the east,
while the world turns toward you.
It has turned toward you since its very
    beginning,
in infinite longing, in infinite love.
And I, a child of Earth, take her as my
    exemplar,
and hold my heart out to you in the dawn.

You have returned, O Sun, as I knew you
    would,
for this is your part in the way of things.
You have your role, and you play it well.
I ask that you inspire me to do the same:
to know the right thing to do
and to do it with passion and joy and
    honor.

Praises to you, Sun in the east;
as you are born from the womb of night,
I praise you.

Leap up, leap up,
young god, young warrior,
rise into the sky as into a battle,
dispelling the darkness that has covered the
    world,
putting to flight the fears of the night.

She[7] has given birth to you again;
again you climb the sky,
again you reach for your glory,
again I stand here to praise you.
The sacred path is fulfilled,
things are as they should be.
Rising Sun, herald of the right way,
I praise you!

A rooster heralding the dawn,
I crow my praise to the Sun that rises.
Amazing! Wonderful!
Every morning, again and again:
Amazing! Wonderful!

Hail to you, Sun, rising in the east,
scattering before you the terrors of the
    night
as a cat among pigeons.
No mere cat are you, though:
a young lion, roaring into the sky,
blazing eagerly into the tasks of the day.
Enflame me, young lord;
suit me for the tasks ahead.

As a queen comes into her own,
entering her throne room,
smiling on all who wait there;
just like that, shining lady,
rise.

You give birth to yourself, Mother Sun.
Each day this great Mystery.

Again the boat sails, carrying the Sun.
Again the wagon rolls, carrying the Sun.
Carry it well and true in its well-worn
    path.[8]

On my left and right stand pillars,
those between which the Sun makes his
    entrance.
And I, like Dawn, invite and welcome Him
    into this day.

When you climb heaven's vault,
your hands beyond counting stretch out to
    all living things,
gently shaking them all awake.
"Arise!" you say, "Day is here!"
and rising we lift our hands to yours:
you who are One, shining.

## Uṣas

Receiving the infant, shining in your lap,
from the hands of your dark sister,
send it on its way to look down on those
    who worship well,
on those whose steps it guides by Ṛta.

## Morning

It is my privilege to perform my morning
    prayers.
It is my honor to do what should be done.
As I rise with the morning, fog lifting
    slowly from my mind,
I pray not to forget these truths.

---

7    From a Wiccan point of view, "She" is the Goddess, and the Sun is an image of the God. From a more polytheistic point of view, "She" is the goddess of dawn.

8    Both ship and wagon are seen, in different cultures and sometimes both in one, as the vehicles that carry the Sun through the sky. There is no reason to see these as contradicting each other; Paganism has room for many images.

I accept the gift of this day
and will make it one to be proud of.

I am born again this morning with this
    morning's birth.

## THE GOD AND THE GODDESS

Mother of All, Father of All:
as I go through the day,
keep my eyes open wide.
May I not miss beauty.
May I not miss joy,
May I not miss wonder.
Keep me awake and aware of the world.

## THE GODDESS

This day is one less I have to live.
May I see it instead as a gift,
Goddess of morning.

## THE ALL-GODS

In the morning, everything is new.
The day's blank slate lies before me,
ready for my writing.
May it be words of beauty I write.
May it be deeds of grace I do.
May it be thoughts of joy I think.
All the Holy Ones, listen:
this is what I pray.

My day begins again,
and again, I dedicate myself to the service
    of the gods.
May it be their tasks I perform.

All-Gods, I thank you for guiding my soul
    and the world through the
darkness into light,
and I pray to you, and most of all to [god's
    name], to whom I am especially devoted,

that you be with me today, with blessings
    and protection.

This day, this morning,
I pray to the Old Gods, the gods of my people,
you have given me blessings on so many
    days past:
grant them to me today.
May I, a faithful worshiper,
flourish in happiness in your concern.

"Was it for this I was born?"
asked Marcus Aurelius,
"for lying in bed in the morning?"
Wake me, move me, get me up,
Gods and Goddesses, Holy Ones,
to go about my proper work,
that which I am meant to do.

Waking in the morning, I think of you,
of you, All-Gods,
of whom my last thought was last night
and toward whom my thoughts will turn,
again and again,
as I live this day.

This day, this morning,
I pray to the Old Gods,
the gods of my people.
You have given blessings on so many days
    past:
grant them to me today.
May I, a faithful worshiper,
flourish in happiness in your concern.

All the Kindreds, I ask of you this day:
May I live a life of Quality.
May I think artful thoughts.
May I speak artful words.
May I perform artful deeds.
May I live a good life under your guidance.

## CERNUNNOS

My lord Cernunnos, I offer you my
worship.
Watch over me today as I go about my
affairs:
keep me safe, keep me happy, keep me
healthy.

## GOD OF BEGINNINGS

The tears of the dawn still sparkle on the
grass as I begin my day.
God of beginnings, bless my beginning.
Open paths before me, make easy the way.
May I go through the day with ease
and end it in thankfulness.

## PERKʷŪNOS, MĒNŌT, DYĒUS PTĒR, ALL-GODS

Each action today, yours, Striker.
Each thought today, yours, Measurer.
Each decision today on what is right,
yours, Shining Sky Father.
Each moment, yours, All-Gods, today.

## SUN

As the day wears on, keep before my eyes,
Shower of the Way,
the path of the Holy Ones,
that I may not forget that it is to them that I
have dedicated my life,
so that every action may be an offering to
them.

Bright youth, newly born, I pray to you.
A fresh day has been given to me;
may I be worthy of the gift.

I stand in the morning
and face the east
and greet the Sun
and a new day.

Maybe I'm awake after a poor night of too
little sleep and disturbed dreams,
but as the saying goes, "I may have risen,
but I refuse to shine."
Sun, you have risen, and as always you shine:
and *such* shining!
Spare some shining for *me*,
your heat my blood's warmth,
gently but forcefully get and keep me
moving.
If I can stay alert until noon I can make it
through the rest of the day,
and I'll think of you when you are highest,
most powerful,
and shining with your greatest beauty,
and pray to you with shining words.

I see, Father Sun, in the skylight above,
the blue you have brought.
And, although I have not yet seen you
yourself,
I praise your necessary presence.

New Sun, newly seen, bring new things
into my life;
bring joyous things,
bring love, and life, and laughter.

Although you're blinding me as I drive to
work,
welcome back, Sun; it's good to see you
again.

## THE ANCESTORS

Your blood is my blood,
flowing out of the past, through me, to the
future.
Through my actions, you live.
Guide me, then, in the decisions I face today,
making clear to me the safe path between
obstacles

and keeping me from false steps along the
   way.

*[With "today" in the fourth line changed to
"each day," this may also be used as a New
Year's prayer.]*

Yesterday has gone to the Ancestors.
Today is a new life.
From the Ancestors I ask the continuing
   wisdom of yesterdays
and from the Gods continuing guidance for
   today.

## FOG SPIRITS

Your creation still covers the land, Fog
   Spirits,
woven from water droplets.
Soon it will be burned away by the
   growing Sun,
but for now it is draped over the landscape,
lending its beauty to this in its proper time.
Though it leaves us soon,
tomorrow it will return in its proper time,
lending its beauty to the morning earth.

## FOR A LIE-ABED

I am here to pray long hours after the Sun
   has risen.
While the day began, I was still asleep, still
   walking
in the land of dreams.
Know this, bright Sun, that though I slept,
   you were
still in my heart.
Now, when I am finally awake, I take up
   my daily
responsibilities.
First, though, I will stand here and drink in
   your warmth
and drink in all the light you give so freely
to arm myself for the day's struggles.

# *Noon*

## EARTH

By your slow turning you have brought
   me to this moment when I can feel the
   power of the Sun,
the power of a Lord at his zenith,
a power that warms me and lights my way.
Mother Earth, this is therefore a moment to
   praise not just Him,
and I do, indeed, praise Him for all his
   splendor,
but to praise you as well, for giving me this
   time when he might shine so brightly.

## HELIOS

Helios in the midday sky,
see what I do justly,
nudge me when I act unjustly.
Judge, but gently,
to keep me on the right way.

## SUN

From high above, the Sun looks down,
the witness of all deeds done by the people.
Lord of Truth, guide me in my actions,
so that all that I do might be worthy of
   your gaze.

You have mounted to your throne in the
   roof of heaven,
you have achieved the heights.
In the midpoint of the day, you rule
from the midpoint of the sky.
Lord of Light, I praise you as you shine!

The great shining eye that sees all things
will see that my deeds are done justly.
I place myself under your gaze
at the high point of the day.

Praise to the Sun, at the roof of the world.
Praise to the Sun, at his point of great power.

Look up, look up, at the glorious Sun,
the world calls to me, and says "Look up!"
From high above, I can feel the heat
    descending,
warming me as I walk here below.
I wish to look up, but my eyes are not
    meant for such power.
I will feel the warmth, though,
and thank you, Lord Sun.

Though you are high above, your heat still
    reaches me,
testing my endurance as I work under its
    glare.
Do not give me more testing than I can
    handle,
and do not insult me by giving me less.

Following your course, laid down in
    ancient times,
you have come unerringly to the heights of
    the sky,
there where you can survey the wide Earth
    with no obstruction.
May all on which you gaze be to your liking!
May all below follow its course as well as you!

Hail to you, noontide Sun, high in the
    southern sky.
A king in full power are you,
sitting high in the heavens' throne room.
And I come to you, as a faithful subject,
to ask you to stretch forth your many
    shining hands
and lay them on my head in benediction.

Your blossom fully open, shining.
Your bloom in full beauty, shining.

Your face in full radiance, shining.
See me from on high, Bright Queen,
watch over me, shining.

High noon and a short pause,
and a short gaze at you,
and then a return to my day
as you go on with yours.

They say that dawn is a goddess.
They say that the coming of night is a
    goddess.
I say that noon is a god,
whose disk blesses and shields.
You whose might is irresistible,
unable to be overcome,
look kindly on me, your worshiper.

You, rising in the morning, in all that glory,
seem in my memory to have been a small
    thing beside you,
shining, have risen to your *greatest* glory,
to your greatest height above our land,
there in the south.
Fill the hands that, empty cups, reach for
    you to fill with some small part of that
    glory,
small enough for a human being to handle.
I bring my light-encrusted hands in toward
    my heart,
where they overflow, filling me with those
    captured rays of yours,
filling me with the life that your invincible
    searing, which none can resist,
gives to living things.
Glory; Glory and unimaginable power,
generated by the joining together of the
    very building blocks of the universe,
creating the very building blocks of the
    universe,
radiating in all directions,

until a fraction of it falls on my upturned
    eyes.
And even this tiny piece of all you produce
    is beyond what my eyes can stand:
I see you through a closed-lid curtain.
May you grant me all the insight I can
    stand;
not just in the world you so obviously
    light,
but even in my submerged soul:
illuminate my darkest secrets,
Sun, Lord of Noon.

## Afternoon

### APĄM NAPĀT

Apąm Napāt, in the beginning of the
    afternoon,
as the Sun begins to descend,
keep me, High Lord, from descending to
    darkness as well.

### MIϴRA

As the watch shifts
I pray farewell to Miϑra,
lord of the morning,
and greet Airyaman,
the High Lord who rules the afternoon.

### SUN

Though you dwindle and descend you are
    still worthy of praise.
These words to you, afternoon Sun.

## Workday's End

With the day over, let me rest, Holy Ones.
I have earned this quiet time by my day's
    labors.
Come and share my ease, come and rest
    with me.

Surround me and support me,
be my rest, my peace, my home.

## Rush Hour

You who guide travelers,
slide me through traffic.
You who grant patience,
help me wait calmly.

### SUN

Although you're blinding me as I drive
    home from work,
it's still good to see you, Sun.
We'll drive together again tomorrow.

## Sunset

### AIRYAMAN AND TRIŠTRYA

Airyaman's time draws to an end,
and now begins that of Trištrya.
He will paint the sky with beauty,
with twinkling points of light,
scattered across the heavens,
which we will look upon in awe.

### THE GOD AND THE GODDESS

I look west and fall into the fading light
    that brings rest
to my soul.
Calm, peace, sleep: bring these,
Goddess of the growing night,
God of the dimming light.

### THE ALL-GODS

As night slides in softly, softly, over the
    resting land,
like sunset's rooster I sing the praises of
    the All-Gods,

and of the Sun whose absence will end in
  dawn.

## AMATERASU

A mirror in the sky, shining, flashing,
and dancing when it rises,
and when it is high,
and one last time as it waits on the western
  horizon,
listening to me.
Amaterasu ōmikami, laugh as you hear
  me,
out of delight that you are well
  remembered,
as I pour out this clean water to you,
having purified myself so that I could say
  these words
and make this offering.

## HELIOS

Helios, to you these oats,
to feed your cattle grazing in brilliant
  pastures
under your all-seeing eye.
Seek out for me hidden knowledge,
conveying it to my sleepy mind
when I doze in your warmth.

# Dusk

The young maiden Dusk is the bringer of
  sweet rest,
deserving of praise.
To you, lovely one, these words.

## MOON

With the darkening of the world would
  come a darkening of my soul,
a shadow on my heart, my self,
if I did not know you would be with me,
  Mother Moon,

or if not you,
then your children the stars, their
  unnumbered eyes keeping watch over
  me in the black of night.

## SUN

The ship reaches its haven,
The wagon its home.
Today's journey is over, and all can rest.
Those who have guided the Sun in its
  journey:
Thank you.
May you guide me as well.

Good night, Sun, as you go to sleep;
I will soon enough sleep myself.
We will both wake in the morning
and share another day together.

# Before Sleep

Gods of dreams, goddesses of visions,
guide me on this journey.

## THE GODDESS

Mother of the World's children,
rock me to sleep
and watch my dreams.

Mother, with your calming hands, smooth
  away the worry lines this day has etched
  on my face, my heart, soothing me into
  restoring sleep.

## MANANNÁN MAC LIR

The slow lapping of soft waves on the sand
  lulling me,
your horses carrying me into dreams
where I awake within a world more real.

## MORPHEUS

Protect me while I sleep, Morpheus,
keep my body safe,
bring dreams that teach,
bring dreams that heal,
bring dreams of comfort and peace,
a peace only a god can give.

# Night

## THE ALL-GODS

The world rests beneath night's blanket
and I sit quietly, finally myself at rest.
All day, I have been the one talking;
my time for silence has arrived.
Speak to me, Holy Ones, and I will listen.
Here I am, waiting to hear your words.

The womb of night will give birth to day
when the proper time has passed.
Though I long for day, in my heart I know
that the way things are is done rightly.
Here in the dark, I remember this
and rest in the sure concern of the Holy
  Ones.

## NIGHT

I speak of darkness from out of darkness,
of night from out of night.
Night I praise, the first of all things,
the blackness within which worlds are
  formed.
In the encompassing embrace of the arms
  of night,
everything was held that has existence.
From under the blanket that she lays
  over us,
everything came forth that has existence.
Birthplace of all, to you I pray:
Worthy are you to be praised.

Outward sight subdued,
may inward sight grow,
in the night, in the night,
Sister of Dawn.

The speckled hen comes to brood
and light-filled darkness spreads over the
  earth.
Silver feathers cover her children with
  warmth and softness,
like a blanket she covers them.
With motherly concern she cares for all
  under her.
This is you, Night,
our sweet rescue from the cares of the day.

Since even with the stars shining from your
  body you are still dark,
how can I hope to understand you
  completely, Night?
I have a small light compared to them, and
  I am only one.
If you cover me like a blanket that will do.
What more could you want?

This night is long,
but it will end,
and animals will stir,
and some will go to rest,
and I will set out on my day's business.
But for now I look at the beautiful stars
that shine in the body of Night,
the beautiful Night,
Goddess of promise.

## RĀTRI

Pinks and red, with trails of purple,
is the cloth that Rātri holds
to wrap the Sun safe against the coming dark
to deliver him, a child,
to her sister Dawn.

Black lady, enfold me as well through the
    night;
deliver me safely to the reviving light,
born from you.

Dawn's sister,
praise to your rising!

Rātri, I praise you with as much joy
as I praised your sister, Dawn.
Your appearance is as beautiful,
roses and pinks and reds flung across the sky,
and your gift, sweet rest, as welcome as the
    activity she brings.
You are not forgotten, Night,
and are well loved,
and I welcome your arrival.

## SAULĖ

Lady Saulė, Lady Saulė,
do not tarry long
where you abide, happy,
among your family,
among Dawn, the Planets, and the Stars.
We are your family, too, lovely Mother,
and have need of you as well,
and eagerly await your return.

## STARS

First star of evening, be my first guide
    through darkness,
passing me from one to the rest,
until morning comes.

Stars that light the night, guide me through
    to dawn.

## DARKNESS SPIRITS

Spirits of the darkness, you are my friends;
though the night's blackness stands as a wall,

you will show me the way through,
my guides through shadows,
my protectors from all terrors.

## Insomnia

From the deep emptiness of a sleepless
    night,
my pleas are sent to the gods of sleep.
To the givers of dreams, I call,
to those who come in the night, not as
    dangers,
but as bringers of peace.
Come to me, as I lie alone in the dark.
Slip quietly through the night and place
    your hands on my brow,
soothing me gently until I slide into sleep.

It seems as if the whole world is asleep.
Although I know that isn't true,
Gods of the night, whose worship I keep,
may I join with those who do.

In the stillness of night, I free myself
from the business of the day and seek
the wisdom of the empty.

## Late at Night

### MORPHEUS

Not yet, Morpheus; I still have so many
    things to do.
A little while, and I will accept your
    beautiful gift.
I'm not rejecting it insultingly:
I simply can't afford to be overwhelmed by
    such an amazing present.
Don't worry, though; when I unwrap it,
it'll be that much more appreciated for the
    anticipating
and my gratitude that much more.

*Chapter 16*

# TIMES OF THE MOON

## *Dark Moon*

It will be a dark night indeed,
for, even though the stars give what light
    they can,
it comes from far away, and is scattered
    and spent
when it falls on the Earth.
Where is the light that comes from nearer,
from our own world's companion, our own
    world's sister?
She hides from us tonight.
Tonight, there will be no Moon.
Tonight, we will have no companion to
    guide us through the darkness.
But though we cannot see you, you live in
    our hearts.
Strengthen us in the darkness:
is that not what darkness is for?

This is a night when the Moon is away
    with her lover, the Sun,
and we will not see her, though we wait
    until dawn.
But when dawn does come, she will be
    there,
and if we do not see her with our eyes,
to our hearts she should be visible.
Dark Lady, open our hearts,
keep them aware of you.

Mysterious Darkness, I pray to you,
you who transform want into plenty.
Even as, in your hidden realm, the Moon
    is reborn,
so, too, might hope be reborn in me.
Queen of Darkness, may the night pass
    soon.
Queen of Darkness, preserve me until
    light's return.

With no Moon's light to break the black
    night,
we wait with patience for change to come.
Pure Moon Goddess, change in me what
    changes in you.
Bring me through dark times. Bring me
    rebirth.

A night that is dark,
a time of change,
mystery of mysteries.
During my dark hours, dark ones,
may I glimpse the mystery
and see ahead of me the newly rising
    Moon.

Dark Queen:
from a time that is dark,
bring back light to my world.

Darkness is for silence.
This I know, Dark Moon.
Just a few words of remembrance, then,
and I will keep the silence with you.

Maiden,
You are dark now.
And in the dark, who knows what
    mysteries are enacted?
For these are women's rites,
and I, a man, have my own mysteries.
But I revere them all, and so tonight my
    thoughts are turned to you.
Lady of Renewal,
renew the Earth.
Queen of Darkness, bring in the light.
Black Void, give birth to the dancing
    Maiden within me
and, from her,
Worlds many and wonderful.

I am told by the ways of the Old Ones
that this darkness is a time necessary for
    the winning of wisdom,
for its germination, its growth.
Forgive me my doubt, Moon in your
    darkness,
and inspire in me that same germination,
    that same growth,
that which you yourself possess;
may I, through my knowledge of you,
win wisdom.

With Her gone from my sight, emptying
    the sky,
I, no longer distracted by Her presence
    outside,
and no longer excused,
look within and find Her there,
find Her light in the darkness,

find She who changes and remains.
May I find fullness in the empty.

## New Moon

Chase your Father, little one;
swiftly he sinks and swiftly you follow him.
Grow in strength and in sureness.
Grow into yourself as the month goes by.

Out of the bright sky, as the Sun goes down,
appears the Maiden who rules the darkness.

Slender Crescent
Young Crescent
Beautiful Crescent:
Welcome back, Moon,
transformed in Mystery,
Maiden.

I pray to her, my eyes facing west
at the end of the day,
at the beginning of the month.
You will not be here with us long;
you dance quickly toward the horizon.
While you are still with us, though,
I will look on you with love.
Hope in the west, prophet of return from
    darkness:
you show us it is possible to go from age
    into the shadowland
and emerge, new yet the same.

When I am surrounded by the shadows,
come to me and remind me of this night's
    lesson
I pray to you, who wear the silver crescent,
not to let me forget.

What is that there, appearing in the purple
    west,
what swims into sight as the Sun sets?
A new Moon is shining.
You have followed the Sun,
and now you are ready to take your own
    place.
Welcome, New Moon,
Welcome, Sweet Maiden.

From out of the brightness, the Maiden
    appears,
dancer, singer, seducer, scattering flowers.
From out of the darkness, the Maiden
    appears,
dancer, singer, seducer, scattering flowers.
Pruning sickle, encourage new growth,
dance and sing and seduce
and scatter your flowers over the Earth.[9]

The world begins in darkness,
and out of darkness springs the light.
The day begins in darkness,
and out of darkness comes the dawn.
The month begins in darkness,
and in the darkness the new Moon is born.
The Wise One goes into the darkness,
and returns the Maiden.
Sweet One of the Silver Crescent:
We invoke your presence here.
Come with your fresh love
and purify your people gathered before you;
Resurrect us, cleanse us, make us new.
Welcome back, little one.

I've missed you in the days of darkness.
Welcome back, to adorn the night sky.

A new month begins,
a new Moon appears chasing the Sun into
    the dying fire
of the western sky,
a new Moon dancing an old dance,
the dance she has always performed,
the same dance in the same sky,
the old steps traced in the old pattern by
    the New Moon.
The Maiden, who is young,
whose art is skillful, perfected by long
    years of practice,
a long stream of new Moon dances.
She dances, intent on the spoor of the
    setting Sun,
dancing Him into his death with Her new
    life's spirit.
She dances into death the old,
dancing into life the new,
as she appears in the darkening sky of the
    world, of our lives,
and returns joy to all who lack.

I see you in the west, as beautiful as a
    young child.

## THE GODDESS

The Goddess has put her child's artwork on
    display:
the sunset sky pinned by the magnet Moon
to the refrigerator of the night sky.

## MÉNŌT

Ménōt who marks the passing of days,
with your sharp edges, cut out this month
from the time before and the time after.
Measure it out to fit the pattern laid out
    for you.

---

9    When the Sun sets, the New Moon emerges from
his brightness where she has been hidden all day. She is
a maiden, but also erotic; the flowers she scatters may be
symbolic of either general fertility or sexuality. She appears out of the darkness as well, out of the three dark
nights of the Moon. She is a pruning sickle, because her
erotic nature is slightly dangerous in so far as it is not in
the service of the community. It is raw power, not yet con-
trolled. Nevertheless, it encourages growth.

## Waxing Moon

As you grow in the sky,
grow in my soul,
soft light of the Moon.

Your increase in size, your increase in
    light, is amazing,
and that I might see it, and be inspired by it
    to my own growth,
amazing as well,
and that's why I'm thanking you.

## Full Moon

Your milky light, Full Moon Goddess,
    feeds your babies,
your children who rely on you for food to
    grow.
Pour down each night, Good Mother,
but especially on this one, when you have
    so much to give.

Queen of Night, your silver wheel rolls
    silently
through the darkness
from sunset to sunrise on this night when
    you are full.
I look on you in awe, and praise you.
I look to you in love, and honor you.

Lamp of the night,
guide my way.
Shine from above me,
a light in the darkness.

As the Sun retreats you enter the sky.
Give birth to the night, Great Mother.
Give birth to your children that fill the
    dark sky.

Give birth to our dreams that will fill our
    sleep.

Your silver disk will light the entire night;
none of the night will be turned over to the
    dark.
Even as your soft light guides my path
    tonight,
may your gentle influence spread softly
    through my life.

Round face of the Mother,
look down on me in blessing;
light my way through darkness.

With such brilliant light, to rival the Sun,
can you be said to move in darkness?
A light for the shadows
a lantern for those abroad,
a guide for travelers:
throughout the night you continue to
    bless us,
faithful Moon.

I pour out milk to the Queen of Heaven,
the Mother of Wonders, shining tonight.
The pool that it forms mirrors you there
as you look down on me.
Accept this milk as a thank you for all that
    you give so freely.

This small bowl of drink is yours, Lady of
    the Moon,
its round brightness reflecting your shining
    wheel.
I place it on the grass, and invite you to
    come with your children to share it.

It is time to be full,
just as it was time to be dark.

With the month duly measured,
with respect for the dark,
I turn to you with joy.

I praise you,
I praise the Goddess shown in you,
bright against the dark.

Change by continuing law into each phase,
    one following the other,
from dark, to waxing, to full, to waning, to
    dark again, and once more into growing,
as I follow your ways, as I submit myself
    to the same laws that govern you.

## THE GODDESS

Whitest Wheel, fullest height,
you shine for us,
Full Moon above.
Guide us, Mother,
Guide us, Goddess,
through tonight's ritual.

Blessed be the Goddess of All
in Her image the Moon.
Threefold is the Moon
and threefold we name her.
When waxing, she is the Maiden.
Blessed be the Maiden.
When waning, she is Dark One.
Blessed be the Dark One.
But when full, she is the Mother
and under this name we call her today.
Come, All-Mother;
Your people are gathered here:
Purified, prepared,
properly dedicated to your service.
Come, Mother of All, and shine within us.
Though all else may be dark,
You will be our beacon.

Though all others shall reject us,
You will hold us in your arms.
Though all else be uncertain,
We will place our trust in your wheel of
    change.
Come, Mother, and be with us.

They say there's a Man in the Moon.
And why not; what man,
or what woman, too, wouldn't want to be
    in the body of the Goddess?
But we already are, we always are.
So says the light of the full Moon tonight.

## ARTEMIS

Your bow at rest,
I praise you, Artemis,
as you shine, full, on me below.

# Waning Moon

The Old Woman takes her place
in the early morning
in the dome of the sky.
Though guardian of the darkness,
and though yourself of advanced age,
you are yet the prophet of the Sun,
promising his imminent rebirth.
Old One, Wise One, Crone in the east,
Anna, I look on you with reverence
and praise you in the moments before
    dawn.

I ask for wisdom from the Old One,
enlightenment in the late hours of night.

The sickle of reaping is low in the sky in
    the period
just before dawn.

The Sun's halo soon will hide it, but still it
  will be there,
at the back of my mind, at the bottom of
  my heart,
poised to perform its acts of loving mercy.
Waning Moon, pass over me, and pass
  on by.
Grant me your wisdom, but withhold your
  power.[10]

Old, dark woman,
growing stronger each night
as each night the Moon dwindles and we
  are spun slowly but irresistibly into
  blackness;
you reach out with your sharpening sickled
  Moon,
to divide, and decide,
to cut straight through me and remove any
  illusions,
any falsehoods and frauds I might harbor,
even unknowingly deep within,
any faults, no matter how dear to my heart.
Please let it be without pain.
But if it has to be painful or frightening,
I'll understand:
the loss of prized possessions is never
  pleasant,
no matter how necessary or wise.

As your sickle sharpens,
cut ever more finely,
shaping me to approach the person whose
  perfection
is appropriate to who I am,
or rather to who I should be,
preparing me for the loss of a light of
  guidance
that will come in the dark of the Moon.

The sight of the Moon may fade:
you will not fade, Goddess.
The light of the Moon may fade:
you will not fade, Goddess.
The dark may come and fill the sky
but it will be a wisdom-giving dark:
for it will be your dark, O Goddess.
And you never fade or fail or abandon us,
O Goddess.

Goddess Moon, as your cup empties in this
  time of your waning,
even disappearing into the dark,
pour your light into me, and I will keep it
  safe until you return,
and I will pour it back in turn.
May we be perfect reflections of each
  other,
your dark my light,
your light my dark.

## MĒNŌT

You gathered light into a ball
and now you unravel it again.
Soon it will be gone, and we will face the
  dark.
But we know it will end in the proper time,
because you are the Lord of Right Measure
and you always do what has been laid
  down for you.

---

10    The waning crescent Moon, as the symbol of the
Crone, is likened to a harvesting sickle. It rises just before
sunrise and is soon blotted out by the brightness of the
Sun. It cannot be seen, but it is still there, just as old age
and death wait for us. The hope, stated in the last line, is
that the sickle will bring wisdom (cutting away ignorance)
but not death. Even in its function of reaping, the waning
Moon brings "loving mercy." There is a Zen story that expresses this well. A student asks his master questions, but
each time the master only hits him with a stick. He finally
grows sick of this and goes to another master. He tells the
new master the story, but instead of giving him sympathy,
the new master berates him for not appreciating the first
master's "grandmotherly kindness." It is just this sort of
wisdom that we seek from the Old Woman. Sometimes we
need to get hit with a stick.

*Chapter 17*

# TIMES OF THE YEAR

Prayers for the times of the year can be especially tricky to write. Many forms of neo-Paganism have a myth of the year, a storyline that runs through all of the seasons, describing the actions of the gods and the goddesses at each point along the way. However, different forms of Paganism disagree on what is being celebrated. For instance, some Wiccans follow Robert Graves in pitting a battle between the waxing and waning years at Midsummer. Others place a similar battle at Beltane. Norse customs and legends surrounding Yule are similar to Celtic ones associated with Samhain. Moreover, there is the obvious problem of differing climates. A prayer that is appropriate at May Day in New Hampshire is not going to be the same for that day in Mississippi.

I've therefore written many of these prayers not for particular dates in the neo-Pagan calendar, but for seasonal events. In that way, they can be applied more easily to different myths of the year and different climates.

I've also included prayers for some secular occasions. Since everything is sacred, there's really no such thing as a secular occasion, no event that cannot be observed with prayer. If it's the goal of neo-Paganism to reawaken a sense of the sacred in everyday life, it's only fitting that we should make the secular sacred.

> Somewhere in this world,
> at some time,
> this day of the year must have been sacred to some gods or goddesses.
> If I don't know which ones or why,
> don't be insulted, but accept this,
> given out of my ignorance but no less sincerely.

### THE GODDESS

Let us remember the words of the Goddess,
that all acts of love and pleasure are her
    rituals,
and let us take joy in this holiday.

### THE ALL-GODS

Holy Ones, whose goodwill crowns the
    efforts of everyone who works hard to
    produce at any season,
bless those whose livelihood depends upon
    this one,
whether it be that which is now beginning
    or now brought to its harvest,
whether farmers, or fishers, or employees
    whose jobs depend on quarterly profits,
bless them, bless their work.

## Birthday

### THE GOD AND THE GODDESS

You who give birth,
You who engender,
bless me today,
my birthday.

A year has come,
a year has gone,
and this child is a year older.
Mother of All,
Father of All,
Divine Parents,
watch over my child as if she were your
    own,
as she begins a new year of life.
Bring her safely through it
and to its end
and to the beginning of a new year of life.
Teach her and love her,
so she may, at the end of this coming year,

be that much more grown up,
that much more ready to take her place in
    the world.
As a parent it is my responsibility to make
    sure this happens,
but I still ask for your help in doing this
    successfully.
Give me the wisdom and patience to
    perform the necessary tasks,
You whose love is cast on all your
    children.

### JANUS

Janus, who opened the way into my life,
open the way for a new year of it.
Make everything that occurs in it
    something of beauty.
These candles lit for me are lit for you, too.

## The New Year

Away with you, dust!
Away with you, grime!
Away with all that brought sadness
in the year that's over.

[God's name], may this be a good year.
I will bless you;
bless me in return.

### THE GODDESS

A New Year is born from you;
praise, blessings, and honors are due for
    this gift!
Hear my words, you who give birth to
    everything.
A newly born year takes its place among
    your wonders,
one more thing for which you might rightly
    be praised.

## HEARTH GODDESS

I light a new fire in a new year;
both pure, both unstained, both clean,
but no more than you. Goddess of the
    Hearth.
Continue to watch and guard,
continue as well to give love and health
as I give this butter, which burns brightly,
our shared food on our shared hearth in our
    shared home.

## JANUS

God of Beginnings, accept this offering,
sweet-smelling incense to make you glad.
Bless me on the beginning of this year,
and bless my beginnings throughout this
    year.

God of the threshold,
who opens up to a new year;
god of doors,
who opens onto a new time;
Janus, who looks both ways,
I pour out this wine to you
and ask you to look behind and ahead
and guide me through the year that begins
    today.

## Deep Winter

Raised against the empty winter sky, the
    barren
limbs of trees and my hands reach out in
    prayer.
I ask from the gods of winter the strength I
    will need
to endure until spring
and the wisdom I require to learn from the
    dark and the cold
the lessons they will teach.
May I receive them without flinching.

Underneath the thick white blanket,
may the Earth sleep, dreaming,
till, rested and refreshed, it bursts free
    again.
Goddesses and gods of land and field,
may it be this winter as it has always been.

## Imbolc

In Ireland, lambs are being born.
But what is happening in the world outside
    *here*?
Telling the old stories is good, but we
    need to remember that if we are to
    honor this season, we need to know
    what it really is.
Goddess of the inside, but also of the tame
    outside,
we ask you to remind us of both.
If we then turn away again, back to your
    sacred flames, it will be knowing what's
    going on beyond them.

When spring is truly here at last, may we
    slide into it unsurprised because of the
    visions allowed by your inspiring light.

In old Ireland, today was the first day of
    spring.
Things are different here, in a different
    land:
the snow is still deep,
with perhaps a short thaw alone to bring
    hope to my heart.
But in my mind, I know spring is coming
    inexorably.
I don't need a groundhog to tell me that;
the earth's message is clear, this year as in
    seasons past.
I will listen to that and be sure of spring,
though the snow may fall.

### BRIGID

We pour out milk and set out bread for
   Brigid,
who dwells, a living presence, on our
   hearth.
This is what was done in the old times on
   this night of Imbolc,
and we who keep to the traditions of our
   Ancestors do it again.

Brigid, Our Lady, queen of our hearth,
goddess who guards the heart of our home,
threefold flame who shines in the center:
we honor and praise you,
we offer you our words of worship.
Queen of Poets, may our lives be creative.
Queen of Smiths, may our lives be useful.
Queen of Healers, may our lives be
   healthy.
Your family is standing before you here,
confident you will do what is right.

## Valentine's Day

### THE GODDESS

With loved for my loved ones,
fill me, Goddess,
on this day dedicated to love.

## Spring Equinox

Look, the ice cracks!
Hear, the snow melts!
Feel, it grows warm!
Spring arrives,
with the summer's gods in her train.

Bunnies and eggs and flowers and
   everything
new and bright and green,
on this beautiful spring day I praise.

### THE GOD AND THE GODDESS

The snow, melting, waters the Earth,
the semen soaking deep into the womb.
Mother and Father, conceive the spring.
Bring to birth the warm time.

### THE GOD

Wielder of the flaming arrow,
look down from your place on high,
and, fitting a shaft to your bow,
let loose your bowstring.
Sink deep into the Earth the shaft of fire,
warming the world, bringing the spring.

### THE GODDESS

The snow sinks back into the Earth,
there to nourish the sleeping life
that waits patiently for its time to come.
Goddess of spring, you have performed
   this miracle through many ages.
Transform, again, the frozen white into the
   pliant green.
Work, again, the ancient magic,
and bring spring to our land.

### DAWN

Dawn brings the Sun over the horizon's
   edge each morning,
winning for light the battle against
   darkness.
Dancer, win for us today the battle with the
   dark of the year:
from this day may there be more light than
   dark.

### DEMETER

I pray to you, Demeter, to remind you of
   the spring,
for Persephone has come home to you,
your little girl, now a great queen.

Show us your joy, mother of grain,
at her homecoming.
Warm the Earth, make the ground soft,
so we may walk barefoot again in the grass
and plant the seeds that will grow all
  summer
until the harvest, when your full power will
  be known
and everyone will see what you have done.
But now it is the time to begin these great
  deeds.
Bring us the spring, that together we might
  produce the harvest.
Warm the Earth, that the plants might grow
so we might display your gifts.
With your tears cried for happiness, melt
  away the winter's snow
and nourish the waiting seeds.

## Eos

Out of the too-long darkened east,
come to us, Eos, illumine the land!
Out of the long-extending night,
come to us Eos, illumine the land!
Out of the frigid, empty cold,
come to us Eos, illumine the land!

## Eostre

Blessed be Eostre, springtime queen,
blessed in all the signs of warmth's return,
blessed in the scent of thawing Earth,
her own true incense rising up in her
  praise.

Born new each morning, you are always
  young,
a beautiful girl, a welcome child.
It is with particular joy that we see you
  again on this morning, Eostre,
that is to say, "She Who Rises,"

for your rising today is not just the rising
  of the day but the rising of the year,
not just the day's dawn, but the year's.
The Sun that follows will be magnificent,
  and our praises of Him will be proper.
But He shouldn't get *all* the glory, Dawn
  Goddess, for you come, too, announcing
  that He's coming, yes,
but worth a prayer or two of your own.
We therefore break our anticipation and
  stop a while to look at this young girl
  you are,
Eostre who brings today this day's dawn,
  which is the dawn of the year,
reaching up and rising, red in the eastern
  sky.

Soft as rabbit fur, Eostre, come!
Pretty as painted eggs, Eostre, come!
With golden hair, Eostre, come!
With winning smile, Eostre, come!
Like the rose of dawn, Eostre, come!
Come, Eostre, bring the spring,
Come, Eostre, come!

I offer you flowers, Spring Goddess,
growth for growth, and life for life.
I offer you dyed eggs, Eostre,
beauty for beauty, life for life.
I welcome growth,
I welcome beauty,
I welcome life,
the new life, returning,
that you bring with us this season.

## Persephone

This is the day that ushers in the time of light,
and it is the coming of a girl who brings it:
Persephone, Maiden no more, gives birth
  to the spring.

## LAND SPIRITS

The warm time is here:
time to work and time to rest,
time to celebrate outside,
time to prepare for the harvest.
All about us, the Land Spirits are singing.
All about us, the deities are speaking.
Help me to listen, all you divine beings.
May I hear your voices.

# Spring

Kite aloft on the winds of March,
carry my prayers to the gods of spring.

## THE GODDESS

May the drops of the spring rain be like the
    hairs of the Goddess
brushing the earth as she turns her smile
    upon it to awaken the spring plants.

In the peepers' call,
sing to me of spring,
Mother of Seasons.

## APHRODITE

When the roses bloom, we know summer
    is here,
season of light and sweat, of heat and
    passion,
*your* season, Aphrodite.
I burn this rose incense to you, sweet-
    smelling.

## ATTIS

Attis is dead!
It is he we mourn,
in the fields, in the home.
He sprang up so quietly,
so full of life,

and we thought, we hoped,
he would never die,
befitting of a god.
But he died,
he died,
and we are alone, without him.
Attis is dead!
Hear us as we mourn,
and mourn with us,
all of you who yet live.
Mourn, the whole world,
for Attis who is dead.

## EOSTRE

The sky is covered with Eostre's cloak,
and the ground is covered with her tears.
She rains down gently on our fields,
Eostre rains down.
Rise up, rise up,
the seed in the ground.
Rise up with Eostre's warmth.

Ground appears—what a wonder!—
    through the snow,
something not seen for months.
And from spot to spot, from green to green,
a trail is growing of dancing feet,
the path of Eostre, who brings the dawn,
and now the dawn of spring.

## KIRNIS

Sweet cherries, tart cherries,
cherries filled with juice,
cause to grow on our trees, Kirnis,
for the enjoyment of this season
and for our refreshment.
After beautiful flowers bring beautiful
    fruit.

## MARS

Spear and shield, spear and shield,
Father Mars, Father Mars,
Dance the steps, dance the steps,
Sing the hymn, sing the hymn.
Bring the spring, bring the spring.
Spear and shield, spear and shield,
Dance and sing, dance and sing,
Pater Mars, Pater Mars.

Your dancers announce the spring, Father
     Mars,
in 3/4 time stamping the waking ground,
stirring it to life.
Even so dance in my soul,
releasing it from sloth.

## PERKŪNAS

Strike hard, Perkūnas, the frozen ground,
opening it for soaking spring rain.
Strike soft, Perkūnas, the waiting fields,
preparing them for the scattering of seeds.
Strike true, Perkūnas, the waiting earth.

## PERKŪNAS AND ŽEMYNA

Perkūnas and Žemyna, joined together in
     lightning strike,
in the first storm of spring that soaks the
     Earth in his seed
that will nurture in her the plants of summer:
for you, praise.

## PERSEPHONE

Softly,
softly pushing the flowers up from where
     you are hidden under the earth,
Persephone,
you're making a dancing ground ready for
     your return,
when you will tread softly, softly,
with your maidens and us.

There's a young girl in my fields
and she's dancing.
She's dancing lightly through them
between the shoots of the plants.
They reach up to her out of love
and she bends down to bless them.
There's a young girl in my fields.
Do you see her?
Sweet Persephone.

## SUN

The bright yellow crocus,
a Sun in the grass,
praises with me the Sun in the sky,
and I with it.

How silently flowers fall from the trees
and cover the Earth like winter's melted
     snow.
Like winter's melted snow, they will go on
     their way,
opening the door to summer's warmth.
Thank you, dear trees, for your gifts of the
     flowers,
and for the teaching that comes with them
     on this day in spring.

The dandelions in the grass, teeth of the
     lion of the sky,
mirror the many-rayed Sun.
I come, crowned with a garland of the
     yellow-bright flowers
and place a bouquet on this stone for an
     altar,
like a child bringing one home to his
     mother.
Look, they are beautiful!
Look, how they shine!
Look, Spring Sun, on your newly bloomed
     image!

## Floralia (April 28)

### FLORA

Each flower that stands in all the world's
  gardens
is a tribute to you, Queen Flora.
Every one that blooms in the wild places of
  the Earth
is an offering both from and to you.

## Beltane

Beltane is a time not for prayer, but to
  dance and sing,
or to pray by dancing and singing.
Dance and sing:
for Beltane!
For May Day!
For the coming of summer!

In and out, wrap the Maypole,
in and out the ribbons wrap,
in and out on this day of pleasure,
in and out to drum and clap.

Warm day
Flower day
Dance day
Happy day.
We are done with Winter;
Winter's waste is cleared away.
Gardens are planted.
Growth begins again,
and we go out from our homes,
happy to be outside again
under the Sun as it warms the earth.

Holy Ones, hear me:
Despite the cold and rain today
I feel the warmth within,
the hidden summer that now arrives.

May it live in my heart until it becomes
  present outside.
This May Day I celebrate the beginning of
  warmth,
even if the weather disagrees.

### THE GOD AND THE GODDESS

The Maypole is His phallus descending
  from the Sky.
The Maypole is Her grain rising from the
  Earth.
The ribbons, multicolored, is Their joy,
  spreading out in all directions.
The Dancers are all of us, weaving the
  Universe into existence.

You share the joy of your marriage bed
  unashamed, Eternal Lovers, with the
  whole world.
Each opening flower, each leaf unfolding,
is your cry of ecstasy.
Each bird or animal mating, each man and
  woman making love,
is not a reflection, pale or otherwise, of
  your lovemaking,
but your lovemaking itself.
Each hug, each handshake, each smile,
between lovers, or family, or friends, or
  strangers,
children conceived today on this Beltane,
on this happy Beltane.

### OPPOSING NATURE SPIRITS

All beings of the air who stand in
  opposition to us,
eagle and hawk, who carry away our
  animals,
starlings who eat our seeds,
crows who eat our dead:
here is your part of the offering;
don't trouble us.

All beings of the earth who stand in
    opposition to us,
wolf and coyote who carry off our animals,
rabbits and deer who eat our gardens,
ants and termites who destroy our homes:
here is your part of the offering;
don't trouble us.

All beings of the underworld and water
who stand in opposition to us,
bacteria and viruses that carry away our
    health,
sharks and jellyfish that drive us from the
    ocean,
grubs and beetles that feed on our food:
here is your part of the offering;
don't trouble us.

All beings of air, earth, and water
who stand in opposition to us:
we have given you your part of the
    offering;
don't trouble us.

*[An offering is made with each
"don't trouble us."]*

# Planting

## THE GOD AND THE GODDESS

I plant the seed in the ground
as the God does in the Goddess,
and all life springs forth:
may it rise here as well
in luxuriant growth.

## POMONA

I know you are goddess of fruits, Pomona,
but I hope you won't mind if I pray to you
    for my vegetables as well,

for all the plants I'm growing in the
    garden,
and that you will work with me to make
    them flourish.
I will give some of them to you gladly in
    thanks.

## ŽEMYNA

I bury these pieces of bread in you,
    Žemyna,
three times three times three times three
    again, many pieces.
May the food I grow come to me as
    profligately.

# Memorial Day

I offer words to the Dead:
may their spirits rest.
The war is over,
well won,
and peace,
sweet peace,
well established.
Your duty done,
well performed,
I thank you.

## GOD OF THE DEAD

Treat them gently, Lord of Death,
dwelling in your land of green gardens and
    water,
of far-extending plains.
May they rest there, after their sacrifice,
their suffering stilled.
We remember, this Memorial Day,
what they gave for our country's way:
for freedom, for democracy and peace.
We give remembrance:
the best gift for the Dead.

## PEACE

Welcome, Peace; with gentle eyes watch
    over the land,
over these honored dead, now at rest,
far from war's horror.
Blanket them with olive leaves,
as they sleep, undisturbed,
and unforgotten by those who stand in their
    debt.

# Gardening

I will need much help in growing this
    garden.
I cannot do it alone.
I ask for help from the Sun: give your light
    so the plants can make their food.
I ask for help from the rain: give your
    moisture to be the plants' own blood.
I ask for help from the soil: give your
    minerals from which the plants will
    form their bodies.
I will give my time,
I will give my care,
I will give my loving stewardship.
All these will I give my garden
and I ask for you others to give what the
    garden will need as well.
We will do it together
and I will not forget your contribution.

Gods of planting and growing,
bless my work today.
Bring together water and soil and seed,
bring to them light and air.
Stir up life with them.
Fill my garden with prosperous growth.
I write my desires for growth for my plants
    on this little board
and push it into the earth,
where it will be heard.

## EARTH

Open with eager joy to my planting my
    seeds in you.

I put these seeds as offerings to Mother
    Earth, into Her body,
and will receive thankfully the food she
    gives in return,
and will thank her when I eat.

## THE ELEMENTS

In the east, where we honor air,
I erect this prayer stick with ribbons of
    blue.
May my plants receive the gases they need
to make their food from the air.
With each flap of the ribbons my prayer is
    said.

In the south, where we honor fire,
I erect this prayer stick with ribbons of red.
May my plants receive the light they need
to make their food from the fire.
With each flap of the ribbons my prayer is
    said.

In the west, where we honor water,
I erect this prayer stick with ribbons of
    green.
May my plants receive the fluid they need
to make their food from the water.
With each flap of the ribbons my prayer is
    said.

In the north, where we honor earth,
I erect this prayer stick with ribbons of
    yellow.
May my plants receive the minerals they
    need
to form their bodies from earth.

With each flap of the ribbons my prayer is
  said.

In the center, where we honor the mystery
  of the spirit of life,
I erect this prayer stick with ribbons of
  purple.
May my plants receive the spirit they need
to form their lives from the non-living;
from air, and fire, and water, and earth;
so they can give life to spirit,
the gift spirit most desires.
With each flap of the ribbons my prayer is
  said.

## SATURN

Golden Age god,
bring the golden grain,
sickled god.

## STORM GOD

Strike with sure aim the waiting earth.
Split with firm stroke the meadows wide.
With blazing axe, with shining blade,
With swift-descending shaft of fire,
prepare and open the fields below
and sow your seed that ours may grow.

## ŽEMYNA

The first thunderstorm has passed.
Perkūnas has opened you to growth.
And so I place the seeds into the ground to
  make my garden.
May they grow well;
may I have fresh food,
that I will share with you.

Bread baked from grain that sprang from
  you
we return to you, Žemyna,
breaking it and burying it,

so you might receive it and give again the
  food from which food is made.
We work together, Mother Earth;
you to grow plants, and we to form them
  into food for all people
and for you who stretch out around us.
Working together, may we grow our crops
  this summer.

## GARDEN SPIRITS

Whether these seeds that I press into the
  ground will grow,
and how well,
is in your hands, Garden Spirits.
Others laugh,
and say it's the Sun, and rain, and the
  richness of the soil that will decide.
But didn't I just say that?

Here in my garden unseen Spirits are
  dancing.
In my moment of blindness of you
may I hear your kind and crashing feet as
  they fall in seasonal rhythm
in your slow but certain circles.

## RAIN SPIRITS

From mountain, from clouds, they have
  come.
The Sacred Spirits, bringing rain, have
  come.
They speak:
From mountain, from clouds, we have
  come.
We, Sacred Spirits, bringing rain, have
  come.
To our children who pray to us, we have
  come.
Plant your seeds now, the rain will come.
Plant corn and beans now, the rain will
  come.

Plant grain and vegetables now, the rain
    will come.
Pray to us, children, and we will come.
We speak:
Sacred Spirits, we will pray and you will
    come.

## Summer's Beginning

### THE ALL-GODS

On this day of cold when it should be
    warm,
at the beginning of summer,
I ask not to doubt that the Gods know what
    they're doing,
that the weather is as it should be.
Even so, I pray for summer's warmth.

## D-Day

Many men, long-trained, well led,
were thrown against the Atlantic Wall,
against a fortress that protected tyranny,
an evil regime,
against the oppressors of people,
to liberate them from occupation:
for them I pour this beer—
    for those who fought on the beaches,
or who landed by air, by glider or
    parachute,
in a hostile land,
and for those who manned the ships and
    boats,
the greatest fleet ever assembled,
who transported them across the channel,
or swept the sea free of mines, opening the
    way,
or drove their boats up to the shore,
to deliver the precious loads,

or who bombarded the shore with mighty
    guns,
protecting the troops,
and for those who flew above,
attacking transportation and troop
    concentrations
and for the planners whose minds were
    occupied,
day and night,
in developing an operation that would
    accomplish its objectives,
with the greatest speed and the least loss
    of life,
and for those who labored in support,
whether loading and unloading,
or typing and filing,
or any of the myriad tasks that sustained
    the forces,
and for those who worked hard,
with great skill and concern,
laboring extra hours to provide the troops
    and sailors and airmen
with their necessary supplies—to all these,
    this beer.
And for those who waited to be liberated,
or who themselves took up arms,
blowing bridges, attacking trains, or acting
    directly against enemy troops,
I pour this wine, red like the blood they
    risked, and sometimes lost.
Thanks to all of you, heroes all,
who freed Europe and allowed us to live
    as we do.
Our words for you, this beer to you, this
    wine to you,
our thoughts to you:
Mighty Dead who will never die.

## Father's Day

### FATHER GODS

May all the fathers of the Gods bless all the
fathers of men on this Fathers' Day.

## Midsummer

With the Sun's fire at its highest point I
immerse myself in water,
at the beginning of the month of the crab.

### THE GOD

Long have you grown,
strong, and hard, and true,
reaching up from the dark Below
until your branch-fingers grasped the Sun:
You, reaching You,
strength holding brightness,
power, burning,
standing in unsullied glory.
Roots snake deep into the darkness.
You spread these, too, just as your
branches;
those seen, these hidden;
those fed, and these feeding;
You basing your body on the Below.
Your branches reach up, pulling your body
with them,
the roots reach down, pulling on your body
as well.
It is time.
Standing in Your glory, the branches and
the Sun,
can you feel the pull downward?
The Dark has its turn.
You needed the darkness to feed your light,
but nothing is free.
It is time to pay, to fill the hungry darkness,
that pulls you down into death.
A true king does not go on the journey
into darkness alone;
he must be accompanied by an honor
guard.
This is yours, Oak King:
You go with the Four,
You go with the Five.
I give them their marching orders:
Air, when he is in the great emptiness, be
his breath.
Fire, when he is in the great cold, be his
warmth.
Water, when he is in the great dryness, be
his moisture.
Earth, when he is in the great stillness, be
his sustenance.
And you, Spirit, when he is in the great
death, be his life.
Stand around in protection, you Four,
protecting the body of the Oak King
until the expected time of growing.
Dwell within, Spirit, protecting his life
until the expected time of growing:
in the time of fading away, do not let him
forget.
These are your orders, you Four, you Five.
You may sink into the darkness,
Oak with the Sun in Your Branches,
with your honor guard about you.

### SAULĖ

Saulė, dressed in gold, with silver shoes,
mother, protector, guardian of all who go
forth under your glowing face,
we stand in the dark, before the dawn,
this midsummer morn,
awaiting you,
looking for you to dance into the sky.
Come, we will dance with you,
welcome Saulė.

## Saulė and Dievas

Saulė, shining Sun,
Dievas, shining sky,
this midsummer day bring blessing to your
 people here.

## Sun

Stand still just a moment in the sky, Sun.
Tarry just a moment in the heavens, King.
Wait just a while on the horizon, Lord.
Stay awhile in lordship over the dark
 before the tide turns toward it,
and receive my offering.
Know this:
A lord without a throne is still a lord.
A king without a crown is yet a king.
And a Sun even in the time of the year
 when He is absent from the sky more
 than he is in it is ever a Sun,
and deserves my honor.
Welcome and dear Sun, Lord and King,
 know this:
through the dark half of the year you will
 never want for worship.
I shall give you deserved gifts.
I shall praise your magnificence.
And I shall pour out heart, words, and
 deeds in continuing worship.

Stop for a moment, Sun, your burning and
 turning wheel's rolling.
Stop to smile down with love and approval
 on the Earth spread broad beneath you.
Smile as you have done since Her birth,
 billions of years ago, when She formed
 from the random tumbling rocks,
floating in your gravitational field;
floating, disorganized, until they joined
 together through their *own* gravitational
 field,

until they formed Her, on whom we stand
 today, looking up at you smiling in the
 sky.
When she was formed, burning and turning
 wheel, your loving gaze on Her brought
 forth life from the dead rock and barren
 dust,
life that changed, that evolved into the
 vast numbers of living things spread out
 across Her,
all tracing their lives back to that one
 common Ancestor whose birth you
 conceived with your rays.
And one of those species is our own, this
 member of which stands here today,
 looking up at you, smiling down on us,
 we standing here on this longest day.
Stop for a moment, your wheel that burns,
 that turns; stop your rolling,
and stand with us, smiling down on those
 who smile up at you.

Lift the Sun on its towering pillar,
as the Sun of the world lifts into the sky;
high and kingly on this day of his height.
Lift hands, lift words, to Lord Sol on his
 throne,
elevated, lofty, shining.

At your height,
at your greatest strength,
I praise you, Sun.
Though you will decrease from here on,
for a while,
the time of greatest warmth,
your gift,
is yet to come.
I will continue to praise you, then,
but not only in the soon-to-be heat,
but in the dark and cold to follow.
But for now, you are bright.

## Summer

### THE GOD AND THE GODDESS

The Sun in the sky on this too-hot day
    pours down its constant message of your
    power, Lord.
The cooling comfort of the water I sink
    myself in equally proclaims the power
    of your Lady.
If I seek her, please don't see it as
    disrespect for you, but as love of Her.
I will long for you on another day,
and turn to you for the comfort I seek from
    Her today.
Lady of the watery womb, I ask you to
    welcome me.

### GRASS

I trim you as a stylist trims hair,
grass of my lawn,
to bring beauty, not damage.

### LLEU LLAW GYFFES

Bright One with the Steady Hand,
who threw so straight, hard, accurately,
hitting the target assigned:
guide my arm today;
give me swift and sure motion
to bring the ball over the plate
when and where, in height, in coverage,
I wish it to be.

## At the Beach

Lift me up, Mother Ocean, as I enter your
    waves.
As I swim in you, keep me safe.

*[With slight changes, this can become a
blessing from a parent to a child before
swimming.]*

## Canada Day

### LADY OF CANADA

Lady of Canada,
your emblem is not eagle or lion,
those creatures that prey on others,
but a leaf, emblem of growth.
May we grow in peace, then,
in prosperity and happiness,
in this our northern land.

## American Independence Day

A few days before he died on the fiftieth
    anniversary of independence, the ill
    John Adams received a delegation of
    the town elders. They were there to
    ask for something to be read at the
    celebrations. Expecting noble and
    high-flown words, they were shocked
    at what he gave them. They perhaps did
    not understand how noble it was, even
    if not high-flown. What he gave them
    was not a speech, but a toast. Today, on
    this glorious Fourth, raise your cups and
    make that toast:
Independency forever!

### LIBERTY

The fireworks are roses in the bouquet
    we're giving you, Liberty.
Hear our love in their explosions.
The sounds of delight in the watching
    crowds are your hymns,
our rededication to you, our offering.

Goddess Liberty,
we pray to you today.
Grant freedom to all your children,
no matter their country.

We take time today to remember
the examples of freedom we have seen in
    our time.
We remember the citizens of Berlin,
who knew that the best use for a wall is to
    dance upon it.
We remember the hole in the Romanian
    flag,
put there by those who overthrew their
    oppressors.
We remember the people who stood in
    Russian Parliament Square
and waited for the tanks to come.
And we remember those who struggled and
    failed,
such as the martyrs of Tiananmen Square,
who, after raising a statue to you,
faced the tanks and lost.
We will not forget.
We will not forget.
Give us the courage
to earn our freedom
and to regain it if it is stolen.
We ask this of you
who are the source of all freedom.

Liberty, your torch shines undimmed by
    the years.
If our eyes have lost sight of you, it is our
    fault and not yours.
We have turned our vision away from the
    heights from which your flames shine,
and seen only that which divides.
Be our beacon, Mother of our nation,
and show us the way again.
Mother of Peoples,
unite your scattered children into one tribe,
one people, one country.

# Lammas

## THE GOD AND THE GODDESS

I place this loaf before the altar,
as first fruits, as thank-you gift,
to you, Goddess, who sends the grain,
to you, God, who *is* the grain:
cut down and consumed on this holy day,
the feast of loaves.

## THE GOD

The feast of bread we celebrate with bread
baked and on our table to be shared among
    us,
but first to be share with the Lord of Grain.
And so I break off this piece and pass it
    among you.
Bless it, each who is here,
that it may be the holly that we share with
    the holy,
placing it in the [field/garden];
and sharing the rest,
eating together with the Holy One.
And this second loaf we give,
turning it over wholly,
after blessing it, each one of us,
separating it out for him alone.
And then we will place it, as well, in the
    [field/garden].
We are grateful to you, Grain God,
we send you our blessings.
Look kindly on us, King of Bread,
and continue to send us blessings in return.

## EARTH MOTHER

Bread lain on the ground,
on which we scatter grain.
We offer to the Earth
in thanks for the gift of the harvest
on the feast day of bread.

## Lugnasad

### LUG

Withhold your lightning spears, Lug whose
    aim is true,
until the harvest is safely gathered in
against the dark and cold that must come,
god of the bright and hot, hear the words of
    one who loves you.

You who brought Bres low,
who won from him the secrets of planting,
who won from him the secrets of growth,
who won for him the secrets of harvest,
it is at harvest that we pray to you
it is today that we pray to you, your holy
    day,
Lugnasad, that is to say, festival of Lug.
We thank you, Lámhfhada, for your
    protection,
for watching over our field against all
    danger,
whether animals who might have eaten our
    crops
whether humans who might have
    encroached on our land
whether Spirits who might have wished
    us ill:
against all these, Long-Arm, you have
    defended us and ours.
And so to you, guider and protector,
teacher and champion,
we pray on this day,
that is rightly called yours.

The spears of Lug are standing straight,
    erect, golden, in the wheat fields.
And when we reap them, we cut off their
    blades with our own.

And when we grind them, we soften the
    sharpness of a god to that fit for the
    nondivine.
And when we eat them, we bring into our
    lives His power,
enlivening us, empowering us, encouraging
    us to thank Him.
And we do:
Lug, thank you.

We are here at the feast of Lug
to honor, praise, and worship the hero of
    the gods.
Lug Lámfada
Lug Samildanach
He whose arms extend greatly
He of many arts
May he be pleased with this rite.
May he be our champion
May all our fields and crafts be blessed by
    him.

Defeat the Dark One,
Bright One, Champion,
your spear bright against the darkness,
a thunderbolt in a clear sky.
Chase away hail and heavy rain
and bring safely to harvest
our grain, our hearts.

Gold shines from the wheat in the field
as your face shines forth with divine light.
May we never forget, Lug, that what we
    may see
as the most mundane of things,
the food that we digest,
is a miracle given to us by the Mighty
    Ones,
and most of all by you, Lug, who know the
    secrets of agriculture
and have taught them to us

that we might have something to offer you
in thanks,
on today, the day holiest to you.

## The Dog Days

In the hot days of August, I am reminded
of you
by the Sun-seared grass now brown in my
yard.
It is brittle and dead now and provides no
comfort when I walk across it.
It is life appearing in the semblance of
death,
for when the autumn rains come, it will be
green again.
Of such small miracles, splendid gods,
is your world made.

Look! The garden is growing well!
Through your help, and through my work,
we have done a great deed, Holy Ones.
We have produced food from seeds'
promise.

## Tomato Season
### TOMATO SPIRITS

I stop for a moment to praise tomatoes,
honoring them by eating one.
Lovely are you Spirits who grow such
things.
First, I praise their shapes—they shun the
easy perfection of the sphere
and take instead their own forms.
Their weight is worth praising, and the
depth of their color.
Before I eat this one, I smell it, taking its
scent in deeply,
finding in me a resonance that tells me that
this is the smell of fertile Earth.

Their skin, though stretched tightly, yields
quickly;
it has performed its duty of containing
treasure with uncommon devotion
and now relinquishes command to me.
With silent thanks, then, I accept the task
and eagerly receive the honor so bestowed,
hoping, by so doing, to honor in turn the
giver of the gift
and the gift itself.

## Late Summer
### SUN

Midsummer is past,
and the Sun already dwindling,
days growing shorter,
nights lengthening.
But there is plenty of time to enjoy the
warmth of summer,
your gift, Lord Sun,
for our pleasure,
and for the growth of our food.
And so I crumble this bread for you in
thanks.

### NATURE SPIRITS

Autumn is circling,
tying knot after knot,
to form its net,
inexorable.
But not yet: now it is summer.
Pokeweeds' jeweled berries,
Lazy Susans' suns:
I praise you,
you and all that is found in this time.
Spirits of late summer,
to you, praise,
you, beautiful,
on this sunny day.

## Summer's End

The door is starting to swing from hot to
    cold.
Although it is still summer, occasionally a
    cool day comes.
The pokeberries are purple, the sassafras
is starting to turn, and the gardens are
heavy with tomatoes.
It is a time to stop and pay
attention:
the Spirits of the land are very busy.
I pray to them at this liminal time to open
    my eyes.
Don't let me wake one day and ask where
    summer has gone.
May I be aware of its going, and be as
    thrilled with it as I was with the arrival
    of spring.

### SASSAFRAS SPIRITS

Late in the summer, with the Sun still
    blazing
I meet with the startling sight of sassafras
    leaves,
turned already to tongues of flame.
They burn away the remnants of summer,
a sacrificial pyre for the year's offerings,
set to summon the fires of fall.
Spirits of sassafras, many thanks to you:
your message will not go unheeded.

## Monsoon

### FLORA

Come to us Flora,
with the rain,
and fill the dry desert with beauty
of flowers and green plants.
Come as you always do
in the right time.

### TARANIS

Thank you, Taranis, for this enlivening
    rain,
pouring from your wheel as it rolls through
    the heavens,
quickening seeds, refreshing plants,
bringing flowers and producing fruit,
this monsoon rain that revives the suffering
    earth,
the dry and waiting earth.

### THUNDERBIRD

From cloud-terrace-topped mountains you
    fly,
each wing beat a roll of thunder,
rain pouring from your feathers to soak the
    prayer feathers we set up in the earth
to call you here, to welcome you here.
Eagle of Thunder, you come to end this dry
    time,
its heat become the lightning that flashes
    from your eyes.

## September 11

On this day,
this day of remembrance,
we commit ourselves anew to freedom and
    tolerance.
For we cannot let hate triumph over love,
nor disdain for respect.
So in the names of all the gods,
ours and the others,
all of those of the dead and those they left
    behind.
We make this oath this day:
to continue the struggle until Justice and
    Liberty prevail in all lands.
And so we remember the dead, today and
    always.

We remember them for what they were, in
  and of themselves,
and for what they mean to us.
And we pray here that they be at rest,
whether in the walled garden of Yemos,
or in the far-off Isle of the Blest,
or on the western island of Tech Duinn,
  where Donn rules,
or again among us, their souls newly
  incarnate,
or in any of the many lands to which each
  of their traditions have led them:
give them the peace they were denied,
  Holy Ones.
This is our prayer today,
this sad day,
this September 11th.

# Harvest

May prosperity ride your diamond-edged
  sickle,
Reaper, Harvester,
as it cuts through this season's grains.
I offer this loaf of last year's grain in
  thanks for this year's harvest.

I offer to the gods of the dark season this
  fruit of the light.

On today, High Harvest,
I think of those who work in the fields,
and offer my prayer to their guardian deities
that they might find rest at the end of their
  labors.

## THE GOD AND THE GODDESS

First spring, exploding life;
now fall, harvest's death.
God and Goddess, you bring life and death,
each as it should be,

dying and giving birth,
together bringing mystery.

## THE GOD

The sweeping of the reaper's blade
cuts quite away your offered head,
the grain from which is ever made
when threshed and ground our welcome
  bread,
this present that we offer you,
from last year's harvest, rightly due,
O Dying God, for whom these words are
  said.

Strike down, god of grain, the grain that
  stands even now,
golden in the fields,
even as *you* were struck down, struck down
  yourself in That Time,
once and again, and always again, in this.

Slain and reborn, each year returning,
on whose death we all depend:
death comes hard to a hunted beast
death comes easy to a fiery leaf
death comes swiftly to the ripened grain,
waiting to be gathered into a sheaf,
its seeds eaten or preserved for planting,
for new life in spring,
the straw burned for light in winter's dark:
It is to you, Grain-God
It is to you, Forest-God
It is to you, Beast-God
It is to you we pray in Harvest Time.

## CORN

Many-seeded, garbed in silk,
you we praise, welcome Corn,
before we harvest you.
True gold, with you we are rich.

## DEMETER

Each time I remove a husk from the
    covering of this ear of maize,
I come closer to the mysteries of Demeter,
that are hidden in the seeds within.

## EARTH MOTHER

The Earth and the work of people have
    together brought the harvest.
We have taken our share, and now we give
    you yours, Earth Mother,
laying it upon you to sink into your
    embrace.

At Harvest it is right to honor Mother Earth
with whom we have worked since spring to
    bring the crops to fruition.
And those of us who do not work on the
    land,
with crop and flock and herd,
have brought, over time, our own work to
    production.
Together, those close to the soil
and those engaged in trade,
praise you, Mother of All,
who brings all things to wonderful harvest:
thank you for all we have received.

## *Fall Equinox*

On one side the light, on the other the dark,
we stand in this moment of balance.
I would prefer the light, but the earth begs
    to differ,
and, turning about the Sun, turns her half
    on which I live away,
away into the dark.
I can't help but grant you the power; what
    use would it be to resist?

I will go with you then, complaining as
    little as I can,
into the dark period of the year,
believing your promise that your turning
    will go on,
and return my half of the world to the light.

I set my face to the dark.
I will travel with the Sun through the dark.
I will go with confidence in the deepest
    dark.
Though about me the dark may grow,
the gods are always at my side
guiding me to light.

## THE GOD

It happened this way:
When the time was right, when the season
    had come,
he came to the deadly place and was
    sacrificed.
Knowingly he came, willingly he came, in
honor and sorrow he came, to do what had
    to be done.
His death made life possible; from it
    sprang the food we eat.
Grain grew where his blood flowed,
animals walked forth from the shade of his
    fallen body.
Like an ash felled by an axe, his body lay
and, with its rotting, nourished the ground.
This is the way it happened, and the way it
    happens today.
For each moment dies and nourishes the
    next as it is birthed by the Goddess.
Each year dies and nourishes the next as it
    is birthed by the Goddess.

Each life ends and nourishes the next as it
    is birthed by the Goddess.

You who die and are reborn, in this season
of death,
we remember your deeds.
You who die and are reborn, in this season
of life,
we remember your sacrifice.
You who die and are reborn, in this season
of life and death,
we remember what happened,
and we praise you in our living, and we
praise you in our dying.

## THE GODDESS

Never will I say, Queen of the Earth,
that your power has ever been diminished.
Today, I saw leaves flying in the wind
and they told me not to doubt.
Though the strong gusts strip the trees of
their summertime finery
and empty branches reach black against the
twilight sky,
my heart will not shudder,
nor my spirits fail.
You are the guide to whom the events of
the world look
and they do not stray from the path you are
continually laying down:
this autumn that transforms the world is a
return to autumns past.
Standing among the fallen leaves,
I praise you,
I pray to you,
I bring to mind your glory.

The world is revolving into the year's dark
half.
Now, while it is still bright, we celebrate
what summer's warmth has brought us.
When our hearts teeter on a point between
happiness and despair,

may we remember this moment,
and how it brought us harvest,
and how it comforted us,
and encouraged us to plant hope's seed in
the waiting earth,
Mother of All.

## EARTH

This is what I know, gods of the universe.
This is what you are telling me
and this is what I tell you:
the Earth prepares for a great change.
Light and dark are equal today, but that
will not last.
The Earth makes its way around the Sun
and takes us with it into the year's dark
half.
We travel with it,
not in calm resignation,
but with wild anticipation of what dreams
may be dreamt
in the night of the world.
May they be good dreams.

## SAULĖ

We strengthen Saulė with prayers, with
offerings,
rising as smoke from sacrificial fires
lit at this time of growing darkness.
Golden woman, we offer as well this gold;
when we wear it, we will be showing how
beautiful you are,
and how beautiful you make those who are
faithful to you.
Even though you may dwindle in the sky
you will not dwindle in our hearts:
Lovely goddess.

## SUN

Half day, half night,
fall equinox.
Half night, half day,
beginning of the dark.
Praise, Sun, on this holy day.

# *Fall*

May their turning be the beauty of my
 life's accomplishment.
May their falling be my letting go of life.
May their raking together be my gathering
 with the Ancestors.
May their rotting into compost be my
 absorption into the Earth.
In their feeding new growth may I see my
 own rebirth.
Dryads, may the glories of your glories be
 my teachers
in this season of the dying year.

## THE GOD

May my death be as beautiful
as that of autumn leaves,
God of sacrifice,
and of coming winter.

## HEARTH GODDESS

With the Sun dwindling,
we must once more make our own light.
Receive this butter, first fire of fall,
and bring it to the goddess who dwells on
 our hearth,
along with our devotion and affection.

## WIND

Wind, I throw these crumbled leaves to
 you for toys.
Make beauty with them and I will watch:
You and I will share the fun.

## MAPLE TREE SPIRITS

The geese are flying
over the maples
that I wish to praise.

The sacrificial fires of maple trees burn the
 summer offering,
the grey sky accepting the smoke offered it
 in honor.
I place this sacrifice before you, gods of
 the year.
May each death on the point of the cold's
 sharp sword
be considered an offering on the altar of
 the Earth.
May each plant harvested be granted the
 status of sacrifice.
May each loss to the end of the summer be
 an addition to your power,
a thread in the pattern woven by you in the
 secret places.[11]

## NATURE SPIRITS

Leaves that are falling from late autumn's
 weeping trees:
I praise you.
Stubble in corn fields, left behind after
 harvest:
I praise you.
Chill of the evening, that comes bringing
 winter:
I praise you.

---

11   The "summer offering" is the offering up of summer
itself, burned by the flaming colors of the autumn leaves.
Each of the forms of life that are dying at this time is
granted, by this prayer, the status of a sacrifice. This prayer
is a gift to those beings who cannot themselves pray; we
pray on their behalf, giving meaning to their deaths.

### Tree Spirits

Cut off from the harvesting of yellow
    wheat,
I, who live far from the farms,
turn instead to the gold of the trees, to the
    red, to the orange,
that feed my soul with beauty as surely as
    the grain feeds my body.
A Pagan, worshiper of the particular, at
    home in the land I find myself in,
praises, not the far-found fields, but the
    trees on my street.

### Wild Geese Spirits

Wild geese flying overhead on your
    journey south,
bear away with you on your thundering
    wings
the cares that have made my summer
    weary.
Cry out my pain, passing over the darkened
    land,
until the air ocean you sail washes it away.

## Apple Harvest

### The God and the Goddess

The apples that fall like the rain that they
    drank, like the cider that will pour out
    when their slurry is pressed,
would not have been possible without the
    Goddess, Queen of Bees and Flowers.
And none of this would have been possible
    without the God, King of Seeds and
    Trees.

When I drink the cider that is the blood
    of life of the apples from which it is
    pressed out,
it is the gift of the Goddess and the God
    that I drink:
their gift, poured out.

### Pomona

Thank you, Pomona,
for this apple, red in my hand.

### Apple Tree Spirits

From each tree in this orchard
I am going to leave at least one piece of
    fruit at its base
as a thank-you to the Spirit of the tree.

## Meal Prayer for Early Fall

With longer shadows, I sit down to my
    supper.
Before me are the products of summer,
the Sun's light become food.
Listen, food and Sun:
I thank you.

## Late Fall

Lock up carefully, Earth's guardians,
and keep life safe until spring.

# Hunting Season

Hunting is a source of some controversy among neo-Pagans. Our respect for life has led some of us to reject hunting. I doubt that any would approve of hunting simply for trophies. And yet, what about hunting for food? If we are to eat meat, we owe it to the animals who die for us to make their deaths a sacred act. It is doubtful that a worker in a slaughterhouse will do this for us. Those who hunt, however, have a chance to take part in the dance of life and death. A properly prayerful attitude makes hunting a sacred act. Through prayer, a hunter is reminded that what he hunts is sacred and that the God was himself the victim of a hunt. (This is a myth that is implicit in various forms of the myth of the year.) The hunter then puts himself and his actions under the control of the God. In essence, it is the God who will be hunting. In this way, the hunter takes the part of the God as hunter, but in the back of his mind is the thought that, as he is the God, so is he the hunted as well.

## THE GOD

The flame on the trees burns away the
    green of summer.
Summer's last heat is put to good use.
Run with the prey as hunting time starts,
race through the forest with the deer, god
    of stags.
The blood on the ground, as red as the
    leaves that fall on it,
flows from your sacrifice as this season is
    born.
In autumn, the dying time, you come into
    your own;

the day comes round for your greatest of
    gifts.
Lord of flame and blood, lord of deer and
    sacrifice,
Lord of autumn and gifts, bless your
    people.

Is it true what they say about you,
Great Lord of Animals?
Is it true that you know what it is to be
    hunted,
to be sought by those who would take your
    life?
I hear that, at the end, you turned to face
    them,
at the moment you knew the time was
    right,
and stood, a willing sacrifice for the people,
awaiting your death.
May it be thus today, Beast Lord.
May no animal come before my weapon
    except as you will.
May no animal be taken by me except in
    the moment that is right.
May we never forget that it is death that
    feeds our lives.

## ARTEMIS

Knowing how much you value your
    modesty
I'm not looking to find you as you go
    through these woods,
Apollo's sister.
But if you could send me a deer or two, I
    would be very grateful,
lovely Artemis.

Artemis who protects both hunters and
    prey,
bringing life to each, in turn,
bring a [deer/rabbit/etc.] to my [gun/bow].

Huntress, I will honor the spirit of my prey
  when it is dead,
as I honor you now, Goddess of Unending
  Life,
with this offering with which I dedicate my
  hunt to you.

## MISTRESS OF ANIMALS

I am going hunting, Mistress of Animals,
so as I enter the forest I set out for you this
  grain,
I pour out for you this drink,
and ask that you bring prey into my sight,
into the range of my [weapon].
If my hunt is successful,
I will also offer to the soul of the [prey]
as was done in the old times,
as it is still right to do.
For a successful hunt, I offer to you now,
and will offer to the animal then, when my
  hunt is done.

## PREY SPIRITS

[God's name], I have a deal for you:
come to my gun, and I will honor and
  remember you.

# *Festival of the Dead/ Samhain*

I pray to all the gods of death,
of darkness, of sorrow.
Though I do not love you, I respect you.
Though I do not welcome you, I honor
  you.
Though I do not invite you into my life,
I know you are already there.

The doors to winter open, for chill winds to
  blow through:
they are the doors through which the dead
  pass, from this world and returning to it
  this night.

End over end in the growing darkness it
  spins,
with no light to flash from its whetted
  edge.
With no light to flash from its whetted
  edge,
it comes as a surprise,
out of darkness, it comes unseen;
it comes in silence, it comes unheard,
until with a thud,
until with a thud it hits our breasts,
and transfixes the summer hearts we had
  not believed could die.
With hardly a hiss of resistance, the sickle
  of harvest cuts away our most beloved
  moments of past warmth.
From the harvest of grain, it comes to the
  harvest of souls.
Its silent coming pulls from us a sudden
  cry, and we mourn.
For the death of the year, we mourn.
For the death of the grain, we mourn.
For the death of the light, we mourn.
And we are shocked to learn that we mourn
  for ourselves:
we mourn for all our losses:
we mourn for every love that has ever
  passed away,
we mourn for every love that never was,
we mourn for every loss we have ever
  known,
we mourn for losses yet to be.
We mourn for all we have yet to lose,
we mourn for all dreams we will never
  realize.

We mourn for the little deaths we have
 known,
we mourn for the little ones to come,
and we mourn for the great one that will
 come at the end.
If there is no one who will mourn that
 passing, all will still be well,
for tonight we will have mourned in
 anticipation.
Tonight, we will have mourned our own
 deaths,
we will have mourned the death of all who
 mourn here with us,
we will have mourned the deaths of all that
 dies,
We will have mourned the deaths even of
 those who die unmourned.
We honor these deaths with our mourning,
that comes in the darkness through which
 Samhain's sickle flies,
that sounds through the thud of our shock
 at its arrival,
that rings out in the silence of its cutting,
that is heard after it is silent again,
that is the eternal mourning of eternal,
 unavoidable loss.
We mourn for all deaths.
We mourn.

It is a time of dark and death, of cold and
 the fading of light.
It was this time that the ancient Irish chose
 as the beginning of the year,
the new coming out of the death of the old.
We mourn that death, and all deaths we
 have known,
all that we have lost, all that we mourn,
this night between old and new.
We mourn death, and we honor death.
With fear and sadness, we leave the old,

with hope and anticipation, we enter the
 new.
We honor the old with a libation to the
 west.
We honor the new with a libation to the
 east.
By drinking from the rest, we honor both
 and bring new and old into ourselves.
Through this night and its accompanying
 ritual, we become old,
we become new.

Where did this cold come from this autumn
 night?
From the grave that waits,
from Samhain's blessing,
soon to come, to land and soul.

## THE GOD

Lord of mounded earth
and of gravestone pillar
king of the land of the dead
and of souls awaiting rebirth:
Praise to you in the Samhain night;
in darkness ever bring me light.

## HERNE

Winding your horn, you come, O Herne,
the Company of the Dead traveling behind
 you,
the Shadow Band,
this Samhain night.
In the wind among branches we hear your
 call.
We hear it, having waited faithfully,
having waited patiently,
for you to bring them here.
Come and sit, Herne, with them gathered
 round

on the ready throne we have established
    for you,
and eat with us tonight, all of you here.

## VELIONA

Veliona, protect the Ancestors
who live there among your care.
Here is pork, well seasoned and roasted
    for you,
to feed and honor you there where you
    live,
and a little more to take, we pray, to our
    beloved dead.

## THE ANCESTORS

As our beginnings are in the Ancestors,
so the beginning of the year is with this
    Samhain.
As we welcome the new year at Samhain,
so we welcome the Ancestors.
We invite you to us on this Samhain night,
this year's beginning,
that year's end,
to join us at our table, Blesséd Dead,
source of our beginning,
promise of our end.

We welcome you, the Honored Dead,
whose lives, now over, led to ours:
Welcome and greetings for those gathered
    here.

Come to us, Spirits of the Dead;
Be honored by our rites,
Be pleased with our offerings.
We invite the dead to join with us around
    the hearth:
We're one family, so it's their hearth, too.
Honored dead, welcome.
Is it cold where you dwell, Honored Dead?

Cold like that I feel when I think of joining
    you,
of joining you, of joining you, on this cold
    night?
Cold like I feel when I think of you joining
    me,
of joining me, of joining me, on this cold
    night?
Or do you feast in the warm well-lit halls
    of the Lords of the Dead?
Do you travel through meadowy plains in
    festival clothes, singing merry songs?
And does the cold touch you, too, when
    you think of joining us,
of joining us, of joining us, on this cold
    night?
When we call you to leave that warm and
    meadowy world do you hesitate,
as we would hesitate to answer *your* call?
Our hall is well appointed, our feast well
    spread,
showing shame to neither host nor guest.
We invite you to it: join us, join us, join us.
Together we will warm this cold night.

Eat with us, Ancestors,
on this night of the dead.
Share our meal with us
and then go on your way.

All of you Dead,
because it is Samhain I am thinking of you.
May I remember and thank you on other
    days as well.

## FOOD SPIRITS

Animals and plants who have given me life
    this year
I remember you, too,
this Samhain dinner.

## Halloween

Tonight, the world turns topsy-turvy,
and children in costumes,
hidden behind masks,
roam through the darkness asking for
    treats.
May you, all you Numinous Ones,
be as open-handed in the coming year as I
    am tonight
to these spirits of misrule ringing my
    doorbell and asking me to give.

## Rainy Season

Drop welcome tears upon the Earth, fertile
    sky.
Awaken it to new life,
feed its thirsty mouth.

## Guy Fawkes Day

### BRITANNIA

Britannia, you saved our kingdom from
    civil war,
bringing to defeat the Gunpowder Plot.
Though it ended in bloodshed, that was
    contained.
We pray to you to deserve our unity.
With bonfires and levity
we remember, we remember, we
    remember,
on the Fifth of November.

## Veterans Day

On this Veterans Day,
I praise all who have served in the defense
    of their country,
whether this or another,
whether living or dead,
whether they were killed in battle,
or died in well-earned peace.
With the aid of all the gods of war,
with the aid of all the gods of peace
with their aid I pray and praise.

I, who didn't serve, pray for the [genii/
    protecting Spirits]
of those who did.
May these words please them,
and may they, thus strengthened,
extend and enliven those who once pledged
themselves for my defense.
It is right to say such things on Veterans
    Day,
and so I make my prayer.

## Remembrance Sunday

"In Flanders field the poppies grow
Between the crosses, row on row,"
and not only do the dead of wars rest in
    Flanders,
but in many places throughout the world,
too many places.
With the wearing of this poppy I remember
    them,
a flower placed on their graves.
All-Gods, bless them, the dead.
Ancestors, they are among you now,
so that when I praise you, I'm also praising
    them.
But today I wish to praise them above all,
killed before their due time:
today I remember you,
all of you who died in war,
on this Remembrance Sunday
I do this.

# Thanksgiving

Here we are, gathered on this wonderful
    holiday, among family and friends,
and all we can think is "thank you."
Thank you to all those whose presence
    made this celebration possible,
and gratitude most of all to the Shining
    Ones,
whom we will continually praise.

All the gods and goddesses
All the Ancestors
All the Spirits of the land in which we
    dwell:
we thank you for all that you bestow,
you who are the givers of gifts.
We thank you today, this Thanksgiving Day.
We remember you and ask that you
    remember us.

## LUG AND BRIGID

Lug, who knows when to plant and when
    to harvest.
Brigid, who gathers families together
    around one hearth.
We thank you for this full table.
We thank you for the family gathered
    about it.
We thank you as it is right this
    Thanksgiving Day
with gratitude and praises:
Lord of the Harvest, Lady of the Hearth.

# First Frost

First frost, harbinger of winter to come,
I praise the Spirits who have brought you
    here,
and the Earth whose journey through space
has brought us to this time.

# Beginning of Winter

First snow, tuck the earth in under your
    feather quilt:
keep her safe till spring.

As the cold time begins,
I turn toward it with courage,
knowing I do not face it alone.
All the Holy Ones are with me;
we will face it together.

Facing the winter
with fear, with trepidation,
this time of cruel ice,
we will trust the Gods
and the mighty Ancestors;
we will sing in the darkness,
we will dance in the cold,
and all will be well.

As winter closes in,
I will fight the coming cold,
the coming dark,
the death around me.
I will fight for life.
And when I fail, as I will,
may it be with grace.
Summer deities,
Spirits of growth and life,
stand by me in my struggle.
Winter deities,
Spirits of the hard and the dead,
be good winners.
Teach, not punish me,
who has only fought for what I love.

Leaves fallen, snow still to fall:
this season has no name.
Even so, I praise the Spirits who watch
    over it,
who prepare the world for winter.

First snowflakes,
flurries,
portents of beauty and hardship:
Welcome!

## THE CONSTELLATION ORION

Bold Orion on the rise,
see the summer fall before you:
guard us in the growing dark.

## SKAÐI

Skaði, bring snow,
to make beautiful the earth,
distracting us from the cold that grips it.
The snow that falls in the winter
will fill the reservoirs on which we will
    depend in summer,
and it is through your gift that we will
    grow our crops.
Goddess of winter, bring us a good summer
through your welcome snow.

## LAND SPIRITS

The leaves may fall,
the grass may die,
but the Land Spirits live,
and to them I pray.
Though some may sleep,
others awake
to face the cold,
to bless the Earth
with the gifts only they can give.
Spirits of rock and tree,
Spirits of running and still water,
Spirits of Earth and sky:
to the ones who now go to sleep,
farewell until the warm time.
To those who now awake,
once again, I greet you,
as the Earth once again enters winter.

## RAIN SPIRITS

Winter rain, are your drops tears because
    no one praises you?
Here are my words for your beauty:
may it be tears of joy you pour down.

# Early Winter

Cry the winter rains to prepare the way,
to mourn the darkness now enfolding.
Cry the winter rains to prepare the way,
to wash pure the world as it lies here
    waiting.
Cry the winter rains, sky overarching,
but soon the sorrows' tears will turn to joy.
Light will return to the covered Earth.
Cry, Rain Spirits, as this time demands.

# Winter

## THE GOD

There is beauty in emptiness,
and in the skeleton of trees against the
    darkening blue of dusk's sky.
When my teeth chatter in winter's wind,
    remind me of this,
God who dwells in the dark as well as the
    light.

## SUN

All through the growing season it was you
    whose light allowed the growing:
How can we not praise you, here in the
    darkness?
All through the growing season it was you
    whose heat allowed the growing:
How can we not praise you, here in the
    cold?
All through the growing season it was
    through your heat and light that there
    was growing at all:

How then can we not praise you, standing
    here in the cold and darkness,
even as our souls cry for heat and light:
You are found even when hidden.

Though even at noon you are low in the
    winter sky, your glory is worth of praise,
and so my prayer.

## SNOW SPIRITS

Tomorrow I will no doubt curse you as I
    drive to work.
I hope you will forgive then, remembering
    how charmed
I was as you fell.

On each flake ride
to the waiting below,
the whitening world,
Spirits of Snow.

With silent steps you come, Snow Spirits,
silently descending, silently landing.
You who silence the world with your
    falling,
silence it so I can hear from you:
I hear silence.

# Pearl Harbor Day
# (December 7)

So many lost, so many dead,
by bullets, by bombs, by inrushing water:
a day of infamy indeed.
May they sleep well, sleep gently,
those whose lives were ended so cruelly,
or who lived with the scars,
of mind and body,
from that day.
Those who rest beneath the waves,

or are buried beneath soft grass,
we remember you today,
and grieve your loss.

# Yule

This is the long night.
This is the cold night.
This is the dark night.
This is the night of last hope.
This is the night of the little spark.
This is the night of turning from darkness.
This is the night of turning toward light.
This is the night of wonder.
The long night is here:
come to us, you Spirits;
together let us fill the long night with light,
calling all beings to warm themselves at
    our fires.

Each candle we light is a star.
Let us light as many as we can, and spend
    time among the stars we've created on
    Earth.
Let us know that their twinkling is them
    smiling, because they know a secret:
the Sun will be coming back, and not only
    returning, but strengthening,
from this day through many,
from this darkest of nights.
On Yule, let us laugh with the stars at our
    fear of eternal darkness,
laugh with these earthly stars we've lit.

Ring the bells of Yule
in the dark night.
Ring the bells of Yule
for the morning light.
Ring in your heart.
Ring in the night.
Ring in the light.

May the wolf be kept far from the Sun,
with bound jaws beyond the walls,
even in the dark night of the year.
May the long winter be far off, and
    Ragnarok delayed.
We pour this mead to the Einherjar,
and to all of the gods of Asgard,
in thanks for summers past
and in hopes for summers to come.

## The God

The child in the Mother's arms
though only just born,
is already too bright to look upon:
the returning Sun,
Golden-rayed God,
shows himself once more,
unconquered by the dark.
In honor of him we light our fire
and pass it from each to the other,
until we form our own ring of flame
mirroring that which returns,
born from Her womb.

## The Goddess

How is it that you give birth to everything,
    Lady,
never once growing infertile?
Even in the cold time, when everything
    seems dead,
each moment is born after its predecessor
and time goes on: you give birth even in
    the poverty
of winter.

## Earth Mother

You were right, Earth,
that the Sun would return,
that the dark would lessen,
that light would grow.
I see it now:

the day is bright that much longer,
each day a little more.
So wonderful, Earth!
Let's be happy together.

## Sun

Around me burn the lights of Yule;
I am filled with their light,
renewed by their light.
I pray to you, new Sun,
Reborn, O Lord, from the dark.

Happy birthday, Sun!
The whole world is spread beneath you,
wrapped in darkness,
as a present for you to open.

The safely contained fire on the hearth is
    a herald in winter's cold of the power
    of the summer's Sun, which will be the
    outside hearth of the sky.
The herald has arrived, if not the One who
    sent it.
On this midwinter's night we are here to
    acknowledge the message of hope,
but also to praise and offer to the herald
    itself, whose glorious friendship is itself
    worth this prayer.

Sink without fear,
without fear in the west, O Sun,
without fear of our fear,
without fear that your children will fear.
For you will rise again,
you will arise stronger.
For you will grow again,
you will grow stronger.
The tide is turning again, we have no fear,
for it's Yule.

*Chapter 18*

# TIMES OF LIFE

Each moment of my life, born and dying away,
I place in offering on your altar, All-Gods

## *Pregnancy*

My words to all the gods:
which of you watches over this child?
Who will protect her, during her whole
   life?
Whom should she worship to ask for this
   help?
Who will be fit for her to worship when
   she is old enough?
I await your answer.[12]


[Patron deity], I am undergoing a great task,
one I gratefully accept.
Be my strength in this time.
[Household deity], a new one has come
   into our family,
welcome her and protect her until her birth.
All the gods and goddesses, your people
   are increased.
Rejoice with me; a new life has come.

---

12    It is never too early to learn if a deity has taken an
interest in your child. After this prayer, sit or stand in silence for a while, listening. It is likely that a deity will enter your awareness, thereby answering your questions. If
not, continue with your life; the answer will likely come in
time. You can say this prayer as often as you need to, until
you receive an answer—every day if you like. If you do
not learn the child's patron before he or she is old enough
to pray, the child can do it him or herself. Once the deities
have made themselves known to you, make sure you make
an offering to them. Install images of them in your family
shrine and pray to them regularly. My daughter is grown,
and I still pray to her patron at least once a day.

## THE GOD AND THE GODDESS

May this child, living for now in the
   womb,
be carried, safely, to [his/her] birth in the
   proper time
into this world
this lovely world,
under your protection,
God and Goddess.

## THE GODDESS

Each moment you experience this,
you who bring each moment through to its
   proper time.
This is my first pregnancy, however,
and I lean on you, asking for strength.
During the time of growing, give me
   strength.
Guide the baby in the way it is to grow,
bring it to health and strength.
During the time of waiting, give me
   patience,
so that my pregnancy might reach its
   fulfillment in its proper time.
You are my model, Mater Dea,
and I look to you for help.

191

## G<sup>w</sup>ouwindā

G<sup>w</sup>ouwindā, I see your soft eyes:
see me standing here.
G<sup>w</sup>ouwindā, I hear you when you speak:
hear me as I pray.
Receive gladly the sweet milk I pour.
A child is coming, lovely one:
release them as I release this offering.

## Juno

Beautiful Juno, of the lovely eyes,
bless all pregnant women,
and all in childbirth,
and all with infants in their arms,
or children playing around their feet.
See these flowers I've set out for you,
the closest I could come, perhaps, to your
    beauty,
and look with gentleness and power
on all those for whom I pray.

## Laima

Laima, are you chiefest of the deities?
Some say that even high-seated Dievas
    obeys your will,
and it is that which he enforces when he
    travels to and fro.
You do, at least, bring babies forth in their
    time
so that they enter the world according to
    that which is right,
to that which must be.
Bless this woman, then, that her child may
    thrive till birth,
and enter the world crying lustily,
as if in a prayer in your honor.

## The Matronae

Matronae Three, sitting so gently,
I will need both gentleness and strength in
    the days ahead.

Aid me as I become a mother:
You know well what that means.
May I know also.

# For a Soon-to-be Father

## The Goddess

I stand on the outside, Mother.
I do not feel the changes, only see them.
I am dismayed, Mother;
I don't know what to do and my body
    won't tell me.
You will have to tell me so I can help your
    daughter.
Teach me, Mother, how to be a father.

# Birth

Which of you Gods, which of you
    Goddesses,
have helped bring this child into our
    world?
Whether one, or a few, or many, or all,
even if I don't know which ones you are, I
    thank you;
those who should receive my thanks,
    please do.

May your pockets never be empty,
may your hands never be closed.
May you receive graciously,
may you give gladly.
May you be a pleasure to know,
may you always be among friends.
Long life, happy life,
beautiful life, useful life.
We bless you today:
may you always be blessed.

Stand about her, servants of the Mother,
singing the birth songs clearly
so that the baby, although deep inside,

may learn what it must know
to do what it must do.
Go before her, Way-Shower,
open the gates, open the doors,
open all ways, that the birth might be easy.

The child moves down the birth canal
on the first of its many journeys.
[Mother goddess], may its journey be
    smooth and safe.

## THE GOD

A father's love seems hard,
Father of All,
but is freedom to do,
is challenge to act.
As you open before my child life's
    responsibility
walk beside [her/him] as Guide.

## THE GODDESS

Seeing the child to whom I have given
    birth
I think of you, forever giving birth to all.
You are the perfect mother, even with so
    many children.
May I be as perfect a mother to this one
    child,
never achieving that goal,
but finding in it not despair but dedication.

You who gives birth to all things, living
    and nonliving,
this child of yours offers this child of yours
    to you.

## THE ALL-GODS

I love my [daughter's/son's] child as much
    as I love [her/him],
so I ask the same blessing on this little one
    as I have on my own child.

As my line continues, all you Holy Ones,
    continue to bless my family,
that we might, out of our happiness, have
    reason to bless you.
All-Gods, bless my [grandchild/
    granddaughter/grandson],
from this day forward, throughout our
    lives.

## AURORA

Aurora,
herald the dawn of this new life.

## HELIOS

Open your eyes, little child,
"Open them," is the prayer of Helios, who
    lights the world.
Open your eyes to the beauty of your life.

## THE ANCESTORS

Spirits of the Ancestors, do you see what
    has been done?
A child has been born to continue your
    line.
Once again, a link is forged in the ancient
    chain
and we are all connected that much tighter.
Bless this child, then;
she carries your memory forward to the
    future.

Ancestors,
Fathers and Mothers,
I place this child,
the continuation of your line,
under your care.
It is through [him/her] that the knowledge
    of you will continue.
It is through [him/her] that remembrance of
    you will be continued.

It is through [him/her] that your honoring
    will continue.
[He/She] is the one through whom you will
    be seen in the future.
Bless [him/her], watch over [him/her].
May [he/she] grow and flourish
that your will may be seen in this world
    again and again.
I place this child in your care.

## Infancy

May the gods walk beside this child
    throughout her life,
guiding her steps into the way proper to
    her,
guiding her way along the sacred path.

### THE GOD AND THE GODDESS

On this baby who rests in my arms,
pour blessings, O Lord, pour blessings.
On this baby who rests in my arms,
pour blessings, O Lady, pour blessings.

### THE GODDESS

Some of [her/his] first hair,
that grew when [she/he] was yet in the
    womb,
we offer to you, Goddess,
burying it in your Earth womb.

### THE ANCESTORS

We bring before you today one of yours,
    people of our past,
one who will continue what you started in
    the long-ago time.
She is one of us, one of the family that
    reaches so far back,
and we will need to guide her until she is
    ready to
assume her full responsibilities.

Be with her and us as we do that; as she
    grows, be at her side to help.
Come to us today to learn who she is,
come and celebrate with us.

## Naming

We welcomed you to life.
We welcomed you to birth.
We welcomed you to your family.
And now, by giving you this name, we
    welcome you to society.
This will be how you will introduce
    yourself to others:
"Hi, my name is [name],"
and they will reply,
"Hi, [name]; glad to meet you."
So this is what we are saying today:
"Hi, [name]; glad to meet you."

We give you the name [name], little one,
such a big gift for such a little person.
Though you are too young to accept it
    yourself,
and to thank its givers,
your parents accept it in your stead,
this name given in love,
by those who look forward to your hearing
    it joyfully.
We speak this name into your ears,
the first time you are hearing it.
You will hear it many times in your life,
from many people with many intents,
but never with as much love
as we speak it now, [name].

### THE GOD AND THE GODDESS

With this word, with your name, [name],
we weave you into the web of words
that together sing the love of the God and
    Goddess.

## The Goddess

You give birth, and know the pains and
    joys of bringing children into the world.
You watch us grow, and know the worries
    parents share for their children.
You bless all in general with the protection
    a mother brings.
Bless this child in particular, whom we
    bring to you today to be given a name,
Goddess, lover of children.

May your name be a bead in the necklace
    of souls around the neck of the Great
    Goddess,
decorating Her beauty,
adding to it its own.

## Parenthood

Holy Ones, see what has happened here!
I have become a [father/mother];
a great mystery indeed.
I do not know in my head what to do,
I know in my heart what is right.
May I know the right thing with all of me
and do it no matter what the pain.
A hard road lies before me, Shining Ones,
a road filled with great difficulties,
a road filled with great joys.
Guide me along it.
Be at my side.

## The God

Father of Worlds, I turn to you in prayer
that you might bless my father,
who took your role here on Earth and
    performed it well.
May I act the role as artfully!

## Childhood and Growth

Prayers are an important introduction to
our religion. They contain principles of belief and guides for conduct and provide a
healthy example of the proper relationship
between the gods and people. Through
them, children may first come to experience the sacred, something that will sustain them through their whole life. Don't
just pray for your children, then; pray with
them.

## For Children

Today my child took her first step.
May it be the first step on the path of the
    gods.
Open the way for her, you who love her,
guide her, protect her, walk beside her.

## Hera

Keep an eye on my daughter, Hera,
as the day goes by,
whether I am with her or not.

## For a Sick Child

[Patron deity], your child is ill.
Bring her to health.
I pledge you an offering of [offering] when
    she is well.

Eternal Balance, see what I place before
    you,
listen to the story I tell:
there is a disturbance here, something that
    should not be.
A child is sick. How can this be?
You know that the business of childhood is
    growing.
Yet sickness prevents growth.
How can it be, then, that this child is sick?

Perhaps you were sleeping and did not
notice.
I have brought it to your attention now,
and I know you will do what is right.
Eternal Balance, Continuous Harmony,
I place my child in your arms for healing.

## Children's Prayers

May I always walk carefully on the path of
the gods
with my eyes and ears open to their
teachings.

### THE GOD AND THE GODDESS

As I grow and learn,
help me, O Mother,
help me, O Father,
to know what is right
and to do only that.

I have a mother and I have a father.
They have mothers, and they have fathers.
We all have mothers, we all have fathers.
And we all have the Mother, and we all
have the Father,
Our Goddess and God, to keep us safe.

### HERMES

Hermes, tricky one,
even as a child you were clever.
Help me with this problem.

### OGMIOS

Ogmios, god of learning,
guide me in school today.
Keep my mind open
and fill it with learning.

### LAND SPIRITS

Land Spirits, show yourself to me
and teach me to love nature.

## First Day of School

Ogmios be at your right hand, guiding your
way.
Rosmerta be at your left hand, guiding
your way.
Cernunnos open your mind, and the
Mothers keep you safe,
as you begin the great adventure of school.

## First Day of School/ Graduation

Brigid, and Ogmios, and Apollo, and
Hermes, and Tahuti, and Vāc:
and all the deities
and all the Ancestors,
who guide children in learning.
Whether I know you and have worshiped
you,
Whether *anyone* has known you or ever
worshiped you,
today's offerings are for you,
to ask you to guide this child in [his/her]
education from this day/to thank you for
your guidance of this child on [his/her]
graduation day.

## School

Your pencils the spears of Lug,
your lunch the fire of Brigid,
your notebooks the tablets of Ogma.
Go to school with the gods,
go to school with the blessings of the gods,
go to school under their protections.

## Coming of Age

Look upon the deities of your home one
   last time.
[pause]
Don't worry, this isn't really the last time.
For the rest of your life you will often
   return to them.
But it will be different; it will be as if
   returning to a home you once lived in,
feeling welcomed, and enjoying the
   memories,
but knowing it is not really yours anymore.
Offer this last time to the deities of that
   time, thanking them for what they have
   done for you.
They won't all be staying. Many will come
   with you, even though your relationship
   will change. Offer to them and invite
   them to come along.
Turn away toward your future now.
There is a threshold in front of you. No
   matter what, and no matter when, you
   will have to cross it.
The question is, will you be dragged, or
   will it be willingly?
If it is willingly, offer to the god of the
   threshold, and then step across boldly,
   with your right foot, to enter a new life
   rightly.


No one asked you if you wanted to grow up:
Nature forced you.
But now, each day you will choose how to
   fulfill this new-acquired responsibility.
Don't blame Nature, but thank Her, for the
   unimaginable gift she's forced on you,
the gift of something to match yourself
   against,
the gift of a challenge to meet.
Relax, though; I know you can do it.

I went over the top first, to clear the way
   for you.
I yelled, "Follow me!" and you did.
You've followed me long enough:
go on ahead.
It's as safe as it's going to be.
I'll watch your back; I'll be covering you.
It's as safe as it's going to be.
Go on ahead with my blessing promise.

At this time of great change, I tell you a
   hard truth:
you are the one who must undergo this task.
I cannot do it for you, nor can any others
   do it for you.
Your magic lies within.
You know what to do.
Look deeply and you will see.
A hard time lies before you, but you go
   under the protection of the Holy Ones
and you go guarded by our love.
Gods of clear sight,
Goddesses of the fierce change,
help your daughter in what she must do.
Be beside her, be with her, be her unfailing
   aid.
Help her to do what she must.


Your whole life has been for this moment.
We have held you close only so that we
   might someday let you go,
made a loving home only so that you might
   leave to create your own.
Do not forget what we have taught you.
May those who have helped us pass on
   these lessons,
help them to make them yours to live by,
and someday pass along.
From generation to generation the ones
   who guide us haven't
abandoned us,

and they will not abandon you,
though you are far from your original
    home in one of your own
created according to all we've taught you.
Go, now, with the blessings of the Blesséd
    Ones
and those of us who love you enough to let
    you go.

## THE ALL-GODS

Balanced on the knife blade,
you come to me for blessing.
And I, your father, say this:
Be true. Be strong. Keep your promises.
Seek wisdom. Love your friends.
Be at peace. Bless your children.
This is my blessing to you.
May all the Holy Ones help you to make
    it true.

# Blessings for a Child Leaving Home

I stand here as your father, in the place of
    the Father of All,
as you prepare to move away and start your
    own household.
Though you may live in another house, still
    the gods will protect you.
Though you may join your life to another's
    family,
still will the Ancestors guide you.
Though you may travel in strange lands,
still will the Spirits there welcome you.
For my father's blessing is not for your
    ears alone:
the numinous beings hear, and they will
    honor it.

Go on your way in safety,
bringing with you the blessings of my
    household gods.
As you have been with us, so will you stay
    a part of us.
May they watch over you until we meet
    again.

# Weddings

I pray to you, goddess of weddings,
who for so long presided over these happy
    rites.
We call to you again;
come to us,
and once more shower blessings
on those who come before you.

May the blessings of all the world descend
    on this couple:
the blessings of Earth, the blessings of Sky,
the blessings of the moving Ocean and of
    the never-still Wind.
From the people of stone, blessings;
the blessings of plants and the blessings of
    animals;
of two-legged and four, of six and of eight;
and the blessings of the footless ones.
From all those who dwell on the Earth
and in it and above it,
may blessings flow.
Join hands,
Join hearts,
Join lives,
Join voices in prayer with those who love
    you,
gathered here on this happy day.

[Name], look into her eyes.
[Name], look into his.

From the beginning of humanity
Man has looked into Woman's eyes,
and Woman into Man's,
and seen the same thing.
Each of you look carefully into each
    others' eyes today,
and each day that you live see what you
    see today
and what has always been there since the
    beginning.

You might think that you've come here as
    individuals, but hoping to be made one.
And so, if your vows are true, you will be.
But you aren't just individuals:
you are every man and woman.
So when you become one, every man and
    woman are made one,
and those watching here aren't just present
    because they love you,
but as representatives of all men and of all
    woman.
In your becoming one, they are made one.
This day is yours, but not yours alone,
it belongs to all humanity, living and dead.
Don't think that this makes you less
    important:
it makes you more.
You are individuals, and nothing is taken
    from that.
Your love, and your need to be married, are
    admired by everyone here;
and everyone here is grateful to you as
    well;
to you as individuals,
willing by your love today to join all
    humanity together,
in the eternally renewing and mysterious
    unity that is our species.

These two are young today
as they place their love in each other's
    hand,
and it may seem odd to wish them old age.
But I do—I wish them to come to old age
    together,
as happy as they are today.
Long life, long love,
may the gods grant you these.

## THE GOD AND THE GODDESS

On this couple who stand before you,
pour blessings, Holy Ones, Divine Pair,
that their union may be as strong as yours,
lasting through all ages.

That there might be love, she formed him
and drew him to herself.
And he, with newly opened eyes,
knew with clear sight his true fate.
And she, with her heart's own true wisdom,
knew that love had passed expectations.
They loved, they love, they will love.
Blessings on love and on all who love.
Blessings from the gods and goddesses of
    love.

God and Goddess, Husband and Wife:
May this marriage be strong.
May this marriage be long-lasting.
May this marriage be productive.
May this love be true and truly made,
as is yours, Eternal Lovers,
As the God and Goddess you join together:
two to each other, and one to all who see
    you,
and in the life you will live,
you, joining together in our witness today.

## AUSTĖJA

Austėja, on the eve of my wedding,
this mead to you,
this honey to you,
these sweet wheaten cakes to you.
May my marriage be equally sweet,
and may the wedding that begins it
be its joyful inception.
Bring happiness on those who witness it,
and make my [bride/groom] a model,
tomorrow and for our lives together,
of how happy a marriage can be,
how honey sweet.

Honey is sweet,
and so is Austėja.
Mead is sweet,
and sweetly we give it to her.
Bless this wedding with sweetness,
Sweet Goddess.

## DIONYSOS

Dionysos, god not only of bliss,
but of faithful and dedicated love,
be both my model and my guide
in my life as a husband.

## JUNO

Marriage guardian, Juno,
wife of Jupiter Greatest and Best,
protector, mother, queen:
I pray to you on my wedding day
to make my marriage as wonderful as
    this day.

# Aging

## THE GOD

Old Man,
I am becoming one, too.
May I not be a stereotype,
yelling, "Hey kids, get off my lawn,"
or spending my time thinking about my
    glory days,
or telling stories exclusively about how it
    was when I was young.
May my stories instead be to impart
    wisdom, hard-earned.
May my todays have their glory, too.
May I be welcoming of the younger
    generation,
who will take my place just as I am taking
    that of those before me.
May I be an Elder, worthy of respect.
May I be a source of knowledge.
May I serve my community in this time as
    well as I have served it up till now.
May I accept by aging gracefully,
for it is a noble phase I am entering,
vital to my people.
Old Man, this is so much to ask,
yet I ask it anyway,
since I have such need,
and there is need for others in my
    performing these tasks well.
You who care about the continuation of
    society
and who knows these things well,
grant them to me,
who come to you for aid.

## THE GODDESS

I have not ended my role as Mother,
only shifted the identify of my children
    from those of my body
to those of my culture at large,

and to do this well I will need your
   wisdom, Crone Goddess,
and your patience as well.
May I not alone turn inward to consider the
   experiences of a fruitful life,
to grow in understanding of all that has
   happened,
but may I be a good teacher to those who
   need it,
that my gifts may not end with me
but continue in the line of which I am part.
This is what you do, Old Woman:
may I do it as well.

## Dying

It is a hard thing to die.
You leave behind everything.
It all stays:
Your family, your herds,
Your fields, your weapons,
Your jewels, your tools.
They may lay them beside you
but you are gone
and there they still lay.
You go into the dark
Where you will be reborn.
No one can say where
or when or as whom.
Doubt comes as you lay dying.
That is the last thing to
leave behind.
Leave it all behind.
Leave it behind and die.
See, your road is ahead.
Go on your way.
It is an easy thing to die.
Like a leaf on the stream
it pulls you on.
Go with it.
It will take you.

Come, I will go with you.
Part of the way I will come
but only part.
There will come a point
where we will separate.
You will go on.
I will go back.
This is the way things are.
My time is not here yet.
Your time has arrived.
Come, I will go with you
as far as I can.
It is a hard thing to die.
It is an easy thing to die.
And part of it we will do together.

### THE GOD

First one to die,
to you I pray.
To you I call,
as you sit between this world and the next:
God of the in-between,
to you my words go out.
As I approach the moment of my death,
as I come closer to the point of
   transformation,
as I grow nearer to the time of ending,
I ask your help.
Grant me the courage to do what I must do.
Grant me the wisdom to understand its
   necessity.
Grant me the peace that you have found,
the peace that is found in the land between
   the
worlds.[13]

---

13   The imagery in this prayer is based on Indo-
European beliefs, in which the Lord of the Otherworld
was once alive. In the first sacrifice, however, he was the
victim. Through his sacrifice, the world came into being,
and, as the first to die, he became the appropriate ruler of
the dead.

Lord of Death, I will greet you soon with
    arms wide open in trust
as I cross the boundary into your realm.
I will enter the world beyond worlds
with my eyes open and my head lifted,
ready to experience its unique wonders,
no less beautiful than in this world I have
    known.
I will go to the Land of Youth,
to rest in your halls, O gods of my people,
to commune with the spirits of those who
    have gone this way
and who wait for me, there on the other
    side.

## THE GODDESS

There will be a time, Old Woman,
when I will see your face, Old Woman,
at the right time, Old Woman,
and not before.
[pause]
And then, Old Woman, I will likely be
    terrified.
All change is frightening,
so the greatest change of all must be the
    most frightening of all.
More terrifying still is that you *know*.
You know the terror you will bring, but
    you still come.
How cruel can you be?
But most terrifying of all is what I will see
    in your face:
love.
You come bringing terror and love.
True compassion might mean death.
[pause]
So I ask you now, Old Woman,
when I am not looking in your eyes, Old
    Woman
that when the time comes, Old Woman,

I might see beyond the terror into your
    love.
Old Woman.

At the end of my life, I put my trust in the
    gods of my people.
Ancient Wise Woman, cover me with your
    cloak
as I walk the last path that leads to your
    land.

## DEATH

Death is a king who cheerfully allows his
    subjects leeway,
accepting healing with paternal humor.
He can do this because he knows that he
    *is* king.
He knows that though he allows us
    freedom
and lets us think we have defeated him.
He is king: a king who will someday call
    us into his service.
And then we will not be able to say,
    "no"—we will be called to account as
    the price for the life
in which we have dawdled.
Death is the cost of life, a cost we will one
    day be required to pay.
May we see life as worth the candle.
and keep our honor by paying gladly.
Have you heard us, Death?
We ask you today not for continued life but
    for noble death;
not the death of a famous hero, perhaps,
but the death of a hero, nonetheless,
whose coin with which he pays his debt is
    his own life,
and who pays it gladly to keep his honor.
Help us to have the honor, Death,
and our payment will make us even more,
a worthy member of your retinue.

## DEMETER

Mother of Grain,
when you wandered the world bereft of
   your daughter,
who had been taken by the Lord of Shades
   under the ground,
a Maiden in the dark,
you mourned, with holy tears,
she who would soon be returned to you for
   part of the year,
to dwell among the dead for months long
   to you.
Demeter, I, too, have had my child taken
   by death,
but without the consolation of return, even
   for a time, however short.
See a mortal's tears, feel them as they fall
   on your breast,
and know them as if they were your own.
You, a mother, see me, a mother,
and mourn with me till the time for
   mourning is over.
And bless my ache, not a heart cut by grief.
Cry, bereft, cry;
move even the gods to tears, to holy tears,
as they mourn with you your loss,
as they mourn with me my own.

## Death

I am not so out of touch with reality that I
think that a dying person can necessarily say
these prayers. They can, however, be said
on someone's behalf, guiding them home.

May I enter the Great Dark with eyes open,
the Great Silence, singing.

## THE GODDESS

It is a great thing to ask, Goddess, Crone:
a good death, a capstone of a well-lived
   life.
Yet to you it is such a small thing, Crone,
   Goddess,
so I dare ask it of you.

Fearful One, when I see your face,
may it be without fear,
may it be without terror,
may it be without panic.
Old Woman, when I see your face,
may it be with understanding,
may it be with courage,
may it be with peace.
Aged One, when I see your face,
may I be brought to wisdom
through your loving-kindness.

## GOD OF DEATH

When it is right for me to enter your
   kingdom,
Lord of Death, Gatherer of Souls,
May I go gently.
May I be a leaf dropping from a tree.
May I be a snowflake falling from the
   clouds.
May I be a drop of dew drying in the light
   of dawn.
Like opening my hands, like letting go,
Like one final gift:
May it be like that.

## INANNA

She is the great Inanna,
she who took the long path,
took the dark path,
took the path of sorrows,
took the path that inclines downward,

took it out of love, the Great Inanna,
to recover her lost love, Dumuzi.
She is the great Inanna,
who was stripped of her jewelry,
who was stripped of her garments,
who was stripped of her power:
she is the great Inanna,
there in the dark land where the dead go.
Great Inanna, be with me when I must go
    that way.
May my losses be regained.
May they be returned.
May I live, though dead,
there in the land to which you went.
Great Inanna, attend to the prayer of your
    worshiper.

## WODEN

You lead the dead on the Wild Hunt,
    Woden;
they follow you to the land to come.
Be my leader, too, after my death,
bringing me to that joyful place.

# For the Recently Dead

You are one of the Ancestors now, [name],
so when I pray to them I will be praying
    to you.
I start today: praise, Wise One;
may you bless your children.

## GOD OF DEATH

Open the way, Lord of Death,
for this one to travel.
Be his guide, show him the right path,
that you yourself traveled in the before time.
You who blazed the trail, leaving your
    marks behind,
teach him the signs to follow.

Make the road clear, removing the blocks.
Speed him on his way to your home.
Accept him into your land.

## THE ANCESTORS

You are journeying across the dividing
    water that lies
between this world and the next,
carried away by the ferryman on your way.
Look ahead of you, do not look behind.
Look ahead of you, where your destiny lies.
Do you see them? They are there, ahead of
    you on the other shore.
Slowly, they become visible to you;
the Shining Ones appear slowly out of the
    concealing mists.
Clearly they appear to you, though hidden
    from our eyes.
Go to them, they welcome you.
Go to them, not stopping for farewells.
Holy Ones in the world beyond,
open wide your arms to receive this one
    who is journeying to you.
Make him a home, bring him to rest.
Farewell, [name].
We who have loved you wish you a good
    journey.

# Funerals

His boat's keel scrapes on the beach's
    shingle.
Leaping from the prow, he is home,
finally home,
where his life began and where it will
    begin again.

May your soul take a soft-footed journey,
on a soft-floored path through the old
    forest

to the Land of Comfort,
where the only tears are the drops of rain
  falling from leaves,
the only moaning deep ocean swells,
the only sighing light evening breezes.
Rest in that land, with the peace you have
  earned.

*[During this prayer, a circle is traced on the
corpse's forehead with a paste made from
powdered red chalk.]*

I anoint you with the red of blood: may the
  blood of life return to you in that other
  world.
I anoint you with the wet: may the
  suppleness of water return to you in that
  other world.
I anoint you with the Sun: may the warmth
  of the Sun return to you in that other
  world.
I anoint you with a red, moist Sun: may life
  return to you in that other world.

To the person who has gone, we say:
"Peace between us; go on your way with
  our blessings."
To those who are here, we say:
"Peace among us; may we live blessed
  together.

I place these pegs in the ground of the
  grave,
encompassing it in a ship.
Gods who steer the dead to their home,
take them on board this grave-ship
and guide them well to the halls of feasting
  where their ancestors dwell.

## THE GODDESS

Mother of All, absorb the spirit of our
  loved one
back into your womb from which he was
  born.
There, reshape him in your place of
  molding,
preparing him for rebirth among his
  people.

His whole life has been like waiting and
  growing in your womb.
The time has come for his birth, from this
  world into another.
Bring him, Goddess, through the pangs of
  this new birth,
there into that other world.
Hold your baby there, draw him close to
  you, feeding him with inexhaustible
  milk from your ever-giving breasts.
Rock him in your soothing arms, until he
  knows the peace of a baby resting in his
  complete faith in his mother.

## AGNI

Like butter in the flames
this body in the fire.
Bring, Agni, into glory,
this one of our people.

## CHARON

Old Man, ferry this one across safely,
bringing him swiftly and without detour
to the other side of the great sea.
Pole your boat here to this place and
  perform your duty.
His fare is paid, his place secured,
so take him aboard and carry him away,
over the sea, following the setting Sun,
to the landing place before the great city

where the Lord of Death rules.
Bring this one before he who sits on his
   throne.
Make his name known to the ruler there.
Make smooth the way, open the doors,
clear the path, unlock the gates.
Charon, this one is starting on a great
   journey.
Stand by him until he is safely home!

## OSIRIS

In the Land of the Dead,
with the trials passed,
with the dangers overcome,
with your heart weighed and found true,
be reborn as Osiris.

Osiris who rules in the land of the dead,
enthroned there in power,
extend your magic to this one who comes
   before you blameless.
[He/She] has not done wrong.
[He/She] has not done that which should
   not be done.
[His/Her] soul has been weighed against
   the feather of Ma'at
and was equal and true to that holy
   principle, that just law.
Welcome [him/her] into your world.
Make of [him/her] an Osiris there.
Cause [his/her] soul to live again.

## THOR

In whatever land our dear one must travel
   in this journey at life's end,
continue to watch over him/her, as you did
   in life.
Watch over the one who worshiped you in
   life,
who approached you in friendship and with
   many gifts.

I place upon [his/her] chest a hammer,
   Mjǫlnir's image:
may it be a sign to you, a continuing prayer
   for your blessing,
a conduit for the guidance you give to the
   one whom we bury today.

## VALKYRIES

May the Valkyries welcome you into the
   land beyond,
you whom we will always love,
with horns of mead, with horns of ale,
into the presence of the heroes.

## YAMA

Lord of the enclosed land,
ruler of the flowery plain,
Yama who first took that path:
bring this one home.
May he flourish in the land beyond.
May he be happy in your land of joy.
May he rest, may he rest.

## THE ANCESTORS

Go your way to the land of the Ancestors,
where they wait for you with open arms,
there on the edge between this world and
   the next.
See; there they stand.
Ancestral spirits, welcome this one
to the place where we all must go.

In the Shining Land,
lit and warmed by the sacrificial fires,
around the sea that teems with life,
all the Ancestors, wise and loving,
wait, patiently but expectantly,
for your arrival.
They will greet you, their friend,
and among all those who have come to that
   place,

you will live, and rest,
until the time comes for once again taking
    up a body.
You know the pain of life, you have
    suffered the pain of death,
and you know the joy of life, the love and
    beauty,
and even the wondering in awe before the
    storms you've faced.
With the farewells of those you have lived
    among,
Under the blessing of the Lord of that land,
By the unfailing direction of the Guide
    who brought you there:
return to among the people of the earth,
once again bringing happiness.

[She/He] is becoming one of you,
    Ancestors:
know [her/him] as we have.
Accept [her/him] into your company,
so that [she/he] may be one of you
as [she/he] was one of us.
[She/He] will be remembered when we
    think of you in times to come.

Receive [her/him] among you so that this
    may be right,
that [she/he] may take [her/his] proper
    place among the company of the dead.
You, [name], farewell for now,
until the next time that we honor the
    Ancestors,
among whom you will now be numbered.

# Chapter 19

# ENDINGS

Return, return, from these changing rites.
Return, return, to your daily life.
Return, return, and with fresh eyes see the
    world.

These rites are over,
this time in sacred time,
this gathering in sacred space.
We go now to our everyday lives,
but transformed by our experience of the
    sacred:
the profane less profane,
the mundane less mundane,
the everyday less everyday,
to our newly opened eyes.

It's always hard to leave a place.
But that which is left is not left behind;
it comes with us as we go,
and never leaves us,
though days and miles do their best.

Our time here is done.
We have worked.
We have worshiped.
We have been in the Land of the Gods
and rejoiced in their presence.
It is good that we have done this.
But now we must return to our land,

the same, but changed by the blessing of
    the Holy Ones.

Hear me, O people:
You have done well.
The gods are pleased
and have granted their blessings.
Go now in peace and know they are with
    you.
Peace, blessed be.

Each outward breath a step from their
    world.
Each inward breath a step toward our own.
But each beat of our hearts their continuing
    presence within us.
Though far way, they are with us now,
and will continue to be so,
securing our lives with each beat of our
    hearts.

The sand castle dissolves when the tide
    comes in.
An ice sculpture melts with warming air.
Our circle dissipates with the ending of our
    rites.
Each remains in the minds of their creators
and in the minds of all who have known
    them.

All gone.
All still here.

Go now, all of you,
each to your own home.
Go in love for the Holy Ones and each
  other,
and come together again when the time
for worship comes around.

Go with the Gods, go with their blessings.
Go with the Ancestors, go with their
  blessings.
Go with the Land Spirits, go with their
  blessings.
Go with the Kindreds, go with their
  blessings.
Go with the Sacred, go with their blessings.
Be under the blessing of the Sacred.
Be ever in its presence.

## The God and the Goddess

Under the God, may we go.
Under the Goddess, may we go.
With the God, may we go.
With the Goddess, may we go.
Continuing in the presence of the God,
  may we go.
Continuing in the presence of the Goddess,
  may we go.
Ever blessing them, may we go.
Ever being blessed by them, may we go.

All we are will be the Goddess,
All we do will be the God.
Transformed by them, but still ourselves,
we will live our lives more truly,
and we will come to them again,
pulled by the need for they who glow in
  the hearts of our souls.

A holy people,
a sacred people,
a divine people,
filled with what we have experienced here:
go now, return to your ordinary life,
you who are ordinary no more.

*Chapter 20*

# FAREWELLS

Holy Ones, Shining Ones, You whose
    power is great,
though you go on your way, may it never
    be said that we have lacked anything in
    our worship,
that we have not honored you as you
    deserve.

Farewell to you, to you who shine,
you, immortal ones, Givers of gifts,
farewell, good friends,
blessers of those who worship you,
who invite you to their table,
who share with you their best,
their libations lovingly poured.

As we called them facing east,
we say farewell facing west.
As the Sun they rose,
as the Sun they set,
as the Sun they will rise again in our lives
when we ask them to come to us.

Turn in silence, in your minds, in your
    innermost hearts,
to say goodbye to those we have
    worshiped.
Turn, and with the mind's clear voice, say
    farewell to those we have worshiped.

Turn again your thoughts and attention to
    those we have well and truly worshiped,
and now, aloud, and with love,
say, "Farewell!"

Go forth, return home,
each footfall a prayer to those who have
    blessed you,
each turn of your car's wheels one with
    Nature's turning,
each means of travel a continuation of the
    sweet blessing
of those we have honored here.

All the sacred beings who have shared time
    with us today,
have shared in our meal,
have received the offerings we have given
    with hearts of gratitude,
have heard the words of praise we have
    spoken,
the songs of beauty we have sung:
we wish you well, departing guests,
on your way from our home to yours.
Go as friends, who, as we well know, are
    great in hospitality,
whose ready invitations to your well-famed
    feasts we await eagerly,
happy to come when called,

to receive with gratitude your inevitable
gifts,
and to invite you to come again to dine
with us.

You go now to your homes,
our friends,
from this place of celebration.
We go now to our homes,
your friends,
from this place of celebration.
As friends we have shared this time,
as friends enjoyed this party together,
as friends celebrated these rites,
each one doing what friends do when they
get together.
We will celebrate again,
as friends do,
here, or elsewhere,
always in a place of celebration.

The Sun sets, and it is night.
The Moon sets, and it is dark.
The frost falls, and it is cold.
But when you come,
there is day, and light, and warmth.
When we call to you from the greatest
depths of our lives,
we know that you will come to us from
love and friendship.
And with this knowledge, we say goodbye
to you,
all you Holy Ones.

Has what I have done here pleased you?
Then please me with what I have asked for.
Has what I have given been welcome?
Then give me what I have asked for.
It is only fair, and you are fair.

Spirits who have spent this time with us,
we know it is now time for you to return to
your homes,
and you know this, too:
this is our last knowing-together.
We give you this food,
to keep you strong on your journey.
We give you this drink,
to quench your thirst.
We give you these words,
to lighten the way.
With gifts and words, we give our farewell,
to you, Revered Ones,
who have blessed us today.
As you go on your way, you go with our
thanks.

We end our rites by saying our farewells
to you,
Spirits who are our dear friends.
We look forward to the time when we
gather again in your worship.
For now, though, we wish you well on the
pathways you will follow.

With these scattered grains I send you on
your way with a gift;
this libation is a stirrup cup to refresh you
for your journey.
Tell all you meet of our generosity!

[Deity], your mouth now closes,
that through which you have spoken words
of power,
accomplishing your will and mine.
This accomplished, your image will once
more
be [wood/metal/clay/etc.],
will no longer be your embodiment.

Yet it will stand in my shrine as a reminder
    of you
and of my dedication to you.

## THE GOD AND THE GODDESS

The God lives inside me,
sustaining and empowering me.
The Goddess lives inside me,
sustaining and empowering me.
Yet for this time, this short time,
they have been before me,
made manifest by my prayers and
    entreaties.
Soon I will see you no more,
yet you will be with me still.
Farewell, most loved ones!

## THE GOD

He turns away, and fades into the forest,
a stag among the trees.
Do not, we pray, stay too far away:
continue to help us
and come among us when again we call.

## AGNI

Agni, we regret that we must extinguish
    you here.
We know, however, that you won't die by
    this,
because you live in all that shines,
and in the hearts of all living things.
Before that, though, this ghee for you!

## IRIS

The Sun, the eye of Zeus, which had
    formed you,
now disperses the mists so we no longer
    see you, Iris.
Still the memory of your glory remains
    with us,
sustaining us until you are next present.

## ISIS

My awareness of your presence fades,
    Mother Isis,
your appearance in my sight diminishes
    and dwindles.
Yet even when it is gone to naught, I will
    hold you in my heart.
I will hear your sistrum in my dreams.

## MANANNÁN MAC LIR

Fare forth freely, Manannán,
on your flower-traveling chariot.
The tide recedes, and you with it,
your horse-waves your train.

## MARDUK

Marduk, I pour one last beer to you
before you go on your way to return to
    your holy mountain,
that you might be refreshed for your
    journey,
and strengthened for your battles.

## NUIT

Not farewell to you, Nuit,
but farewell to me,
as I am absorbed in your infinite body.

## ODIN

No Valkyrie, I pour out this stirrup cup to
    you, Odin,
as you mount the eight-hooved steed on
    your way to travel the world,
this mead, as if it were the source of poetry,
    which you love.
Only may you leave behind your
    inspiration and protection.

## PAN

You go, Pan, into the wilderness,
you who embody the wild.
Your enemy-scattering call will not be
    heard for a while.
But we will listen for hooves on rocks until
    you come again,
to leave behind blessings.

## PERKŪNAS

Leave with one last roar of thunder,
    Perkūnas,
with one last lightning strike.
Leave us today, to come again
swiftly to overcome any dangers
that will threaten us in the future.

## VĀC

Vāc, receive this ghee as you go,
your voice echoing in my ears.

## VENUS

May beauty be ever in my mind, Venus.
May love be ever in my heart, Venus.
May you be ever in my life, Venus.
May you never be far way.
May you always be prepared to hear me
    when I cry out.
Farewell, Lovely One, Farewell!

## LAND SPIRITS

Return to mountain and river:
you know the way.
Return to forest and field:
you know the way.
Return to desert and scrub:
you know the way.
Return to rock, to tree and bush and grass,
to animal, and insect, and bird:
you know the way.
Return, return, return to these, your homes:
you know the way.
Return, return, return to us when we call
    from our need:
May you know the way.

*[Perhaps throwing a handful of grain with
each "Return." May also be used as a
litany.]*

## NATURE SPIRITS

Spirits of the land,
who have gathered about us as we
    worshiped,
we once again do you honor,
as we are about to return this place
to your uninterrupted control.
    Thank you for allowing us our time here.
May there ever be peace between us in this
    world we share.
Nature Spirits, we thank you!

## Chapter 21

# DISSOLVING THE SPACE

Deasil, I drew the border,
Widdershins, I dissolve it,
disestablishing my sacred space,
dissolving my magic circle.

Spirits of [Air/Fire/Water/Earth], go on
  your way,
to your home, to that blesséd realm,
leaving blessings behind in the peace
  between us.

I smooth out the break between this world
  and the next,
zipping it up,
sewing together the halves of this seamless
  garment of the world we love.

A home is sacred ground,
where gods dwell.
So we do not return from sacred ground,
where gods dwell.
We remain on sacred ground,
where gods dwell.
To those gods who have come to be with
  us in this home,
where gods dwell.
believe us when we say that you will
  always be welcome in this home,
where gods dwell.
To the gods of this home,

believe that we are glad you dwell here.
And we show our belief, and our love as
  well,
with this poured-out milk and offered
  bread,
showing our happiness at living in a home,
where gods dwell.

The space that we have transformed from
  profane to sacred
we transform from sacred to profane again.
losing nothing thereby of the sacred gifts
  the divine beings have conveyed to us,
losing nothing of the knowledge of the
  mysteries we have acquired,
losing nothing of the memories of that
  blesséd land that lies beyond ours,
that supports and sustains.
May those gifts,
may that knowledge,
may those memories,
support and sustain us as we go about our
  everyday lives:
We are those who have dwelt in the sacred
  land
and will again.

# Directions

Having completed our sacred rites,
we send the Lord of Air away,
grateful for his help.
Having completed our sacred rites,
we send the Lord of Fire away,
grateful for his help.
Having completed our sacred rites,
we send the Lady of Water away,
grateful for her help.
Having completed our sacred rites,
we send the Lady of Earth away,
grateful for her help.
All of you, Lords of the Elements,
All of you, Ladies of the Elements,
to all of you we say that we are grateful for
    your help.

[In this prayer, milk is poured into a bowl
and then cast as offerings in the directions
as noted. This prayer is complemented by an
opening prayer found in chapter 8.]

We stand, pillars, in the center of the
    world,
while all else turns about us.
In the center, Cosmos gifts Chaos.
It gifts it with order and with peace.
May there be peace in the south
May there be peace in the west
May there be peace in the north
May there be peace in the east,
the place of prayer, the place of light,
the place of the Holy Ones.
And may there be peace in the center,
where we stand, pillars,
while all else turns about us.

We ask from the east the gifts of the east.
We ask that they become us.
We ask from the south the gifts of the
    south.
We ask that they become us.
We ask from the west the gifts of the west.
We ask that they become us.
We ask from the north the gifts of the
    north.
We ask that they become us.
From each direction we ask the proper gift
to bring with us as we leave this place.

Bright Ones of the east, farewell!
Bright Ones of the south, farewell!
Bright Ones of the west, farewell!
Bright Ones of the north, farewell!
Bright Ones of all directions, farewell!

The Spirits who have come among us from
the [east/south/west/north],
attracted by our rites and the power we
    have raised,
we thank you and give you our farewells
until once again you come to join us.

Numina who dwell in the [east/south/west/
    north],
thank you for the help you have given us in
    our rites.
May you go on your way with our thanks,
but come once more when we call to you
    again,
when we have need for you.

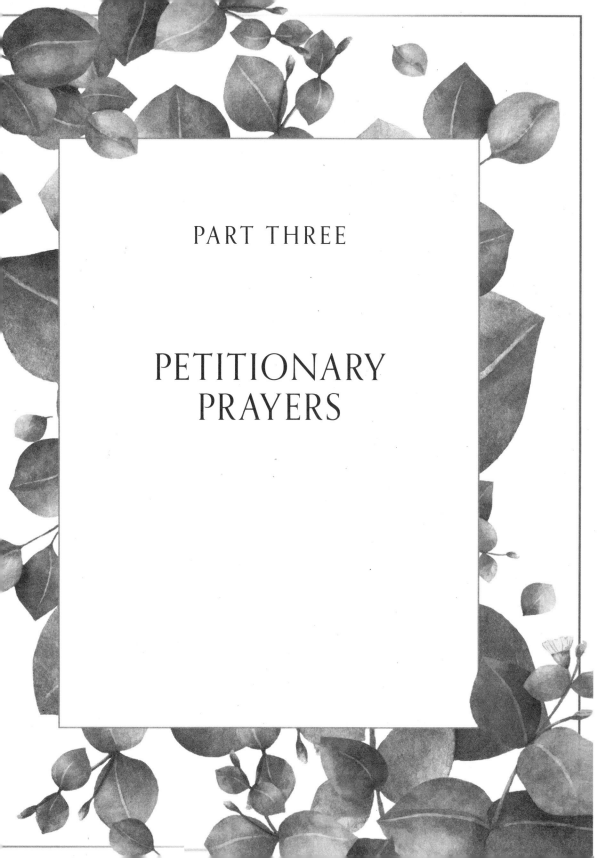

PART THREE

PETITIONARY
PRAYERS

*Chapter 22*

# PETITIONING THROUGH
# PRAYER

The work part of a ritual can vary greatly. We saw some of the major purposes a ritual can have in part 1. There are many others, however, some personal and not suited to group ritual, and some more appropriate to occasions when the rest of a ritual needs to be simplified, or even eliminated; while driving, perhaps, or waiting on the tarmac. Others, such as divination, can be parts of rituals dedicated to other purposes. I've given these prayers their own section to make it easier to find ones for specific occasions without cluttering up the main ritual part of the book.

Another reason for giving them their own section is that they are petitionary; that is, they ask for something specific. Some of the prayers in part 1 are also petitionary, but in this section petitioning is what they're all about.

People are often criticized for petitioning through prayer. In fact, it is because of this kind of prayer that prayer in general is most often criticized. The usual objection is that petitionary prayers reduce religion to a cosmic "gimme." We ask the gods and they give; if they don't, we lose faith in them and turn to other gods or Spirits. This makes the gods our flunkies who must toady to us if they know what's good for them.

Petitionary prayer can be so much more than this, though. I've already discussed prayers of thanksgiving and praise. These go a long way toward creating a good relationship with the gods and can be incorporated into petitionary prayers. Praise shows the gods, and reminds you, that you appreciate the gods, that you don't see them as your employees. Thanksgiving shows the gods, and reminds you, that you don't consider what you ask for to be your right, something they have to give you.

One way to prevent the "gimme" attitude that is not acceptable is to limit petitionary prayers to intangible things. Some of the prayers in this chapter ask for what might be described as material blessings—fertility, prosperity, health. Others ask for what might be called spiritual blessings—comfort, awareness, wisdom. It's one of the points of Paganism, however, that the material is no less valuable than the spiritual. As Pagans, we don't point our noses to the sky and say, "Well, I only pray for spiritual things." The material is just as sacred as the spiritual.

We shouldn't pray for an excess of things, though. Excess is a drain on the Earth. Pagans try not to be a drain on anything—not if they are true to their path, that is.

Pray for what's right, for what's good, for what's deserved, and let no one but the gods tell you that it's wrong.

Petitions don't have to be for your own problems, of course. After all, your concerns are tied in with those of others. For instance, the rain that is prayed for will benefit other farmers, and peace will be a gift to everyone. Still, most of the prayers in this section of the book center on the well-being of the person praying. It has been like that for millennia and is still the most common intent for spontaneous prayers.

There may be cases where petitions are specifically for others, though. Prayers for healing often do that. A prayer with an individual intent can easily be adapted for the benefit of others; this can usually be done simply by changing "me" to "this person," "my friend," "my patient," "all humanity," or a specification by name.

I've divided this section by intent. Because of the overlap of purposes, I've combined more than one in some chapters. For instance, many travel prayers are for safety, so I put them in the same chapter. "General Requests and Offerings," the first chapter of the section, is for prayers that are general in the sense that more specific petitions can be attached to them.

THE BIG BOOK OF PAGAN PRAYER AND RITUAL

# Chapter 23

# GENERAL REQUESTS AND OFFERINGS

To the east, to the south,
to the west, to the north,
to above and below,
I send my words flying.
From the east, from the south,
from the west, from the north,
from above and below,
may blessings come flying.

Surrounded by all the numinous beings of
　earth and sky and water,
I pray with confidence, for I know their
　help is certain.

I place myself at your service,
gods of my people.
Open me to your wishes,
make me a conduit for your will,
bringing forth your desires in the human
　world.

With this gift I establish hospitality with
　you.
I am your host this day;
be my host another.

I bring greetings to the gods of this place
from my people, from my family, from me,
and not only greetings but gifts of
　friendship.

I give them to you to establish between us
　the sacred bond.

We have been hosts today, and know you
　will be ours in the future.
It's been this way at least as long as there
　have been people,
and will continue to be,
even those who have forgotten you treating
　each other in the sacred way you and
　we do.

When I speak, may it be divine words.
When I think, may it be divine thoughts.
When I act, may it be divine deeds.
May what I do be divine.
May what I am be divine.
May I be divine, be divine.

My divine self asks my divine self to
　remember itself.

The first offering I make is the life of this
　wood.
I offer to that offering with this offering,
[oil/butter] to feed you.

Giver[s] of Gifts,
I give in return,
with reverent heart,
this [offering].

With this gift I maintain my relationship
    with the Gods.
With this gift I maintain my relationship
    with the Ancestors.
With this gift I maintain my relationship
    with the Land Spirits.
With gift and with gift, relationships are
    established and maintained.


Each of you has your gift,
and each your preferred offerings.
Since I can't give everything,
I give you this,
asking for gifts from those who are pleased
    by it.


Refreshed by this drink, find power and
    reason to help [me, us, etc.] to [petition].


I'm not trying to buy your affection with
    this, but to show you mine.


I pour out words of praise to you with this
    drink.
I remember you;
remember me when I need you.


With [these words/this offering/etc.] I pray
    to you today, [god's name].
I have prayed to you in the past, and will
    praise you in the future.


All the Kindreds, be honored in our midst.
We pour out our offering to you,
like living water,
like grain from a bag.
Drink deeply of the gifts we give.


Around me, all the gods of the land are
    watching—
May I do what is right.

I give from my own store to you,
the gods of this place.
Remember my generosity and be my
    friends.


Accept this gift, Holy Ones,
and keep me in your minds,
as I will keep you in my heart.


Holy Ones, Mighty Ones, I ask for your
    blessings today,
that I might be blessed with holiness and
    with fortune,
that my family might be blessed with
    holiness and with fortune,
that my community might be blessed with
    holiness and with fortune,
that my country might be blessed with
    holiness and with fortune,
that my planet might be blessed with
    holiness and with fortune.
Send them forth, you who are holy.
Send them forth, you who are filled with
    fortune.
Send them forth, upon all for whom I pray.
Send them forth, send them forth.


Blessed one, come near to me and hear my
    prayer.
You who have, since ancient times, listened
    to my people's words,
hear my prayer now.
Great is your power, and perfectly is it
    applied,
with artful skill, with respect for beauty.
My own might is little indeed;
yours is beyond imagining.
Use your power in my interests:
grant me my wishes, accomplish my
    objectives.

I place myself today in the hands of the
   gods,
knowing that their protection comes with
   a price.
For those who wish the help of the old ones
must walk their path with all their hearts.
This I promise I will do.

Even the stones make it clear to me that
   everything
partakes of the nature of the gods.
The buildings that surround me speak of
   the skills
that have been given to us by the gods in
   ancient times,
that are being given to us in these days,
that will always be given to us
by the Mighty Ones.
Remind me of this daily, you who give so
   much.[14]

Only a few words for you today,
Gods and goddesses, Ancestors and Spirits,
but all these are praise and thanks.

May I live a life of piety,
of regular prayers,
of regular offerings,
of regular turning to the Holy Ones for
   their friendship;
to give, to receive, to thank,
in continuous relationship with the holy.

---

14   The world of the Pagan includes more than the
products of nature. The gods not only produce the natural
world; they give culture. Athena, Ogma, Thoth, Coyote—
in every Pagan society, there is at least one deity revered as
the originator of skills and learning. To make too strong a
distinction between natural and artificial would not, therefore, be the Pagan thing to do. We are, after all, ourselves
part of nature, and so are our products and skills. One way
to prevent these products and skills from causing exces-
sive damage to the others with whom we share this planet
is to revere the deities who gave them to us. In this way,
we are made constantly aware of their sanctity and, thus,
of the responsibility they demand from us.

With this gift I establish hospitality with
   you.
I am your host this day;
be my host another.

Spirits of the elements, I stand in your
   center,
a being that shares in all your ways;
hear me, help me.
Spirits of the land, I praise the land's
   beauty,
and I do not separate myself from it;
hear me, help me.
Spirits of the Ancestors, I continue to walk
   the path you laid down;
hear me, help me.
Deities of my people, I worship you with
   words and actions,
as from ancient times;
hear me, help me.
All of the numinous beings that crowd
   about me,
I am a fellow traveler on the ancient path;
Hear me, help me.
Hear me and help me, Shining Ones,
you who do not cease from watching:
send me aid when it is most needed.

Here on a stone, in the midst of trees,
I place an offering to the gods of this place.
Though I don't know your names,
I know you are here
and I wish for your friendship,
for me and my people.
Accept what I give you
and do not forget me.

All of you Holy Ones
All of you Sacred Ones
All of you Numinous Ones:

We give this libation to you,
All of you Kindreds.
We worship you today.

Spirits of this place,
whether you are gods or goddesses,
spirits or the dead,
accept these offerings from one who
    wishes only to
be at peace with you.
Today I am your host
and I give you a host's gifts.
Tomorrow the turn may fall to you
and you will be the hosts.
Remember that I have acted as hospitality
    requires,
and reciprocate when the time is right.
May the gods help us always to do
only that which is right.

Walk beside me, Lord of Strength,
as I undergo trial.

Listen to me, you who grant wisdom:
The stories that have been told about you
    from the
times when our race was young have
    taught me
that you are the clearest of thinkers and the
    best at deciding the proper path.
I find myself now with a choice to make
    and I do not know how to make it.
Without a clear road before me, then, I turn
    to you for help.
Path-Marker, Way-Shower, what should I
    do?
I ask that you give me a sign to help me
    decide.
Come to me with your clear counsel; come
    to me with advice.

Come to me, whether in a dream, or in
    the chance remark of a stranger, or in
    my own deliberations.
May my decision reflect your calm
    wisdom, and my life become thereby a
    pleasure for you to see.

*[The exact deity to whom this is directed will
depend on your tradition.]*

A pure smell of incense I send to the pure
    gods
to delight their noses, to please their senses,
to prepare them to receive a request not so
    sweet.

## THE GOD

If I should hesitate to approach your altar,
there in the hiding shadow of threatening
    pines,
the pillars of your cathedral:
Know that I am more afraid of what might
    be lost
than desiring of what might be gained.
Lord of Light, here Lord of Shadow,
show me the light in the shadow,
teasing me from my ignorance,
and from my fear.

A mighty bull in the field,
a penetrating mind at work:
choosing the appropriate mode, you find no
    opposition.
Lord of talents, be with me in my efforts.
Bring my plans to fruition.
Controller of the riches beneath the Earth,
fertilizer of all life upon it,
distributor of the wealth that arises from it:
Lord of the Earth, Lord of Wealth,
when sharing out your bounty,
do not forget me, who is faithful in your
    service.

## THE GODDESS

Mother, help me,
I am calling to you!
My need is great, but your power is greater.
I know you will prevail over the troubles
   that beset me.

You who gave birth to all things,
give birth to what I desire;
bring it to pass.

## THE ALL-GODS

It's not really so hard to see the gods, is it?
You open your eyes and there they are.
But I'm fooling myself if I think that
   seeing you is enough.
My deepest of gazes won't go deep enough
   to see all of you.
You are truly amazing, all of you.
The least among you is incomprehensible.
You are a different kind from me.
But are we so different?
We can meet as friends over the offering.
Perhaps you will be the greater,
but we will be friends, nonetheless.
Look what I have brought for you:
here is food.
Let's sit down and eat together like friends
   do.
Someday I will sit at *your* table.
Today, sit at *mine.*


You set before us a banquet, All-Gods,
and we ask for table scraps.
Today my prayer is, "Open my eyes."

All-Gods, may one of you hear my prayer
and help me in return for my gratitude.

## AGNI

*[with an offering of ghee]*

May this be to you as food, Agni;
Agni, may this be to you as drink.
Priest of the gods, go,
strengthened by my offering, to them,
carrying my prayers in your hands,
speaking them with your mouth.

May Agni, priest of the gods,
carry this offering to them.

If your tongues will speak my words
I will feed you with butter;
you will grow strong and carry my prayers
   to the gods.

Lord of undying fire that burns within us
   all,
my prayer is sent to you, from my heart to
   yours.
As you are enflamed, so may I be also;
filled with the fire that rolls out from your
   hidden home,
that golden-walled palace enclosed by
   living water.
Burn away my weaknesses.
Light within me a raging fire of strength.
Cause me to burn with zeal to perform the
   acts of the gods.

Agni, I offer my words to you,
as if golden butter poured on your flames,
feeding you, strengthening you, giving you
   life.
I ask you to convey my prayers to the gods,
Priest of the gods, who speaks honeyed
   words.

## APᴀM NAPĀT

Apǫm Napāt, you seized the Xᵛarǝnah,
the glory of kingship,
to hide it under the waters of the sea
    Vourukaša
to protect it from the depredations of the
    unrighteous
who sought to claim it for their own,
undeservedly.
I come before you today, declaring myself
    worthy
to receive some of what you grant to those
    whom you favor,
whom you determine properly appointed.
I declare myself purified of wrongdoing
that you might show me favor,
that you might give me a portion of the
    power to rule
that which is in your keeping.
May I rule over my passions,
May I rule over all my life,
May I rule over all tendencies toward the lie,
May I gain, as well, the power to influence
    others,
in small groups or large,
to bring them to follow the truth as you
    teach it to me.
And may you give me the power to discern
    the difference between that
and simply what I want myself,
so that I can do what is right,
rather than what is convenient,
what's proper,
rather than what is self-serving.
May your power in me, the glory, the
    Xᵛarǝnah, the power to rule,
enable me to serve the aša.

*[The aša is the cosmic order, the Truth.]*

## APĀM NAPĀT

Apām Napāt, shining in the sea,
the Waters attend you,
watching over you as mothers do their child.
You burn without fuel, self-sustaining.
It is you we propitiate
when we want pure water that enlivens us.
To you this ghee,
a ladle-full on the flames,
small before you, Napāt of the Waters.

## APHRODITE

Foam-born Cypriot goddess,
bring me love
as I have brought you this gift.
Pour it out for me as I pour this wine for you.

## ARIANRHOD

Bestower of widespread names,
Giver of means of defense,
Provider of loved ones:
you can withhold or grant, Arianrhod—
be gracious to me.

## ASHERAH

I anoint you,
your devoted follower performs this act of
    worship.
Protect the one who does this
and make [his/her] actions prosper,
bringing to fruition all their affairs
under your caring hand.
I stand in your presence
and ask this;
I pray to you,
and it is done.

## THE AŚVINS

Buried by adversity, I call upon the Aśvins
to come here quickly on their swiftest of
    horses
and free me from the pit into which I have
    fallen.
I have learned how they do this from the
    hymns and the tales,
and ask that they do it for me.

## ATHENA

This well-wrought cloth, Athena,
goddess of weaving,
to bring you the beauty you most desire,
not that of outward appearance,
but of the deed well done,
the craft well accomplished.

These olives for you, Athena;
I hope you approve of my offering,
given with loving heart.

## AUSTĖJA

Bee-queen, honey-sweet, Austėja,
I pour you mead:
bring grooms to brides
bring children to parents
bring people together in happy
    communities
under your protective wings.

## BES

Bes, you look a bit ridiculous,
but you are dead serious.
Bes, you look weak,
but that is the last thing you are.
Bes, you look like an Outsider,
but you are deep inside.
You protect children
and women in childbirth
and pregnant mothers.
You protect the future of our people
and even of our species itself.
We paint you on cribs and doors
and wear your image around our necks
because we know what only you can do.
And so we offer to you as well:
Bes, I give you this beer and bread.

## BRIGID

Brigid, Brigid, fire.
Brigid, Brigid, poet.
Brigid, Brigid, healer.
Brigid, Brigid, smith.

Inspiring one, Brigid, Brigid.
Loving one, Brigid, Brigid.
Welcoming one, Brigid, Brigid.
Protecting one, Brigid, Brigid.

Brigid, who guards children, Brigid.
Brigid, who warms the homeless, Brigid.
Brigid, who watches over the helpless,
    Brigid.
Brigid, who wraps her arms around the
    bereft, Brigid.

Brigid, Brigid, hear our prayers;
our prayers hear, Brigid, Brigid.
Your children call upon their mother,
upon their mother, Brigid,
upon you, Brigid, Brigid,
upon you, upon you, Brigid.

## CASTOR AND POLLUX

Zeus's boys, ride quickly to me:
I am in need of your help.
Save me from danger,
you who listen to desperate prayers.

## CATHUBODUA

As beautiful as a crow's eye,
bright among black feathers,
come, Cathubodua, to those in danger,
those who stand among their foes,
who search for victory:
Come with fierce comfort to all in distress.

## CERNUNNOS

Lord Cernunnos, opener of the door,
guide to the ways between,
gatekeeper of the gods,
open for me the pathway,
that all I wish for might be accomplished.

Open the doorway to truth for me, Cernunnos,
You who look this way,
You who look that.
May I see all sides of this matter
so that I might choose wisely.

## ČISTA

I offer to Čista, who guards the pathways,
    who guards the traveler, those who offer
    to her.
May I travel smoothly through all that
    separates me from the pure, the divine;
with prayers, with offerings, with thoughts
    and deeds, I will worship the numina,
as she herself, as Čista indeed, is indeed
    honored by those whom we worship.
So let her, worthy of being heard, hear our
    prayers;
so let her, worthily hearing, pass them on,
so let her, hearer of the worthy, pass the
    numina's blessings on to us.

## THE DAGDA

Turn away, Ollathair, from me the blasting
    end of your thunder club,
extending instead the one that blesses.
See: I have made porridge for you,
something I know you like.
Receive it and give in return.

Famous glutton that you are,
this offering can't come close to satisfying
    you.
Still, Good God, may it be pleasing in
    quality if not in quantity.

## DIOSKOUROI

By the star on your brows guide me
    through portending darkness, Zeus's
    boys.
On your strong horses' backs carry me
    through hard times to come,
White Foals.
From death, from poverty, from lack of
    means, save me,
Saviors of Men.

Zeus's boys, Saviors at Sea,
Helpers of all in all distress:
through the waves of danger
that surround my days,
the little boat of my little life,
guide me, sure stars, in all I do.

## EARTH

Dark and warm and strongly scented,
shaping the seeds and roots of all living
    things,
be firm beneath my body that lies on you
and honor my faith by filling me with
    exactly what I need:
I won't ask you for more than that.

Small blue dot in the solar system,
vast beneath our feet:

Mother Earth, in your place and from mine
    I pray to you.

## EARTH MOTHER

We return a portion of the earth's blessings.
May she continue to grant them,
and may we continue to deserve them.

## FIRE

The grass grows from the rotted death in
    the earth.
The cow eats the grass and makes milk for
    her calves.
The milk contains the cream, and the
    cream the butter,
and the butter contains this fuel that shines
    with the Sun's gold
and with which we feed you,
fire of transformation.

## GAṆEŚA

Pom, pom, your footfalls shake the trees,
your weighty head forcing trunks and
    tendrils aside,
your tusks cutting through foliage, making
    a way.
Gaṇeśa, Gaṇeśa, open the way for me.
Gaṇeśa, Gaṇeśa, remove my obstacles.
Gaṇeśa, Gaṇeśa, carry me on your back,
bringing me through difficulties to success.

## THE GREEN MAN

From the tree leaves eyes are peering,
    smiling.
But when I turn my back, it seems like
    they're looking with distrust.
So I leave this for the Green Man to prove
    my good intentions.

## HATHOR

Heavenly Cow,
rain your blessings down on your people,
like milk pouring from above.[15]

## HEIMDALL

High One, Heimdall, winder of the horn,
Ward and watcher of the way to Asgard,
standing at the border of the Bifrost
    Bridge:
may our prayers go through to the sacred,
may the rainbow join us to the sacred.

Do not wind your horn, Heimdall:
no enemy approaches you.
Let your warning call be still:
I am your friend.
And I am friend as well of those you guard,
standing ward on the Bifrost Bridge,
the gods and goddesses who dwell
in their high-walled home.
I come not to offer danger but instead a gift:
golden mead, poured out liberally.
May my generosity gain me a hearing
before the Mighty Ones.
May my words go over the rainbow and be
    heard.
You hear them first, god of the great ear,
and to you I give this first prayer
and pour this first offering.

## INDRA

Indra, soma-fueled, laid low oppression,
snapped restriction,
with his vajra laid low the legless one.

---

15   This prayer to Hathor may be addressed to other
goddesses envisioned as a cow, such as the Irish Boand
("giver of cattle") or cow-eyed Hera. While being compared to a cow may not seem exactly flattering to us, it
was thought to be so by the ancients. This was, of course,
especially true of those people whose economy was based
on cattle.

Today, through prayer and offerings,
through poured-out libation,
may I please him,
that he might free me from all obstructions
that might hold me back from success,
    from prosperity,
from happiness.

## Indravayu, Mitravaruṇa, the Aśvins

This cup of unmixed tea I set out for
    Indravayu,
that which awakens and enlivens
to these two of great power.
This cup of tea mixed with milk I set out
    for Mitravaruṇa,
The cow's gift given to me I now give
to those of the true laws.
This cup of tea mixed with honey I set out
    for the Aśvins,
sweetness for those of the honey-soaked
    goads,
to the two who rescue and heal.
To you three, you six, I set out these cups,
to refresh and empower you,
mighty gods.

## Iðunn

If it doesn't give unlimited life like your
    apples, Iðunn;
still this cider is sweet.
So I offer half to you;
we share in its blessing.

## Janus

I'm beginning something
so I'm looking to Janus with hope,
and pouring him this wine.

Janus is the blesser of the opening door.
Janus is the blesser of the setting forth.

Janus is the blesser of the arriving safely.
Janus is the blesser of the closing door.
As the god of beginnings has, from the
    beginning,
blessed our beginnings,
As the god of endings has, to the ending,
    blessed our endings,
I can confidently pray to you, Janus
    Pater,
to him my praise and petition.

## Jupiter

Iupiter Optimus Maximus
Jupiter, Best and Greatest
From your seat above the sky
Look down to me.
Smell the sweet scent rising to you.
Hear the holy words reaching to you.
Answer my prayer, Most Holy One.

## Liber

Fill, Liber, my life's cup,
with the wine of free conviviality,
as I fill this cup with sweet drink
and set it before you.

## Life

My heart the fire of offering.
My flesh and bones the offering.
My blood the libation.
But whom to offer to?
To life this continual offering,
on this day,
on all days,
in thanks and love.

## Lug

A spear with flames streaming like waves
    of a brazen sea in ripples along its
    length

appears before the eyes of my mind, my
   heart, my soul,
held by a man whose face shines with the
   brilliance of a flowering Sun,
from whose fingertips and from each hair
   on whose head leap bold lightning
   strikes,
jagged scythes through the Cosmos that
   strike down all who oppose him,
each flash like the spear he holds, of stiff
   and flowing molten bronze,
that he will direct with his sure arm to its
   true target.
Lug, you know the target I have in mind,
the walls, and those who man them, who
   stand in my way,
who press on me with many threats to my
   own true actions:
as you are true, and your aim, so am I in
   my purpose.
And that is why I dare ask you to loose
   your spear against my adversaries.
Help one who will be properly grateful,
speaking of the power you wield in
   gatherings of men.

## MANANNÁN MAC LIR

Lord of the mists,
clear away the fog,
and show me all things laid out before me.
Son of the Sea, smooth waves of
   confusion.
Manannán, Chariot Driver, carry me to
   truth.
Open the way, Sailor:
be my compass, my sextant, my charts,
my rudder that shapes my journey,
my keel that keeps my sailing true.

## MARS

Mars, if I say, "Take that hill,"
may those in my chain of command do so
   eagerly,
not because of fear of punishment, but
   because they
know I will be there, too,
ahead of them, leading them, as it is right
   for me to do.
Mars, an officer goes first and eats last:
give me courage and strength to do so.
Remind me ever of my duty.

## MATI SYRA ZEMLJA

Into this hole I made in the dirt,
I whisper my needs to Moist Mother Earth.
Against it I press my ear
to learn her answer.

## MATRONAE

Matronae three, seated in state,
to receive and to give:
receive these words,
give in return blessings,
Mothers worthy of honor.

## MIϴRA

Great friend,
Lord of contracts,
Miðra of wide pastures:
my offering today is like a hand stretched
   out to you in friendship.

## MITRA

My friend is in need, Good Friend,
Mitra who draws people together
and binds them with friendship's bonds.
And so I pray to you on my friend's behalf,
who, ill and struck down by disease,
cannot pray for himself.

Bring healing, release the bonds of
   suffering
for my friend, God Friend,
Mitra who draws people together.

## Moon

Throughout the day, you will be observing
   my actions:
help me to make them worthy of your
   notice.
You who measure the sky, dividing it into
   sections,
do not be too strict in your judgment.
Friend of the honest, be my friend.

## Nāsatyas, Indra, Sarasvati

This honeyed milk to you, Nāsatyas.
This sweet drink to you, Indra.
This pleasing draught to you, Sarasvati.
To all of the gods, this draught of sweet
   honeyed milk
I set out in offering to please them
for their pleasant consumption.

## Nechtan

Nechtan, if you find me worthy,
let me have a drink from your wisdom-
   well.

## Nike

Out of opposition,
rescue me, Nike.
From greatest desperation,
free me, Nike.
Over enemies' contention,
make me victorious, Nike.
Whenever I compete,
may I emerge as winner,
Winged Nike, fleet for success.

## Ninurta

I pray to the bringer of fertility to the land,
Ninurta, whose father is the wind.
I pray to the promoter of life in the land,
Ninurta, whose mother is the wind.
I pray to the defeater of the slain heroes,
Ninurta, whose power is the wind.
Bring protection and prosperity to us
on the wind that blows from the south.

## Nymphs

Nymph[s] of this [grove/field/stream/etc.],
whose dancing, lightly brushing the earth,
contributes to its beauty,
to you this wine poured out,
to you this bread put out,
to you this cheese gladly given.
Beautiful one, bless me as I bless you.

## Pan

Pan of the fields, these words.
Pan of the fields, this wine.
Pan of the pasture, this milk.
Pan of the pasture, this bread.
To you between the wild and the tame,
I offer these that culture can give nature,
and my devotion, which I know you will
   welcome.

## Perkʷū́nos

Perkʷū́nos, whose serpent-slaying
is world-creating,
is world-redeeming,
be with me in this day's rituals.

Perkʷū́nos, you held back your storm,
so we were able to have our [barbecue,
   party, wedding, ritual, etc.] outside,
as we had wanted.
So here is some mead, which I know you like,
as I had promised, to thank you.

## POSEIDON

Between high and low tide, I build a small
    cairn
of water-smoothed stone
and place on its top my offering
to be taken by the waves of the returning sea,
your steeds, Poseidon Hippios,
carrying them to you.

## RAVEN

When I hear the clacking of your beak,
the rough laughter from your throat,
I hope, Black-shrouded Flyer, that the joke
    isn't on me.

Okay, Raven, it was you, wasn't it, who
[kept my car from starting, tripped me,
    rained on my parade, etc.]?
Me, I don't get the joke.
Laugh if you want to, but take this salmon
    and don't do it again.

## RHIANNON

It's quite obvious, really,
but at the same time a marvel:
a woman on a pale horse,
a woman who cannot be reached by great
    exertion.
Impossible to reach, she is easy to attain.
We need only call and ask for her love.
So I call to you, Rhiannon;
out of my need I call to you.
I call to her—look, she stops.
Listen to my needs, Rhiannon,
fulfill them:
Please listen to someone who loves you.

Show me the way to the Otherworld,
riding before me on your pale horse.
I will not tax mine, Rhiannon,
by seeking of my own to catch you.

I ask you nicely for this gift,
and offer oats and barley for her,
and mead for you, Sweet One.

## RIVER GOD

Bull-horned god,
as I cross you
I give you these words and this coin.

## SUN

As spears, as swords, as arrows,
the Sun sends out his rays,
as weapons from the hands of a mighty
    warrior,
to strike down falsehood and untrue ways.
As spears, as swords, as arrows,
Send out your rays,
as weapons from the hands of a mighty
    warrior,
to strike down falsehood and untrue ways.

## SVANTEVIT

Anything there is you can see, Svantevit,
from one of your eyes,
or two on each side.
Look my way, then;
see this cup of wine I place before you,
and see what I need
and grant it in return.

## TARANIS

Against all opposition to new birth,
Taranis,
cast your conquering lightning.
Over all obstructions to growth,
Taranis,
roll your thundering wheel.
Into all conditions of choking drought,
Taranis,
bring your fructifying rain.
God of destruction, bring to us creation.

## Týr

Týr, I thank you for your sacrifice,
a hand given to sustain the world,
even though you knew it would only be for
    a while.
Help me to make sure I don't waste a
    single precious day
for which you gave such a precious gift:
not just your hand,
but the oath that you swore with it,
your honor, your truth.

## Unknown Deities

Whatever deity or Spirit or Ancestor
whose presence I feel in this place:
take this offering as a gift in return for your
    blessing.

These trees are the pillars,
the roof the intertwining branches,
with the scent of leaves and needles
    underfoot rising as incense.
To which god or gods is this temple built?
I don't know.
I place this offering, then,
and pour this libation,
to the unknown divine present here
and to the Spirits of this place.

## Vāc

Vāc, it is through you that I can pray at all;
it is through you that I find the words;
it is through you that I string them together
into jewelry that I place around your neck.
It is through you that I bring beauty to you:
listen to this prayer,
be pleased with it.

## Velnias

Velnias, co-creator,
shape the world into a benevolent place,
with all that is good for man.

Maybe this cat is you, Velnias,
come from the world below.
Maybe this crow is you, many-named one,
come with a message for me.
Maybe you have come from your realm
with an Ancestor's words.
Speak: I am here to listen.
I ask only that you speak the truth.

## Viṣṇu

Hail to the Measurer, who laid things out,
putting this one here and that one there,
putting each in the place it belonged.
Hail to the determining one, who
    established laws,
that all things might run smoothly,
that all things might perform well.
God of establishing, I pray to you:
may you fashion the world in such a way
as to bring me happiness,
as to bring me prosperity,
as to bring me peace,
as to bring blessings on all of your
    worshipers.

## Woden

All who wander without direction:
to these, Woden, be a guide.
All who puzzle without solution:
to these, Woden, be a guide.
All who search without finding:
to these, Woden, be a guide.
All who inquire without answer:
to these, Woden, be a guide.

All who seek without out obtaining:
to these, Woden, be a guide.
God who understands:
to those to whom the journey is worth the
   cost,
even not arriving,
to these, Woden, be a guide.

Grey-hooded wanderer,
guide the movements of my life.
Grey-haired ponderer,
guide my thoughts as my wandering
   goes on.
With your one eye, see the right way for
   me to go,
and with but a tipping of your mead,
give to me the wisdom to know what
   that is.

## Žemyna

Beer for you, Žemyna. [pour]
Beer for me, Žemyna. [drink]
Beer for all of us, Žemyna [pass to next
   person]
that we might all be joined together to
   worship you
and all the gods.

## Zeus

If ever I have poured out libations to you,
or crumbled honey cakes in your honey,
accept this offering to you now
and look kindly on me.

## The Ancestors

Ancestors, listen to me—Remember how
   you prayed to *your* ancestors?
Well, now I'm praying to *you.*
Your prayers were respectful and so are
   mine.

Your prayers were for favors and so are mine.
I only expect what you expected
and what others will expect of me when I
   join you.
Family helps family.

Ancestors, whose death has brought you
   close to the gods,
bring these prayers of mine, these offerings
   of mine, to them without losing any
   along the path there,
and in the same way, bring their gifts to me.
Take some part of these offerings in
   payment for your services, and some
   part of the divine gifts as well.

The ground on which we stand,
the starter block of our race;
the slate on which we write,
the pattern behind our lives.
You who lived in the times before us,
who laid down the way on which we travel,
who established traditions that guide our
   people,
whose blood flows red within us,
whose genes have engendered us:
a gift for you, a small one in return
for the great ones you have given us.
Even the greatest, life itself, is your gift to us.
A gift, then, from life to the dead.

## Earth Spirits

Do you hear me, Earth Spirits,
as I go walking?
Do you hear my footfalls,
drumming on the dirt?
Do you hear my breathing,
mixing with the air?
Do you hear my heart beating,
weaving in the rhythms?
Do you hear my words of prayer,

asking your attention?
Do you hear me, Earth Spirits?
Hear me, hear me, hear my voice.
Hear the one who walks among you.
Hear my words of peace and friendship.
Hear my plea, grant my wish.

## FOREST SPIRITS

You there, in the shadows of the edge of
    the forest.
You there, in the shadows behind the grey
    stones.
You there, in the shadows beneath the
    spread branches.
You there, in the shadows, I give you my
    words.

I don't bring incense:
you have incense already—leaves and
    needles underfoot.
I don't bring libations:
you have libations already—streams and
    springs in the depths.
I don't bring sacrifices:
you have sacrifices already—the deaths
    of plants and animals in your hidden
    places.
I've brought instead something you don't
    already have:
prayers spoken in a human voice,
prayers are my gift.

Within the tangle of bushes and vines,
among the stones and under fallen trees,
the Spirits of the forest are waiting for me.
I go to them with gifts as tokens of
    friendship.

## LAKE SPIRITS

You who live in the depths of this lake,
I sit and think of you
and honor you as you deserve to be
    honored.

## LAND SPIRITS

Spirits of this place,
of nature and culture,
who dwelt here before us,
before all people;
those amongst whom
we make our way,
we make our homes,
we make our lives:
we come here in friendship
with open hands.
Watching ones, welcome us!
Welcome us as we come here among you.

The people of Earth bless you,
people of spirit,
coming to you with our strength
to use if you wish.

Spirits of this place,
I honor you with these gifts.

I cast grain on the dirt.
I feed the Spirits that live there.
I scatter these offerings around me.
I give to those who live in all directions.

Here, wild ones,
bread from my home, cooked on my hearth,
my gift to you.

For the time that I am in your realm,
Spirits of the [Forest, Plain, Desert, Sea,
    etc.],

I ask to be family.
See, I feed you as family would;
See, I pour out welcome drink to you.

## MEADOW SPIRITS

*[with an offering of jewelry]*

I'm told you like pretty things, Meadow
Spirits.

## NATURE SPIRITS

Spirits who dwell in the land about us,
all those with whom we dwell in peace,
those in whose presence we perform our
rites,
bless them, and us, as we offer to you.
Nature Spirits, accept our offering.

## RIVER SPIRITS

The Spirit of this river is a snake winding
through the land,
its breath rising.
I feed you with this; feed the land.

## ROCK SPIRITS

What being, what Spirit, has come to me in
the shape of this stone?
Or is it the rock itself to which I pour this
out?
I pour to the numinous before me.

## SPIRITS OF THE WILD

Let this line of meal that I trace here on the
forest's edge
be a dividing line between your world and
mine,
Spirits of the Wild.
May our border be a place of giving.

## TREE SPIRITS

Your skin hard and rough against mine,
I trace with my fingers the patterns of your
bark's folds.
Is it your words to me?
Do you hear *my* words to you?
At least know the meaning of this offering.

Chapter 24

# ABUNDANCE

## *Prosperity*

### THE GOD

Your phallus as sharp and firm as the tines
    of your crown,
not gold, but antlers;
not jewels, but a rod of flesh is wealth.
They fertilize the Earth,
and with it my self.

As coins pouring from your lap,
rain down your gifts on me, Prosperous
    One.
As plants turning green in spring,
bring me fertility, Lord of Grain.
As cattle returning to the pastures,
send riches into my life, Great Bull.

### THE ALL-GODS

Health and wealth, Keepers of Treasure,
    give your worshiper.
May this little offering be returned a
    thousandfold.
May my blessings be countless,
scattered out from your storehouse with
    sweet-scented hands.

### ATHENA

Sprung full-armed from the head of Zeus
with fully formed faculties,
nimble Athena, who guides the craftsman:
turn me onto a productive path.

### CERES

Increase our crops.
Cause to increase our crops.
Bring rain and Sun to increase our crops.
May your earth be fertile to increase our
    crops.
May your earth be fertile to cause to
    increase our crops.
Mother Ceres, may our crops increase.

### COMMERCE

Commerce, who links people together,
forming from them a community,
and then forming from communities a
    greater one—
from many one—
for the enrichment of all:
Respond to my prayer by enriching *me*,
I who take part in your communities.

### COYOTE

Hey, you, Coyote,
thanks for your gifts.
Don't forget to keep on giving.
We can always use more.

## DIEVAS

May you come, dog-drawn, to our land,
　Dievas,
your wagon laden with fertility for our
　crops.
Scatter it widely.
Scatter it freely.
Scatter it with an open hand,
just as we, open-handed, offer to you.

## EARTH

Mother of earth and people and plants,
bring grain and milk for these children.

## FORTUNA

With the next turn of the wheel, Fortuna,
bring me luck.

## GᵂOUWINDĀ

From your heavenly udders,
round as the earth,
white as the Moon,
pour out inexhaustible milk for your children
　who stand here with upraised hands.
We have offered to you, Gᵂouwindā,
you know we have,
and now we wait expectantly for your
　loving gifts,
Provider of Cows.

## KAMI

May the Kami of this [tool/weapon] shine
　[its/her/his] power,
like that of a lightning flash in the black,
like that of a fire in a fireplace,
like that of the Sun from rising to noon,
showing the way through difficulties,
smoothing the path between me and my goal,
shoving aside all the obstacles between me
　and my path.

## KANE AND KANALOA

Kane and Kanaloa, you came over the sea:
bring us fish in abundance.
Kane and Kanaloa, you came to this land:
cause our crops to grow.
Kane and Kanaloa, here is some whitefish
　for you.
Kane and Kanaloa, here is a coconut for
　you.
Kane and Kanaloa, bring prosperity to us
and to the sea and to our land,
with fish and crops in plenty.

## KANE-KUAANA

Kane-kuaana, though this is not your land
　by custom,
still I place it,
and myself,
and my family,
and all in my culture,
under your protection, looking to you for
　prosperity
in the form of fish,
plentiful fish,
fine-tasting fish.
In your honor, I light this fire:
see it and send your blessings to it
and to the one who has lit it
and to those for whom he asks blessings.
I have not oppressed the poor, but given
　aid to them,
and I will give them more out of the riches
　you send.

## LAIMA

Laima, appear as a swan before me on this
　pond
that I might grow rich.
I will not catch you, but watch you swim
　freely away:

give me in return the freedom that wealth
brings.

## LUG

You wrung from Bres the secret of
  planting,
the secret of harvesting,
when to do each,
and gave to Ireland bountiful grain,
overflowing prosperity.
Help us, Artful One, to produce our food,
to bring growing crops to fruitful harvest,
to fill our storehouses, that we might eat
and more than full, that we might sell,
and be prosperous,
and praise you, Lug, who know so many
  things
and are the true king,
whose righteous rule makes his people
  prosper.

## MARS

This ram, Father Mars, to you,
that you may be increased in power
that I might be increased in power
for prosperity and protection.

## PŪṢAN

Pūṣan, this gruel, as if a goat, I offer you.
May this new commercial venture be
  profitable,
O you who protect.

## ROSMERTA

Give me but a sip of your well-filtered
  mead,
dearest Rosmerta, and fill my life with
  gold,
and sprinkle the mead about the world to
  fill it full
with the gifts of your inexhaustible hand.

Commerce's bride, bring prosperity to me
  and to all.

## VELES

Out of the mound
the cattle come
through your agency, Veles,
granter of wealth,
who dwells beneath.
And for that we thank you,
and with this offering ask
that you continue to bless us.

Veles, from your underground world may I
  obtain wealth;
of [metal/coal/oil/gems, etc.]:
grant it freely and without danger.

## VELES AND PERKONS

Dweller beneath the hill,
Veles, bless all that grows in the dark;
Dweller on the peak,
Perkons, bless all that flourishes in the
  light,
that all of my enterprises may grow and
  flourish.

## VULCAN

Vulcan, to whom fish are given.
bring some to me,
and I will offer some to you in gratitude.

## *Work*

### THE GOD

With this flag-decked tree I top this
  structure,
its skeleton done,
its flesh yet to be completed.
Lord of heights,

Lord of trees,
Lord of all that stands erect:
we pray for safety in our construction.

## THE DAGDA

An Dagda, good at all things,
increase my skills at all I attempt.
May all I produce be of high quality.
I will do my best:
I ask that you make it better.

## HEPHAESTUS

Though crippled, you possess great skill in
    compensation.
Hephaestus, of power and skill, show
    sympathy for my own shortcomings
and guide me, and aid me, to produce
    works with quality.

Naked to the waist,
leather-apron-girded,
Hephaestus performs his work,
with hammer blows shapes the unshaped,
with strength and skill forms beauty,
with hard work produces quality.
May I, you who are smith of the gods,
through my hard work be equally
    productive,
creating in the end results that I can be
    proud of,
and that will bring me recognition.
Work is noble and ennobling, laboring one:
well do you know it;
well may you aid me in mind;
well may I perform.

## HERMES

Herald of Zeus, you bring together one and
    another;
as a small child you gained through your
    cleverness

the friendship of Apollo,
with whom you were at enmity.
So, too, bring this conflict to a peaceful
    resolution
by finding that thing each one desires
and the other is willing to give,
and conveying that knowledge to us,
to we who are negotiating.

## KUPA-AI-KE'E

Kupa-ai-ke'e, with fire I form this work.
Kupa-ai-ke'e, with water I quench and
    temper it.
Kupa-ai-ke'e, with hard blows I work the
    design,
soften my mind,
to create:
may what I create be beautiful and
    functional.

## LUG

I place this coffee, Samildánach,
before you,
to enliven and please you,
and ask that you, in gratitude,
help me to get a job.

God of all skills, Samildánach,
may my skills win me a good job.
Winner of battles,
may your long arm reach out and do this
    for me,
and from my first paycheck I will buy an
    offering for you,
and give it gratefully and willingly.

Lug, of arts and skills,
as your spear,
so my hammer:
May it fall powerfully and accurately,

and may my work be performed with
   beauty
and without delay.

I sit [stand] before my place of work
and spread my tools before me.
Lug Samildánach,
grant your blessings on my tools
that they might serve me as well
as the parts of my body do.
Master Craftsman,
grant your blessings upon me,
that my work might bring beauty
to all the world and all who live in it.
Orderer of Chaos,
grant that all that I do might be in accord
with the will of Nature,
so that, by doing my work,
I might do the will of the gods.

## MERCURY

God of communication,
may my job interview go well.
God of commerce,
may I receive a good job offer as a result.

During today's negotiations, make me
   eloquent,
Mercury;
ease the way, remove all obstacles,
opening the path for a smoothly
   accomplished deal,
opening the path for a profitable outcome.

Bring customers to my store, Mercury,
Customers ready to buy, God of
   Commerce,
Customers with open purses, God of
   Exchange,
Customers who will see my wares and buy
   them, Merchant God,

Customers who will add to my property,
   Bringer of Wealth,
so that we will both be happy:
they, because they have found what they
   wanted,
and at a fair price;
I, because I will have increased my
   prosperity
and practiced my livelihood.
This is my prayer to you today, Mercury,
a prayer from someone engaged in the
   business that pleases you well.

## TVAṢṬṚ

Tvaṣṭṛ, guide my chisel as I create from
   this [wood/stone].
May I form by Ṛta,
May I create satya;
may the Good and the True be the result of
   my work.

Craftsman of the gods, Tvaṣṭṛ,
make of me a well-honed instrument.
Shaper of the unformed, Tvaṣṭṛ,
rub away every rough thing.
Former of beauty, Tvaṣṭṛ,
make me, make all I am and do,
fit so that when people say:
"Look, there goes one to serve the Holy
   Ones,"
it will be in admiration not reproach,
showing everyone how talented you are,
if you can create glory from the raw
   material that is me.
Tvaṣṭṛ, I know you can do this,
for you are the great crafter.

## TVAṢṬṚ AND PŪṢAN

Protect these road workers,
Tvaṣṭṛ who knows what it is to shape,

from those who hurtle past in cars,
  unheeding.
Protect those who tend the ways,
Pūṣan, god of the ways,
and make their work safe and easy and of
  quality.
Inspire their minds, you two,
to solve problems that arise.
Empower their arms, you two,
with the necessary strength.
Tvaṣṭṛ, Pūṣan, may they work safely
to create well-wrought roads.

## VULCAN

When the gods want the best,
in strength or art,
they turn to you, Vulcan.
And so do I:
not for you to do the work,
but to guide my arms.
Although my work can't equal yours,
may it be the best possible for mortal man.

The strong arms that drive the hammer
  against the metal on the anvil,
causing the crash that deafens my ears
  among the liquid flames of the volcano
  where your smithy is hidden,
end in clever fingers, which create fine
  work to cause as much marvel for their
  artistry as your rougher work for its
  utility.
Guide my work, both rough and fine,
  Vulcan, and the praise that I receive
  from others will be praise of you.

## EARTH AND WATER SPIRITS

Through long time fine soil has been laid
  down by water to make the clay with
  which I form this vessel.

Every liquid poured into or from it will be
  a libation to earth and water.

# *Rain*

The rain will fall just like this [mead,
  beer, milk, etc.; depending on the deity
  addressed]
if you like my offering.

## THE MARUTS

What is the clattering noise I hear, as tree
  limbs against each other?
It is the Maruts, coming in splendor,
  bringing rain.
What is the glittering fire I see, as of clouds
  hiding lightning?
It is the Maruts, coming in splendor,
  bringing rain.
What is the awe-inspiring presence I feel,
  as of the clashing of armies?
It is the Maruts, coming in splendor,
  bringing rain.
Splendorous Maruts, come quickly,
  bringing rain.

## STORM GOD

Rain, God of Storms, send rain.
Not the lightning that obliterates
  everything it hits,
and not torrents that wash away the dirt
  from our plants and our homes,
but rain that falls gently,
lovingly even,
soaking into the ground where it can be
  used by living beings.
Rain, Storm God, send rain.

## SUN

The hard Earth lies vulnerable beneath the
  onslaught

of the Sun's rays,
too weak from thirst even to raise her
   hands in prayer for relief.
I do it for her, then; I raise my face to the
   Sun:
shining disk, wheel of light,
your power is indeed great, your place of
   honor is assured.
I come to you as a herald, asking for peace.
Withhold your darts that are keeping back
   the rain clouds.
Allow them to come and quench the thirst
   of their sister below.
Establish peace between yourself and the
   Earth:
a true king knows when to relent.

## THUNDERBIRD

Lightning in dry air over the burnt land,
   hey!
Fire in the dry air over the burnt land, hey!
Rain clouds in the dry air over the burnt
   land, hey!
Thunderbird, trailing fire in his wings,
   comes.
Thunderbird, carrying roars in their
   beating, comes.
Thunderbird, bringing rain to the burnt
   land, comes.
Thunderbird, we will turn wet faces to you,
   hey,
when you pass over us.

May the roaring flapping of your wings be
   the thunder accompanying the storm.
May the cutting flashing of your eyes be
   the lightning accompanying the storm.
May the rhythmic clacking of your beak be
   the rain's music as it falls, be the storm,
that will come as you fly to us,
as you fly, Storm-Bringing Thunderbird.

## CLOUD SPIRITS

The sky is weeping great tears in sorrow at
   the earth's drought.
Weep on, overreaching clouds:
Your sorrow will return life to the earth.

## RAIN SPIRITS

The rest of my neighborhood is soaking
   their lawns each day with water from
   distant lakes,
but I am waiting for rain.
Grass at this time of the year is *supposed* to
   be brown and brittle; I know that.
But grass is so beautiful when it is green
   and soft.
So I'm waiting patiently for you to return:
but hurry.

*Chapter 25*

# MIND AND SOUL

## *Thought*

### THE GODDESS

Listen, she says, just listen:
Still the rambling thoughts,
quiet the restless mind,
stem the stream of words,
and listen for a moment.
Just a moment is all I ask,
is all I need, for you to hear me,
just one.
Listen, she says.
Speak, and I will listen.

As Maiden of the waxing Moon, enliven
    my mind.
As Mother of the full, give maternal
    guidance.
As Crone who brings the dwindling light,
    bring final wisdom.
Under whatever phase, in whatever guise,
you who are the constant Moon,
teach this child of yours this moment's is
    and ought.

### THE ALL-GODS

Piece, by piece, by piece, fills the pot.
Step, by step, by step, reaches the goal.
One, plus one, plus one, and the infinite
    sum is attained.

Patience, Old Ones, Patience:
You know how to wait with patience.
I ask for patience that I may wait.
May I wait in patience.

Yes, but . . .
No, but . . .
When I form opinions, may I always
    remember "but,"
because, All-Gods, that is often where truth
    is found.

### APOLLO

Remove from my mind all illusion, Far-
    Seeing Apollo.
Light me a path through confusion,
    Ordering Apollo.
For true is the speech from you to each
    who asks for your help, Apollo.

### ATHENA

Knowledge alone will not suffice:
with wisdom to use it bless my mind,
Athena, whose skillful touch is sure to
    those who worship you,
with well-wrought words,
with well-crafted deeds.

Knit together the fragments of my tattered
    mind,

that spread, Athena, through my life,
into one complete cloth,
beautiful, whole,
and ready to be shaped.

## CERNUNNOS

May I see both sides,
weighing them fairly before striking out
    with a decision, Cernunnos,
drawing my strength from the tension and
    peace of the middle,
just as you do, Cernunnos:
the power you wield in the service of our
    purposes
comes from the purity of its time and
    intent.
Make me more like that, Cernunnos.

Wisdom is found in between, where the
    view is best.
Lord of the in-between, lead me to
    wisdom.

## THE DAGDA

Grasping your thunder club firmly,
descend into the depths of my inner ocean,
and there, Good God, overcome the many-
    armed monster
that floods me with stifling water.
Destroy it so my mind will stop producing
    only confusion,
so there can be fertile mind,
needing only seed and care to grow
    wonderful, beautiful, creative ideas.

## DYÉUS PTÉR

I stand here on the summit of your high
    mountain, and think of you.
Surrounded by the sky, lifted up into the
    sky itself,

the awesome clarity of your focused vision
    comes closer to me
and I am more aware, myself, of your law's
    urgings.
Dyéus Ptér, lord of all that is right, of all
    that is just, of all that should be;
Dyéus Ptér, judge and king of the world, of
    all who live and all that is,
Dyéus Ptér, advise me; make the right path
    open beneath my feet,
make my eyesight clear, that I may always
    see as far
as I do from the top of this mountain of
    yours.

Clear my muddled mind,
Dyéus Ptér,
God of clarity.

## FIRE OR FIRE DEITY

Fire's teeth cut.
Fire's heat burns.
Fire's light shines.
Fire's tongue teaches.
Fire, help me decide the truth.

## GAṆEŚA

Patient as your ponderous feet,
make me, Gaṇeśa.

## HEKATE

Your torch has brought me here.
Your knife bars the path.
Burn, cut away,
Wisdom-bringer.

## HELIOS

You, Helios, see everything through your
    light that shines on us.
I open myself to that light;
I welcome you to my most inner places,

to shine in my darkness.
Each hidden secret,
each unknown shame,
each unrecognized flaw,
all that is in me that I have pushed deep away,
and denied the existence of my
 responsibility for:
fill these with your unrelenting scrutinizing
 fire,
show them to me with irresistible clarity.
And when I run from these terrors, leave
 me no place to hide.
When I seem to rationalize, leave me no
 explanation,
and when I seek to excuse them, leave me
 nothing on which to base my excuses.
And when I submit myself at last to the
 truth you display,
may it be a purifying river of molten gold
 into which I am thrown.
I will burn:
but oh, how I'll shine!

## JUPITER

Sceptered, enthroned,
with eagle crowned,
you rule, greatest Jupiter, over the cosmos.
May my actions be such as will win your
 approval.
Guide me, Father, in my decisions.

## LUG

Fear is cut through
by the spear of Lug.

## MANANNÁN MAC LIR

With a swift shake of your cloak,
 Manannán,
separate my thoughts from regretted
 memories,
leaving only a not-understood gratitude.

Fog-ridden is my bedeviled mind,
mist-filled my thoughts.
If it be the shaking of your cloak, son of
 the sea,
shake it again, banishing the mist,
clearing the cloud-covered sky to show me
 the guiding star
that shines from your divine brow.

## MARS

May fear and shyness that block the
 bridges I try to build to others
be themselves blocked from entering my
 mind, Mars,
you who binds people to others and
 protects the peace of society.

## MÉNŌT

Measuring is true.
If measuring is true, it must fit.
Does this fit?
It doesn't.
Ménōt, may my mind fit.

Ménōt, make me remember the
 unremembered.

Measuring time,
Measuring space,
Measuring well,
you always find the right answer.
No surprise that, since the answer only
 exists because of the measuring,
as that made by your ever-turning wheel
that rolls through the night sky.
True measurement brings light to the
 darkness.
True worship of you, Ménōt,
opens our minds and dispels ignorance.

Moon, who measures out time and space,
who puts this here, and that there,
this then, the other in its own time,
who orders that which is as it should be:
teach me to divide properly all I
    experience;
teach me to divine all I need to know,
that my life may be true,
that I may live in the Truth.

The confusion in my mind,
Measurer of the Sky, of Time:
bring order to it.
You divide the unmeasured,
and put each thing in its proper place:
do that as well with my suffering-causing
    thoughts:
Heal my soul.

Mḗnōt who measures time and space,
you are therefore lord of numbers,
wise in mathematics,
the way they are arranged,
knowing in the principles that lie beyond
    all that is:
the laws of the universe are in your mind.
It is to you, then, that I direct my prayers:
words for numbers and an understanding
    of them.

## THE NORNS

The two-eyed Wanderer came to your
    terrible well.
Away from it came the One-Eyed, the
    Rhymer.
Even he came to seek the wisdom only you
    bestow,
earning his place through Mimir's Gift,
even as he had won the runes riding his
    Horse.
Norns, I cannot give such a gift,

nor do I seek as much as he won,
but I ask a little, only a little,
in making this decision.

## OGMA

Ogma, creator of writing,
as I read may I understand and learn.

Write my memories, Ogma,
well into my mind,
stroke by stroke,
word by word,
line by line,
clear and strong.

## SKY GOD

Anger brings confusion.
Make my mind as clear as your most
    cloudless sky:
God the Firmament.

## SUN

You whose rays cross the empty spaces,
bringing light to the darkened land,
revealing the night-concealed:
cut through, O Sun, the fog of my mind,
the mist that stands between me and the
    truth.
Remove, Light-Giver, Way-Shower,
the blinds that keep me from knowing
    things as they really are.

## THOTH

When I open this book, open my mind,
    Thoth,
let the thoughts in.
But as the thoughts enter, Thoth,
inspire my discrimination;
may I consider but not be manipulated by
    these ideas.

Ibis-headed one, Tahuti,
may I read this book with a bird's clear
    sight,
Weigher of Words.

## VENUS

Show me, Venus, the way to show my love
    to those whom I love that they may
    know.

## ZEUS

As clear as your cloudless sky,
my mind, Zeus, my mind.

# Speech and Inspiration

All the gods of my people:
hear me.
Let it be your words I write.
Let it be your words I speak.

When I speak, may my words be as clear to
    my listeners as yours would be to me, if
    I only knew how to listen.

Speak my words,
comes the god's hidden voice.
When I open my mouth, may this be true.

## THE GODDESS

Thinking carefully, attempting clarity, I
    ask the
Goddess for inspiration.

## AGNI

If your tongues will speak my words
I will feed you with butter;
and you will grow strong and carry my
    prayers to the gods.

## APOLLO

Each word you speak a song,
each line a symphony:
so, too, today my speech,
Son of Leto.
Give me a clear mind to receive your
    wisdom,
and a mind filled with the skill to use it
    once given.

Apollo, inspirer of all who speak,
may each word I say today be like an
    arrow into the minds of my listeners,
as if launched from your never-erring bow,
and inform, educate, and persuade them.

God of eloquence, teach me to pray.
Open my mouth that the words might come
    forth.
Open my heart that the words might ring
    true.

A true song is one inspired by the god of
    truth and music,
whose lyre shines like the lucent Sun.
May the song I am writing be a true one,
    Apollo,
and in its singing, all will know of your
    perfection.

Player on the lyre,
fill my fingers as they [strum, pluck, bow]
the strings of my [instrument].

Apollo, lover of music,
may I sing beautifully today.
May beauty rise from my singing—beauty
    and truth.

May the music of the spheres
resound in this song I am writing.

God of the Logos, fill it and me
with the beautiful Order.

A guitar, not a lyre;
a pick, not a plectrum;
may I nonetheless make beauty that will
    please you, Apollo,
not worthy of a god to create,
but perhaps good enough for one to hear.

## APOLLO AND HERMES

Apollo, Lord of Truth, may I see into the
    truth when I perform my research today.
Apollo, Lord of the Good, may I create
    beautiful theories from it.
Hermes, god of trickery and speech, may I
    see beyond the obvious, no matter how
    attractive,
and convey it to others in attractive words,
although under your friend Apollo's
    watchful eye.
May the attractive be True,
may the True be the Good.

## THE AŚVINS

May my words be honey, Aśvins
sweet to the ears of my listeners,
accomplishing my goals easily.
Nāsatyas, saviors,
may speech be my salvation.

## ATHENA OR MINERVA

With one small reflection of the mind
    of creation whose home is in your
    helmeted head,
gift me, Maiden, as I set about this creation
    of my own.

## AUŠRINE

As the many colors of your miracle
    rainbow extending from earth to heaven,
so, too, may my words be here today.
Aušrine, who brings the shining Sun,
bring the Shining Ones to hear my words,
and may my words, through you, shine to
    please them.

Rising from the mists,
with your brother-husbands in attendance,
bring divine light to me,
Aušrine, young and lovely,
and my words to them,
the lovely Holy Ones.

## AUSTÉJA

May my [singing/playing/performance]
    today, Austéja,
be as beautiful as the humming of your
    bees,
as sweet as the honey they make.

## BRIGID

May I be filled with the fire of Brigid,
the threefold queen who inspires the [artist,
    writer,
craftsman, healer, etc.].

May Brigid place her fire in my head,
her liquid flame flowing from my mouth,
burning with truth.

Make my words sweet enough to call you
    here,
and sweet enough to praise you when you
    arrive,
Sweet Brigid.

## BRIGID, THE DAGDA, LUG

Sweet gods and goddesses,
give me the right words to say.
Inspiring Brigid, skillful Dagda, Lug of
    smooth speech:
pick out from the many words just the right
    ones for this occasion
and feed them to me.
I will do the rest.

## DAWN

Any time is yours, young Lady, whose
    entrance announces with wordless
    prayer a new light.
Dawn within me now; with words as sweet
    as your morning song, awaken in me my
    own voice,
let it rise to your ears, let it rise to the ears
    of the Holy Ones,
let it rise as your sweet mead that flames
    on the morning horizon.
Any time is yours, welcome child:
may this be a time for you to dawn in me.

Just as you rise in the east, Maiden of
    Dawn,
raise in me poetry;
just as you bring the Sun,
bring from me dazzling words.

For us who wander blindly,
in ignorance or despair,
blossom in the darkness,
your rose petals pushing back the night,
as you rise in our hearts
most beautiful Dawn.

## DIONYSOS

I wait in the dark for the curtain to rise,
for Dionysos to arrive.
Bring music and dance, ecstatic god.

As if they were ranging across your
    mountains
with drums, with cymbals and tambourines,
picking out a rhythm for stamping feet,
as if their instruments were crying "Eo, eo,
    evohe,"
as if each note was a prayer to you, god of
    ecstasy,
Dionysos, bless this band who are about to
    perform,
and bless as well those who listen,
and join them together, each with each,
and each with the band.
Make this concert a ritual in your honor.

Dionysos, who leads the Maenads in
    ecstasy over the hilltops,
through meadows and fields,
guide my feet as I dance.

## HERMES

Such a small thing is a pen.
And yet, how broad and empty a sheet of
    paper.
I would get lost, my words cast into an
    endless sea,
if it were not for you, Hermes,
for you guide both those who travel
and those who tie together words.
I have need of both these things, wingéd
    words god:
with your help may I express myself with
    clarity,
never losing the way,
with you to lead me if I do.

## INDRA

Indra, having stolen, as an eagle,
the sacred drink, the soma,
from the Asuras,
the snakes who raise themselves against
    the gods,
became strong.
I, in drinking these Waters of Life,
derive for myself not only strength,
but inspired sight.

## KU-KA-OHIA-LAKA

Ku-ka-ohia-laka, smooth my movements
and make them precise and correct.
May they flow gently in the correct
    courses,
a powerful stream in a streambed.
May my dance be beautiful,
well adorned and simple,
to convey what I wish,
all the while bringing pleasure to those
    who watch,
and to me, the one who dances.

## MÉNŌT

Though ecstatic utterances gush freely
    from the well that burns,
unless cooled by your ordering, they are
    mad jabberings.
No matter where I find my words, I turn to
    Ménōt to help me shape them,
to form a song of beauty from them,
inspired, but well put,
measured out to fit.

Ménōt, may my notes tonight
be precise, and accurate, and well timed,
just as you dependably cross the sky.
May my songs be beautiful,
just as you are beautiful when you shine.

Ménōt, may all go well.

Ménōt, you are god of numbers and their
    relations,
and so, god of music, measured sound.
I ask that my singing shine out of the silent
    spaces
and bring order to the world.

## NECHTAN

Pour for me, Nechtan, a single draft,
of wisdom, of inspiration;
whether you serve it yourself,
or delegate to your cupbearers is yours to
    choose.
I only swear myself trustworthy, willing to
    take the risk.

## ODIN

I pour this mead,
the mead of inspiration brought by wingéd
    Odin,
in three draughts.
I pour once.
I pour twice.
I pour a third time.
Through drinking the remainder
may I find inspiration,
words that fly like eagles.

Even if you have to use deceit to break
    through my armored walls to find there
    the inspiring drink my outward-facing
    eyes had never known was there, grey-
    cloaked wanderer, your face only half-
    hidden by your drooping hat, befuddle
    my mind so I don't remember the tales
    well enough to recognize you; slip
    through before I can put up my fearful
    senses.

I want you to bring the drink of poetry to
    me to swallow, but knowing the stories
    of what your own wisdom cost you, I
    think I'm quite justified in being afraid
    of what you'll want from me.
I'll look aside, then, avert my gaze, and
    you can sneak up on me, and rip out
    the hidden poetic madness in one quick
    motion, and then hold it out to me as if
    it were not your eye-payment, but mine
    instead.
Show me my unknown talents for
    inspiration, Odin, and I will know what
    else I need, and so be willing to pay the
    cost, even if it be as great as that you
    paid without hesitation.

## OGMA

Deviser of alphabets,
be an unobstructing conduit of ideas
    between me and my readers,
Ogma, through whose gifts, speech
    becomes seen.

## OGMA [WHEN DIVINING WITH OGHAM]

A stave, and a stave, and then one more,
of those named after you, Ogma,
revealer of wisdom, I draw.

## OGMA, BRIGID

I take up my pen and invoke Ogma:
God of writing, make my way smooth.
I take up my pen and invoke Brigid:
Inspiring goddess, enflame my words.

## OGMIOS

May the words of this book
go from the page to my mind
as if, Ogmios, on your golden chains.

## PAN

Pan, be in their drums,
Pan, be in their guitars,
Pan, be in their basses,
Pan, be in their bodies and voices,
those of the band about to perform.

## SARASVATI

Sarasvati's strings be found in my voice,
stream through my fingers,
vibrate in my heart.

May music flow from me as smoothly as
    you flow on,
Sarasvati, goddess of the holy river.

A sweet river, as of milk,
Sarasvati, with amṛta in her hands,
gives gifts, protects, inspires.
She is worthy of praise,
beautiful in her arising:
My prayer to her for true words.

White river, poured-out stream,
Sarasvati, carry words from the divine
    lands to my lips;
may the sacred find its way into my
    speech, my prayers,
may the gods be called in words they
    themselves have inspired.

## SILENCE

I would pray to Silence,
but I won't.

## SPEECH

Semantics of all words,
Syntax of all sentences,
Former of utterances:

Speech, may all I say express perfectly my
    will,
and that of the Holy Ones,
binding us together in one speech-
    community.

## Vāc

Vāc gives me the words to praise her,
words given by Word,
but leaving some to join myself with other
    people,
and to praise other gods.
I thank her for the joining and praise,
hoping it will continue,
her words pouring into me to pour out again.
And I have to wonder whether the gods
    thank her as well
for providing the means to praise them.
Gods, let's join together to praise her.

With each new word, I learn a new thought,
a new way to praise Vāc.
Help me, speech.

In my speech today,
may I be eloquent,
Vāc, who inspires and guides those who
    speak.
With beauty may I speak.
With clarity may I speak.
With effectiveness may I speak.
May my words, goddess Word,
be well formed, well delivered, and well
    received.

I pray to Word in simple words,
for simpler words,
for words more true.

Sitting in front of my computer's screen,
my fingers prepared to strike the keys,

I pause a moment to ask inspiration
from you, O Vāc:
may my words flow freely.

May my words today, Vāc,
that I speak today, Vāc,
flow smoothly today, Vāc,
be of beauty today, Vāc,
be wise and filled with truth today, Vāc.
May all these things be so today, Vāc.
I ask these from you today, Vāc,
your worshiper today, Vāc,
May you grant them to me today, Vāc.

## Writing God

You whose fingers hold the pen,
or stroke the keys,
whose output of words flows continuously,
and never ceases,
and never ceases to amaze:
God of Writing, inspire me as I begin to
    write,
be my model.

## Zorya

Lark, little lark, do you hear what I am
    saying?
Fly, little lark, and sing, with your beautiful
    voice.
Fly to Zorya, to little dawn
and tell her we are here,
here asking, here waiting for her to come,
with the gods in her train.
Zorya, we call to you, with beautiful
    words,
words of praise, words you love well.
Come to us here, be the first to arrive,
be the first to arrive of the Holy Ones,

to help us pray to the others as well,
our prayers to them, their gifts to us.

May our prayers be as beautiful as the
    songs of the lark
we send on her way to ask you to come.

## THE ANCESTORS

Mother and Fathers who went before,
Watch over my words as I tell the old
    stories,
that they may be passed on rightly.
Make me today's link in the chain that
    reaches on,
from nights around the fire beneath African
    skies
to the end of humanity
and beyond.

## COMPUTER SPIRITS

As the electrons travel my neurons,
so, too, in this computer.
As my thoughts are divine,
so, too, with this computer.
May we write well together,
spirit with Spirit.

## ENERGY SPIRITS

Each Sun ray,
Each water drop,
Each gust of wind,
Each colliding atom,
Each Spirit that formed coal, or oil, or gas:
Each keystroke is a hymn to you.

# Divination

I [choose these runes/place these cards/cast
    these coins, etc.] to know what is, and,
    from that, what will be.
May this small thing be a true reflection of
    the great thing,
so that by understanding this, I might
    understand that.
God(s)/Goddess(es) of prophecy [or their
    names],
may I read correctly what I am shown.
I ask your help in seeing only what is true,
not just what I want to see.

Speak to me as you follow the wind,
leaves of oak above my head.
Follow perfectly the waves of the air-ocean,
making known to me their invisible
    pattern.
Out of the well of the world they flow,
carrying the wisdom that is her gift.
Carry it to me also, give to me, oak Spirit,
the knowledge that you have,
the knowledge that I seek.[16]

Weaving goddess, who knows the woof
    and warp,
who sees the pattern before the cloth exists,
form from my actions here that which
    will be
if the threads remain as they are now
    arranged.

---

16    At the oracle of Dodona in ancient Greece, the
movements of oak branches were used to determine the
advice of the gods. In this prayer, it is explained that, since
everything is connected with everything else, then from
any one thing, any other thing may be known. Since leaves
reflect the wind, they are a perfect example of this relationship and are thus a good choice for divination.

Spirits of these tools of divination, my
    question is this:
[Question]
Answer, and I will listen.

May the deity of this moment guide
    my reaching fingers toward the true
    divination tokens.

[God's name], in the next words I hear,
speak wisdom, speak truth,
make clear the path that lies before me,
that in the days to come I must walk.
May the words of strangers not be idle talk,
but words from the source.

## THE GODDESS

The World, which speaks,
the Goddess, whose words they are,
whose body is the world,
is the Earth who gives our own bodies their
    birth,
is speaking to us in words that seem mad:
mad words of a mad priestess,
as the cryptic utterances of the Python of
    Delphi,
sitting on the tripod over the cleft,
breathing the fumes, tasting the laurel she
    chewed.
Mad words of uncertain meaning,
difficult to interpret,
dangerous to follow,
but even more to ignore,
and always true.
These are the words, the type of words, the
    World speaks,
the utterances of the Goddess;
these are the words we must listen for,
and listen to,
though they come to us half-heard,

hints from the edge of sound and sanity,
blown to our ears on the fluttering wind.
Though obscure, though the seeming
    ravings
of a disordered mind,
they are still Her words.
I doubt them:
in my doubt, may I listen.
I lack faith in them:
may they speak to my soul.
I do not trust them:
may I know them to be true.
May she speak with sure words
and may I listen with sure understanding,
or if I do not understand them,
with wonder, with amazement, with awe,
    with love,
to the words she speaks.

## IRIS

Descending from heaven on iridescent
    wings,
you bring the commands of Zeus to my
    earth, Iris.
They are hard to understand, though,
so I ask your help so I can follow them.

Wrapped in rainbow-hued robes,
bring the words of Zeus, who alone speaks
    with the Fates,
to me in this divination.

## ODIN

Speak to me, Odin, through the casting of
    the runes,
and I will listen.

Odin who speaks in riddles and hints,
speak clearly through the runes I draw.

## OGMIOS

Ogmios, cover me with your hide of
    prophecy,
and bring me wondrous dreams,
wise dreams,
true dreams,
from the knowing dead.

## BIRD SPIRITS

May the flight of birds carry divine
    messages to me
that I will understand:
may they be present,
may they be clear.

## NATURE SPIRITS

When nature speaks to me, may I hear.
May I know the language of birds and
    animals.
May I understand the sounds of swaying
    grass
and the creaking of tree limbs.
May I perceive the tiny sounds of stones as
    well as the roarings,
the murmurings, of water.
May I come to know the music of the
    spheres
sung in the empty space between the
    celestial bodies.
May I hear in them the epics they have
    been telling each other
since the beginning of time.

# Chapter 26

# WELL-BEING

## *Health*

Just as this offering strengthens you,
strengthen my immune system against this
  disease.

Healing gods, guide the hands and minds
  and caring hearts
of nurses and doctors upon whose healing
  skills I depend.

On the waves of rhythm,
on the beat of the drum,
may my soul fly to the world above
to bring back health for the soul
of the one whom I am here to help.
Fill me with the power to cure,
O drum,
to find my power animal again
so that we might travel together to the land
  of healing.

## THE GODDESS

Mother of all that lives
and all that dies,
promote life,
defeat illness and death,
in this one who comes to you with love.

## THE ALL-GODS

The All-Gods expel this illness from you,
disease, and pain, and tiredness, and
  suffering,
ill-health, and depression, and body aches.
These seek to destroy the order of life.
The All-Gods despise disorder and will
  defeat them.
You can be sure of this:
it is their way.

## AIRMED

You gathered from your brother's grave
herbs of great power,
Airmed, daughter of Dian cécht.
This herb is of great power,
Airmed, daughter of Dian cécht.
May it heal me with part of your great
  power,
Airmed, daughter of Dian cécht.

Airmed, who knows where the healing
  herbs grew,
may this medicine be like them.
May your future praise come from a
  healthy worshiper.

Airmed, provider of healing herbs,
goddess of medicines,
may I find an open pharmacy,
and may it have the drugs I need,
that I might be healed.

## APOLLO

Flights of arrows descend from your ever-
 turning bow,
onto those who look toward you from
 below.
Flights of arrows that bring disease or
 healing
onto those who look toward you from
 below.
We who look toward you ask that they be
 causes of healing,
that their killing power be directed toward
 illness.
Do this and we will always have good
 reasons to praise you.

Woken in the night by a pain in my
 stomach
I pray to you for cease of its prodding
and a return to healing sleep,
Apollo of the shining bow.

Apollo who heals,
who sees only the truth:
may this [medical procedure] go well.
May it be easy.
May it be effective.
May it work as it should.
May it be accurate.
May it tell what it is designed to tell,
and may what it tells be a message of good
 health,
sweet health,
like the smell of these bay leaves I burn
 for you,
the smoke of which rises to please you
who desire only sweet smells, healthy
 smells,
Apollo who heals,
who sees only the truth.

## APOLLO (AGAINST CANCER)

Apollo, God of the Logos,
of the Truth that is behind the form,
whose lyre sings forth harmony.
God of the pattern that is,
and thus of the shape that should be:
you are rightly called Great Healer,
returning life to its proper place,
setting it firmly within the natural Order of
 things.
Rain down your unfailing arrows on this
 illness;
pierce the crab's hard shell,
cut it cleanly about its edges,
drive straight through its heart and carry it
 away,
leaving a purified body behind.
I have always revered the Logos, Son of
 Leto,
and dedicated myself to it.
You know that, God of the Bow,
so when I pour out this libation in your
 honor
I know you will look kindly on me and
 answer my prayer.

## APOLLO OR BRIGID

With your vivifying flame, fill with vitality
 this loved one who lies here ailing,
Bright One who heals.

## ARTEMIS

Artemis, you love your hounds that sport
 about you,
just as I love my own dog(s).
Just as you take care of them,
take care of mine,
Lady of the Beasts.
Goddess of animals,
accompanied by a leashed dog,
Artemis, lover of beasts.

## ASKLEPIOS

It was an honor for you to be struck down
   by the hand of Zeus,
a great honor to be so treated,
the greatest of honors to be so feared by
   the gods.
You were breaking the natural order of
   things, keeping men from death,
so you were punished.
Zeus treated you justly, Asklepios,
and I have no quarrel with him.
I don't ask for immortality, then,
but only for health in the time allotted me.
The gods may know what that time is
(or maybe they don't; maybe it is in the
   hands of a Fate beyond them),
but I do not.
So I ask you, Asklepios, for health while
   I live.
End this sickness that weighs me down.
You have the power and need only use it.
Give health to one who confidently
   worships you.

As I touch this patient,
may my fingers be each like your staff,
   Asklepios.
As I speak this prayer, giver of true
   diagnoses,
may be words be like the lapping of the
   gentle snakes that surround it.
May everything I do to heal [name] be
   exactly what you would have done if
   you were the doctor here.

You lift your snake-entwined staff, great
   healer,
and send out healing knowledge.
You know each drug and its effects,
each technique and when it should be used,
each symptom and what it means,
each illness and how to treat it,
each patient and what to do.
May my hands be yours.[17]

To my waking mind send knowledge,
Asklepios, son of Apollo.
Sharpen its diagnostic skills
to see with unfogged vision this illness's
   cause,
and the way to cure it lay open to me,
god of physicians.

## BRIGID

Brigid who guides a healer's hands,
whose fire inspires soothing words,
be with me as I greet this patient:
may diagnosis and treatment be true.

## DEATH

If I give this to you, Death, will you go?
Will you return on your well-marked path
   to the enclosed place?
Will you stay far away for many years left
   unlived?
Will it be a payment for your time waiting?
Take this, then, and go.

You have your own place, Death,
and this is not it.
There you rule as king;
here we are the most common of people.
There you dwell in a noble palace;
here we live in a simple house.
There you enjoy sparkling riches;
here our poverty shames us.
Go to your place, Death,
and wait for us there.

---

17   This prayer to Asklepios is for a doctor to pray
before each day's work. Only a little change would be
needed for it to be used by a patient or a patient's friend.

We have heard your message, and we will
  respond.
But we are busy here, Death.
We have many things to do.
Be patient, we will respond,
but only when the time is right.
Return to your home, Death,
and wait for us to come.
For you it will be only a little while.
For us it will have been a lifetime.

## DIAN CÉCHT

Dian Cécht, son of the Good God,
defeat this disease as you did the monster
  of Berba,
who had snakes for a heart,
and let life's river flow on.

## DIAN CÉCHT AND AIRMED

Dian Cécht, may my doctor's knowledge
  be yours.
May [he/she] diagnose correctly and
  prescribe rightly.
Airmed, may whatever medications are
  prescribed be the right ones
for the job, and accomplish their tasks,
  returning me to health.
Dian Cécht and Airmed, may what is done
  be the right thing to heal me
quickly and safely.

## FIREBIRD

Firebird, who dwells on the Tree of Life,
bring some of its fruit to me,
to heal my sickness,
to return me to health,
and I will praise you.

## GUAN YIN (FOR SOMEONE WITH ALZHEIMER'S)

As my [loved one/father/mother, etc.]
  descends into the fog of Alzheimer's,
Guan Yin of the beatific smile,
with each moment draw [him/her] closer
  in the strong and gentle hug of your
  encircling arms.
In this troubling time, may [he/she] find
  your peace.

## KU AND HINA

Before the upright stone I have laid an
  offering for you, Ku.
Before the rounded stone I have laid an
  offering for you, Hina.
Beneath the upright tree I have laid an
  offering for you, Ku.
Beneath the spreading bush I have laid an
  offering for you, Hina.
At the top of the mountain I have laid an
  offering for you, Ku.
At the bottom of the valley I have laid an
  offering for you, Hina.
I have offered there to Ku.
I have offered there to Hina.
I have offered there for health and life,
to the engenderer and bearer, I have
  offered.
May life and health come from them.

## MOON

We pray for light's power to heal this
  person.
Not *your* light, though, Sun.
The fierce purity of your blazing would
  harm more than heal.
Another time we will come to you with
  respect and offerings.
Tonight, we turn to Luna of the soft light.

With this bowl of milk, we ask you to pour
   your own healing swiftness over this one.
Swathe [her/him] in your sweet unguent;
with it draw anything inimical to health out
   from [her/his] body.
You are dependable in your constant turning
so we feel confident to depend on you for
   this.

## Comfort

Maybe I have as many troubles as there are
   grains of sand on all the beaches of the
   world.
But there are more of you than all the
   grains of sand on all the beaches of all
   the worlds in all the universes.
With your irresistible power you can crush
   them into powder and wash them away
   if you want.
Please want to.

I place myself in the center of the turning
   world:
the center is still.

For every person,
for each one, single,
of unfathomed worth,
who cries at night from hunger,
from fear,
from soul-eating loneliness;
for each and for all who suffer amidst
   rejoicing,
or starve amongst plenty,
or stand alone, while others live with
   families and friends about them:
Today, I am praying for them.
You Gods, each and several of every power
   and disposition,
I place these people into your care.

## THE GOD AND THE GODDESS

May I not forget in the midst of despair
that all things are born from the Goddess
   and God,
so that even the trials that come to afflict
   me
are the children of those who are my
   blessed parents.

## THE GOD

He walks at my side,
armed with sword and staff,
and in the darkest of nights,
my fears fly before him.
He looks into my eyes,
sitting with empty hands,
and in the brightest of days,
my cares are as nothing.

I raise my hands in prayer to the God,
to him I pray, Lord of the Earth.
He who was the first of any to die,
the first of any to be reborn.
He who rises with the Sun each day
and sets with it each night.
Out of my darkness and death, I call
and pray to you,
Lord of All.
Out of my need, I send my voice
with honor and longing,
in hope of intercession.
Grant me my prayer, Mighty One,
you who know what it is to suffer.
Grant me my prayer, Antlered One,
you who are the great giver.

Old fierceness is what you show us,
fierceness no less strong because it's old.
For the age is not in your body, but in your
   eyes;

a little tired, perhaps, from having seen so
much.
But like so many fathers the fierceness is
love.
Fierceness isn't always motivated by
cruelty;
a father's fierceness may be of respect,
not letting us win games by throwing them,
but making us beat you fairly,
thereby gaining our own respect to match
yours.
Sometimes silent, like fishing beside each
other,
sometimes talking on a long road trip,
there is so much in those eyes.
Men are often bad at putting things into words
but express their love no less through deeds,
even though that may be hard to see:
even to dangerous work,
he is speaking his love.
The man who carries the heaviest suitcase,
even though he's sick, too,
is speaking his love.
The husband and father who goes each day
to health-destroying work,
is speaking his love.
If we don't see this, it's *our* fault, not his,
and although you are a god, you are purely
a man,
and show your love through deeds.
Not a soft love, but love so hard it
sometimes doesn't seem like it's there.
But the fault is *ours*.
So when I come to you, looking for
comfort,
I don't expect hugs, or soothing touches,
I expect comfort, sure, but the comfort
comes in these words:
"Okay, let's work to fix this—we'll do it
together."
And we will.

In [my/our/their] darkness give light,
Lord of Brilliance.

God of justice, may I not complain
at what fate has brought to me.
Cleave my night with your lightning-axe,
dividing my troubles into ones I can bear.

Destroy all fear in me,
Lord whose sharp-tine antlers carry all
faults away,
carry them in tatters.

## THE GODDESS

With your soothing fingers,
wipe away the lines that worries have
etched on our faces.
Surround us with calm,
let us rest in the glow of peace,
as if we were encircled with the Moon's
own light.
Let our concerns and tensions drain away
from us,
pouring as water into your Earth.
Accept our troubles
and transform them into wonders.

I drop my fears into your ocean
and watch them sink from sight.
I place my fears on your broad Earth
and see them rot away.
I put my fears into your hands
and they are no more.
When you offer your arms to me,
Great Mother,
your hands hold nothing but love.

Her love is perfect, and perfectly She
expresses it.
Loving all, She gives all love,

with Her, all things are done with her love
    for all.
And yet—and yet—and yet—I'm
    suffering.
She loves all, but She doesn't love each.
So many have died so I could live,
unless I die, so many will never live.
And yet—and yet—and yet—and yet,
    Greatest of Lovers,
may this be my day.
May Your love for me be Your love for all.
May I see your smile
and smell your sweet breath as you say:
"Peace."

Mother, can you hear me crying?
Gather me in your infinitely encompassing
    arms,
hug me to your soft breast,
and whisper, "There, there;
all will be well.
All will be well, but for now cry.
My clothes have been wet with tears before
    and will be again.
So for now, cry,
and all will be well."

Inside the tadpole, the frog.
Inside the caterpillar, the butterfly.
Inside my pain, happiness.
I don't doubt your ways, Goddess of
    Nature,
nor do I want to criticize you,
but they're hard.
Send me strength and comfort, until I see
what will come of the way things are.

Adrift in the unseen waves of the infinite
    dark I float at ease,
resting trustingly in your enveloping arms.

I'm crying,
lonely,
my tears Your ocean's waters.

Not true, not true, not true, not true, not
    true, not true;
it can't be true.
All I want is for you to hold me and say,
    "Even if it's true, it will be okay."
Please, Mother.
Please.

Broken and tired and scared and scarred,
I sit empty,
and wait for Her to fill me,
and wait for Her to dive deep into my
    emptiness,
and return clutching my lost self tightly,
and return it to me with smiling eyes,
with soft hands open and soothing.

The Goddess sits beside me as I wait for
    your night terrors to subside.

Sitting here, looking at the Moon, at the
    Lady whose changing is yet regular,
    assured, and reliable, I ask her to give
    meaning to the mess I'm in.
Spinner of the Night, may the web I find
    myself in trap blessings.

If you have any fears, bring them to Her,
to the Mother of All,
She whose presence is soothing,
whose hands hold love.

## THE ALL-GODS

All-Gods,
each god,
joined together in perfect relationships:
I hunger for friends to fill my lonely days,

and it is to you whom I turn to for help.
Bring me in contact with the right people
and advise me on how to do the rest.

## BA'AL

Depressed, my spirit low,
I call to the Lord of Mountains,
to Ba'al who dwells on the heights
to lift me up.

## CATHUBODUA

Black goddess, free me,
Cathubodua,
as a white skeleton from disappointment
    and distress,
leaving shining purity behind,
a shape ready on which to rebuild a life.
Lovely dark one, crow goddess,
I call to you from my sadness.

## CERNUNNOS

You are still: may I be still!
You are firm: may I be firm!
You are at rest: may I be at rest!
The steady center of the turning world,
axis mundi, Lord:
Your antlers are heavy,
you bear them solidly.
Your antlers reach up,
they lift you straight.
Upright and calm in the midst of the
    tempest,
you provide peace to those who ask for it:
hear my prayer, raging god!

I saw him.
I saw Cernunnos in the eye of the
    whirlwind.
I saw the one with antlers sitting in the axle
    of the midst of the world's turning.
He was the very force of calm force;

still, but ready to lash out in any direction;
balanced on the cusp, the nexus between
    one moment and the next.
I saw him
and this is what he told me to tell you:
be at peace.

You with the antlers,
It is always still where you sit in the center
    of the whirling storm.
When the winds whirl about me,
be the rock to which I cling.
I pray, Lord Cernunnos, for a share of your
    peace.

Calm, still Lord, may I be calm.

In the center of the storm, there is calm.
In the center of confusion, there is peace.
In the center of exhaustion, there is rest.
Cernunnos, sitting in the midst of the
    world,
lead me to the center
and grant me the calm and peace and rest
    that are found there.

## DAWN

It matters not that the Sun shines on those
    around me,
or even if it's highest on the brightest day
    of the year,
I am still in darkness, my soul open and
    aching.
I cry for the light, the truest light,
I cry for it to fill the hole within.
Dawn, open your gates in me, and bring
    the dawn to my soul,
unlock the gates of my heart,
and create a path where people might walk
    through open doors.

## EPONA

A white mare, a vision, a goddess on
   horseback,
suckles a young colt:
Gather me, Epona, in your maternal arms,
and carry me away from troubles in your
   caring embrace,
on the back of an envisioned white mare,
   striding.

## HATHOR

Our mother, Hathor:
bring us children.
Inexhaustible udders:
give them prosperity.
Ever-loving cow:
may your lowing be always the loving
   murmur
of a soothing lullaby.

## INANNA

As you went in quest to rescue Dumuzi
   from the land of the dead,
from the hand of your sister,
from the hand of Erishkigal,
Inanna, Rescuer of the Despondent,
raise me from my depression,
from the darkness with which I am beset,
from the shadow that surrounds my soul.

## ISIS

When Osiris was slain, and divided into
   pieces scattered over the land,
you went and found them one by one,
   recovering, Isis, the lost,
a wife's love driving you on.
Search out all I have lost to time and age
   and sorrow,
and return it to me, each bit, one by one,
with a mother's love.

Queen Isis, my lady, my goddess,
since ancient times the bringer of comfort,
who mourned for your husband the Lord
   Osiris:
be with me now in my time of loss.
Grieve with me now in my time of loss.
Comfort me now in my time of loss.
Wrap about me your soothing wings,
Blankets to warm me from sorrow's cold
   hands.

## MANANNÁN MAC LIR

Manannán, play a strain of soothing on
   your harp
to dry the tears of those in sorrow
before they even begin to fall.
"Peace, peace," the sound of the strings,
play, Manannán, a soothing strain.

## MATRONAE

Mother who holds children in her arms,
nursing them tenderly,
their source of nourishment:
great is your love, great is your care,
and great is the need with which I turn to
   you.
As if I were your own child,
for that is what I am,
answer my cries of help.

## NUIT

Fearful things surround me, and fear rises
   in me:
Absorb both fearing and feared into your
   all-containing body, Nuit,
and leave me free.

## ODIN

Pierced and hanged, with bleeding eye,
inspire me in my suffering time
with hope for wisdom at its end.

## PEACE

Come to me, Peace,
as you would to the world.
As you would calm strife,
calm my mind.
As you would banish weapons,
banish my self-doubt.
As you would bring happiness,
bring it to me.
Come, Peace, bring peace,
to me as you would to the world.

## Perkʷū́nos

My voice might not be as loud as yours,
but it comes from my essential being, too.
May it rise through the crash of clouds and
    into your ears, Perkʷū́nos,
you who obliterate all that stands in your
    way.
May I be filled with the booming
    brightness you hurl and not by my fears.
May my body tremble with the strength of
    your arms and not my weakness.
May all I do be with your unfailing
    accuracy and your power that cannot be
    withstood.

## SUN

Feeling the shadow creeping upon me from
    behind
I pray to the last of the light to sustain
    me through the darkness with the
    knowledge of your return.
Keep me in this awareness:
Dark follows light, as it must,
but it must as well surrender to light when
    the proper time comes.
Just as you, setting Sun, may I know the
    proper time to come out of my sorrow as
    that time arises.

## ZURVAN AKARANA

Zurvan Akarana, to you I call, from the
    turning world,
toward the center I face you,
who stand like a pillar in the still point,
enwrapped with the turning,
surrounded by the changing.
It all happens about you;
you are not aloof from it,
you are there in its midst.
You do not reject the changing world,
nor do you transcend it,
but by standing within it, you find the still
    point.
Axis mundi, to you I call, from the turning
    world.
May I, though engrossed in the great
    changing,
find, even as you, the center.

## BIRD SPIRITS

Hey, you up there,
you, bird up there,
up there, bird.
Look down here.
Look and see me,
me down here.
Take my cares away from here.
Away from here, far away.

## PEARL SPIRITS

An irritated oyster gave birth to this pearl,
    which is so softly beautiful.
Pearl, produce soft beauty from the
    hardship of my life as I wear you.

## WIND SPIRITS

The wind that blows through man's empty
    halls
is the wind that blows through the empty
    deserts

is the wind that blows through the
   emptiness of all empty spaces
is the wind that blows through my own
   empty time.
But if you blow, wind, then there can be no
   emptiness.
Blow in my heart and keep this lonely one
   company.

Blow, Winds, through my life,
carrying away sadness; then still, leaving
   peace behind,
which I will remember was from you.

## Safety and Protection

Encompass me about with your protection,
Holy Ones of old.
Stand about me on all sides,
warding away from me all dangers,
keeping away from me all harm.

Stand about me, you protective Spirits,
on all six sides establish your guards.
From all dangers, no matter from what
   quarter,
whether from above or below, keep me safe.

### THE GOD AND THE GODDESS

My Lord at my right hand, my Lady at my
   left:
be with me throughout my life,
watching over me by night and by day.

### THE GOD

Sword's blade, spear shaft, lifted shield:
defend me.
Strong-armed, thick-sinewed, full-muscled:
defend me.
Your antlers as weapons:
defend me.

### THE GODDESS

Your arms are strong, Mother;
they can hug a child
or restrain one from harm.
Wrap them about me:
I trust you to know which is needed.

### THE ALL-GODS

I invoke the help of all the gods,
be you gods of earth or of sky;
whether of nature or of the busy city,
whether of the deep within or the vastness
   without:
all of you, I call out to all of you,
all of you I invoke,
and ask all of your help:
each to protect each of those at war,
in harm's way,
each to watch over those sent by our
   country into war,
those who have need of you.
We have need of you,
all of the gods,
each of the gods:
this is my wartime prayer.

### APOLLO

Your bow's swift arrows:
are they of blessing or destruction?
Show your blasting face to those who
   need it.
Show your blessing face to those who
   deserve it.
Whether beating down mercilessly
or shining benevolently,
bring what is right to each, Apollo.
Whether by fighting off enemies
or singing them to peace,
be my protector
and I will always speak sweetly of you.

## ARES

Spear against shield strikes fear in those
  arrayed against me,
but not in me,
because you and I are brothers, Ares,
in arms and at the table.

## THE AŚVINS

We are dear to you, and you to us,
divine physicians, horsemen, Aśvins,
to whom I pray with upraised arms,
to the saving gods,
who rescue from danger,
whose protection I ask.

## ATHENA OR MINERVA

Armored one, with the aegis on your breast:
to you, praise,
from you, protection.
The one deserved, the other hoped for.

## BA'AL

Protector of cities,
protect mine, Ba'al.
Here is a cake for you.
Protector of peoples,
protect mine, Ba'al.
Here is another.
Protector of your worshipers,
protect me, Ba'al.
Here is a third.
And here is beer for you.
Protect, Ba'al, as a king does.

## BAST

Ubesti, protect your child.
Perfumed one, protect your child.
Preparer of the dead, protect your child.
Whether Sun or Moon, protect your child.
Clearer of pests, protect your child.

Lioness, protect your child.
Mother of Many, protect your child.
Protect me, Ubesti; with sweetness
  surround me.
Protect me, Ubesti, from all that threatens.
Protect me, Ubesti, by both day and night.
Protect me, Ubesti, from waste and from
  want.
Protect me, Ubesti, with raging strength.
Protect me, Ubesti, as a molly her kittens.
I give, I ask, you bestow in return.

## BES

Small in stature,
great in power,
little Bes,
faithful protector
of families and children:
watch over and guard;
this is my prayer.

## CASTOR AND POLLUX

On either side of my AFV ride,
sons of Zeus.
May my treads be as well placed and
  unfaltering as the hooves of your own
  steeds.
May each piece of ordnance that flies from
  me be like your spears,
as sure in aim and as certain in destructive
  power.
Bring me through this battle successfully,
  Dioskouroi;
may my mission be fully accomplished.
Then, when you have brought me back to
  base unharmed,
I will offer to you in thanks.
This is my vow to you, Castor and Pollux.

Saviors at sea,
Sons of God,

Divine brothers:
Watch over this ship as it sails into danger.
Protect it and all who sail on it,
that we may return home safely to port
when our mission is accomplished.

## THE ELEMENTS

If wind blows you away, you will be
    protected by Air.
If flames rise around you, you will be
    protected by Fire.
If waves overwhelm you, you will be
    protected by Water.
If gravity drags you down, you will be
    protected by Earth.
In all of these dangers, Spirit will never
    abandon you,
as you lie within the protection of the
    elements.

## EPONA

This rose garland I place around your
    statue,
Epona, protector of the young.

## GUAN YIN

Guan Yin of the gentle hands,
with arms held wide in benediction:
come between my enemies and me
and join us together in peace.

## ISIS

Goddess with the enfolding wings,
wrap them about me, Isis; keep fear and
    danger at bay.
May I mount your throne and rest there in
    peace.

Queen Isis, wrap your wings about my
    family and me
and bring us through danger in safety.

## MANANNÁN MAC LIR

Wheel wells not awash,
rims not even damp,
on a flowery plain a chariot comes to me
    here in my boat.
Amazement not even relevant, since gods
    perform miracles,
and you, Manannán, are most certainly a
    god.
If the waves on which I sail can never be
    flowers under my keel,
may they at least be your horses carrying
    me safely,
with still manes.

## MARDUK

Marduk, whose mace is ever ready to crush
    the enemies of those who worship you,
of your faithful servants,
of we who pour out this beer,
who lay out this bread,
before your image.
Destroyer of Tiamat,
Defender of cities:
Protect us,
protect those who offer to you today.

## MARS

Listen to my prayer, Father Mars,
that comes with this libation of unmixed
    wine.
Protect me, and all I am, and all that is dear
    to me,
and I will offer to you regularly in thanks.
I pour out this libation now and will pour
    many in future years.

## MOON

You move among the stars as a shepherdess
    amongst her sheep,

guiding them, keeping them from straying.
Mother Moon, softly light my way,
keeping me from danger as well.

## MORRÍGAIN

A snake that is not a snake,
A dog that is not a dog,
A cow that is not a cow—You are not these
    things, Morrígain,
and I am not sure I want to know what you
    *are*.
If my offering pleases you, though,
protect rather than destroy.

## OCEAN

All life began in you;
preserve my life while I sail on you.

I draw myself under the seen,
entering your hidden water world.
I rise up to where your waves reach over
    me,
where sense meets the incomprehensible.
May this gift of honor to you inspire a gift
    in return:
may you keep me safe when I sail on your
    surface.

## ODIN

Twin wolves stand, All Father,
at your throne, one on each side,
well-trusted servants and true.
As you watch over those who watch over
    you
I ask that you watch over my dog(s),
their domesticated kin.
And so I offer to Odin,
and to Geri and Freki,
in praise and supplication.

## PEACE

Far from home,
living with fear,
I pray for Peace to pull all the world into
    Her embrace.

## POSEIDON (AGAINST AN EARTHQUAKE)

Still the earth beneath me
and I will pour you a libation of wine,
blue-maned hurler of the trident.

## RUDRA

Turn aside your storms, send them away.
May peace descend in their wake.
Rager, Rudra, Lord of Lightning,
withhold your chaos,
pass by this place, leaving it in calm.

*[Sometimes it's appropriate to pray to a deity
to stay away. Perhaps if you ask politely, they
will listen.]*

## SKAÐI

Your skill on skis, Skaði,
is well and justly renowned.
Protect me on the slopes today.
May my time on the hills be fun and safe.

## SPIDER WOMAN

Spider Woman, weaver of beauty;
Spider Woman, laying patterns on the
    world;
Spider Woman, binding all things together:
wrap your threads lightly about me in
    protection.

## STORM GOD

Striker, axe-bearer, splitter, hammerer:
protect me.
Bolt-caster, cleaver, smasher, way-clearer:

protect me.
Warrior, victor, overcomer, protector:
protect me.

Break their shields, hammerer;
dissolve their defenses, stormer;
remove their courage, thunderer.
Fight beside me as my comrade,
win through with me to victory.

*[This prayer is as appropriate in the board-
room as on the battlefield.]*

With your quick-sent lightning and
    penetrating rain,
make the Earth fertile, storm-rider,
    hammer-wielder.

Wield the lightning on my side, Thunderer,
and I will ensure that my cause is just.

## SVANTEVIT

Svantevit, with your four faces,
one for each direction,
guard me from dangers no matter which
    one they come from,
and, watching well, may you find me
    acting rightly,
and thereby deserving of your attention.

## THOR

Wielder of the hammer,
red-bearded one,
Thor, protector,
to you I call.
I stand in the midst of a storm
and ask your protection.

You who bear the flaming hammer,
to you I pray:
fight on my side against all my opponents.

For with you on my side, who can stand
    before me?
Remember my devotion to you, Lord of
    Thunder.
As I work to your honor, may you work
    also to mine.

## THOR AND ODIN

Arriving won't do you any good unless
    you arrive safely,
but arriving safely won't do you any good
    unless you arrive at the right place.
Be blessed with the company of Thor, for
    safety.
Be blessed with the company of Odin, the
    Knower of the Way,
for safe arrival at the right place.

## VARUṆA

As I have sought forgiveness from,
and given compensation to,
those I have wronged,
I seek forgiveness of,
and burn this butter to,
you, Varuṇa:
may your snares that enclose wrongdoers
    pass me by.

If we have done that which is wrong,
breaking the laws of gods and of men,
may Varuṇa's snares still miss us.
Next time we will do better.

## VULCAN

Vulcan, be with them,
those who are repairing the wires
and returning electricity to my home and
    so many others.
Protect them from foul weather and
    dangerous currents,

and make their hands and minds swift and
    sure
to restore power quickly.
Vulcan, send your blessings,
as I do, too.

## ŽEMEPOTIS

Žemepotis, protect the land
and all the buildings
and all the animals and people
of this one who prays to you.

# Travel

Guide us to the right path,
protector of the way.
Steer us toward the proper goal,
guardian of the path.
Open the road that should be traveled to us,
Lord of going.[18]

May you walk with me,
as I go on my way,
walking yourself in front,
clearing the way.

Guide to travelers,
for your help I pray,
that you might be with me
as I go on my way.

I give greetings to the gods of this place,
I, a traveler, offer up prayers.
From my land to this one, I have come,
meaning no harm to any who dwell here.
Land Spirits, I pray to you;
though I do not yet know you, I honor you.

Lord of Trees, I pray to you as I enter this
    forest.
Watch over my steps while I am under
    your care.

This road is all roads:
my prayers to this road are to all roads on
    which I will travel.

On the open road
open me to all I encounter
Lord of All Ways.

Lord of the Pathways,
go before us on this trip,
and bring us safely and happily to our
    destination,
we who are your grateful followers.

This road I step on joins with all the other
    roads, forming an irregular net over the
    Earth, as if we could capture Her, an
    absurd and forlorn hope:
the net is only a decoration for her, like a
    golden hairnet on a beautiful woman.
So as I set myself on the road,
as I begin my traveling,
I make this offering to the Lord of Paths,
and I make offering to Earth.
But this net, and all roads, ends at the sea.
So surprisingly, as I begin this travel across
    the land, I make offering to the Sea God,
    who receives all roads in the end, and
    thus encompasses all travelers on them.
Rider on the Waves, may the enclosing be
    of protection, not incarceration.
And even the sea is in the care of the Earth,
    lying across Her like a jewel around the
    neck of a beautiful woman,
and even the Sea God Her child.

---

18    This may be used to help smooth a journey, but it
may also be used to help smooth a life. The way and the
path are images of how things should be and for how we
should act.

So I make this fourth and final offering
   before setting out to the Earth,
ending my prayer where all roads and sea
   and traveling begin.

Both Healers and Guides,
go with the ambulance I'm pulling over
   for.

## THE GOD AND THE GODDESS

Lord of grain and animals,
Lady of fruits and plants,
may I find a place to eat off this exit.

## ATHENA

Goddess who finds the way like an owl
   through the dark,
you found one for Odysseus through
   adversity,
over a hostile sea:
show me the right way to go;
bring me, a lost one, home.

## CASTOR AND POLLUX

Dioskouroi, Saviors,
bring me through this storm:
safely on the shore I will offer to you.

Across the sea, on swift-running steeds,
come Zeus's boys, saviors of sailors,
the stars who guide us safely to harbor,
who still the waves that threaten our vessel.
To those who supplicate you, come, twin
   sons!
Come with aid to win us home.

## EARTH

Wide-Extending Earth,
who cares for her children as mother
   should:
be smooth, be without obstruction,

beneath and before me,
as I travel on this journey.
Bring me to my destination and home
   again safely,
to contentment.

From the air I can best see the land below,
the land below, spreading out,
spreading out, Mother Earth,
Mother Earth, your airborne child praises
   you.

As I speed through the night
you are speeding, too, Earth, toward dawn.
We are traveling together.
May my arrival at my destination
be as certain and free from difficulties as
   yours.

Driving on this road, linked to others,
in a net laid over you, Earth,
I am traveling one thread in my woven
   fate,
which is lived in your constant presence.
May all I do bring you honor,
weaving a beautiful cloth for my life.

## THE ELEMENTS

Air, be wind for his sails.
Fire, be Sun on his face.
Water, be smooth ocean beneath him.
Earth, be the island from which he sails.
All this on a safe journey to his desired
   destination.

I put you in the hands of the ones whose
   realms
are in the elements.
I put you in the hands of the Air Beings:
may they protect you when you enter their
   lands,

when you think, may you be safe and true.
I put you in the hands of the Fire Beings:
may they protect you when you enter their
    lands,
when you act, may you be safe and true.
I put you in the hands of the Water Beings:
may they protect you when you enter their
    lands,
when you feel, may you be safe and true.
I put you in the hands of the Earth Beings:
may they protect you when you enter their
    lands,
when you are still, may you be safe and
    true.
I put you in the hands of the Spirit Beings:
may they protect you when you enter their
    lands,
when you are, when you do, when you are
    in the midst of all,
may you be safe and true.

## GAṆEŚA

Dancing Gaṇapati,
Trumpet the jet engines' roars of my plane,
clearing the way.

## HEKATE

My prayer today is to Hekate:
may the fire with which I bless you be one
    of her torches,
going before you to guide you on your
    way.
May she whom even Zeus honors, and who
    receives a portion of every prayer,
hear this one;
may she provide a light, not just of
    protection until you reach your
    destination,
but to illuminate you that you might
    not miss the beauty of the journey in
    anticipation of your goal.

## HERAKLES

Wanderer,
Laborer,
who never rested until you laid yourself,
live and in pain,
on your own funeral pyre,
lit by a friend,
from which to rise, once mortal,
to a seat among the immortal gods.
Traveler, aid those who travel;
aid me on my way.
Succeeder in trials,
bring me to success through your
    invincible strength:
closest of the gods to man.

## HERCULES

Returned from a voyage,
and safely home,
I offer to Hercules,
as they did of old
at the pillars of Gades.
Thanks to you, Travelers' God,
whom I honor with this gift.

## INANNA

On each step of this journey set out before
    me,
guide me, Inanna, you who know of
    dangerous ways.
You traveled to death, and know that way;
keep me from it though threats may
    surround me.

## LUG

On rails kept long and straight and clear of
    obstruction,
laid spear-like across the land,
guide this train, Lug, with technology's
    long hand.

May it travel smoothly and arrive safely.
To the Samildánach I pray.

## Manannán mac Lir

May my car flow through the undulating
    traffic as effortlessly as your chariot
    over the flower-plained ocean,
Manannán mac Lir,
you whose waves are horses.

Oirbsen mac Lir,
smoothly sailing, and safely to shore,
God of the journey, to you I pray:
go before me, clear the way.

Manannán, guide my flight today.
May my airplane's wings rise like sails,
like wings of gulls.
May the air be smooth,
be like a flowered plain beneath your
    chariot wheels.

## Poseidon

A horse among horses be this boat,
under the protection of the god of horses,
god of the sea, of white-maned horses.

Poseidon, Earth-Shaker, Lord of the Sea,
your undeniable power moves against this
    ship,
which moves, in response, from side to
    side.
This great ship, proud accomplishment of
    human mind and muscle,
    is at your mercy.
We who sail on the surface of your depths
acknowledge your power, and your
    mastery of this realm.
That is why we turn our prayers toward
    you,
to the blue-maned deep-dweller,

who can stretch out his trident-armed hand
and make the flat sea-surface grow
    mountains and canyons,
foundering the ships that cross it,
or who can, if he wishes, still the churning,
and smooth the way of the wave-cleaving
    ships.
Lord of waters, we pray to you,
scattering offerings overboard.
Take them and not us.
Receive them gladly and give in return
calm seas and safe passage,
until we return to land
with gratitude for your kindness.

With your trident smooth the waves
that beat against the hull.
With your horn scatter the winds
that threaten my passage.
Earth Shaker, calm the water beneath my
    boat.

## Rán

Preserve, Rán, my boat as I cross the sea;
withhold your net from bow and stern,
keep keel and rudder from clinging danger,
speed me to my destination.

## Sea

Happily arrived in harbor, I offer this
    thanksgiving coin to the sea.

## Space and Time

Time is Space, and Space is Time;
Space-Time is the fabric of the Cosmos.
I'm a little embarrassed to invoke such a
    thing for such a little reason, Lord of
    Space and Time, but it's like this:
I'm late for an appointment.
As the time grows less, may the space
    grow less rapidly.

I'm not asking you to bend the rules of
   physics,
just to make the way smooth for those
   ahead of me,
so that it might be smooth for me,
so that I'll arrive in time, or at least not too
   late.

## WODEN

All-Father Woden, protector of travelers,
guard us, guide us,
bring us through
in safety and ease
on our journey today.

A companion makes the way shorter,
or sweeter,
and the load lighter.
Walk with me, Woden.
Even when I don't see you, I'll know you're
   there by the mysteries spoken in my heart,
from the wisdom-patterned sound of my
   feet against the ground,
echoed by yours.

A road-weary traveler, trudging beside me,
lifts hand to hat as if in salute;
his one eye winks, and laughter follows.
Woden, Lord of the Way,
do not lead me lost,
make my road right,
Old Rambler, you.

Grey-hood, as you wander the world,
spare a thought for the those who, like me,
wend their way today.
Bring us safely and directly to our
   destinations.
I think of you as a friend when I say these
   words, Woden;
smile on me as one of yours, too.

Ahead walks, cloaked in snow-cloud grey,
the guide to pilgrims who make their way.
Do not, pale Woden, I deeply pray,
mislead my feet from their sacred goal.
Guide of travelers, it lies to you;
my faltering steps, their strength renew.
This power is yours if the lore is true:
hear my words and guide my soul.

## AIR SPIRITS

The Spirits of the Air play about this plane
   as it flies.
May they seek their fun in keeping its
   flight smooth
rather than tossing it around;
may they compete among themselves as to
   which of them can best succeed in this.

## FOREST SPIRITS

Into the forest, laughing,
guide my feet, Spirits of Nature;
into its depths, conduct my heart;
into its mysteries, initiate my soul.

## HOTEL SPIRITS

I pray to the gods and Spirits of this
   temporary home,
this [hotel/motel/bed-and-breakfast/etc.] in
   which I find myself spending [the night/
   these nights].
I honor you as if I were honoring the
   Spirits of my own home,
and offer to you this drink that I have
   brought to you.
Please consider every prayer that I make in
   this room to be addressed
in part to you.

## LAND SPIRITS

Spirits of the land we're driving through,
hand us off, each to the next,

smoothly as we go.
We honor each of you with this prayer.

## RIVER SPIRITS

Proud River, I give you this respectful
thought as I cross this bridge over you.
Even if I myself don't endure struggles as I
cross, [river name],
I remember that those who built this bridge
did,
and consider [these words/this offering] an
addition to theirs.

# Before Flying

## AIR SPIRITS

As I enter your realm, Spirits of air,
as I mount to the clouds in this airplane,
I place myself in your hands.
There, among the vagaries of the winds,
I won't be afraid, because I know you are
my allies.
As I fly today, be at my side.
Protect me until I land again safely.

# For Military Flyers

Ride beneath their planes, protecting
Spirits,
raising up their wings with your own.
Guide their weapons, warrior Spirits,
bringing them to their targets with accuracy.
Be with them throughout their mission,
Spirits of power,
that what must be done will be done,
that it will be done well.

# For a Business Trip

May I go and return in safety.
May I go and return with profit.

May I go and return accomplishing my
goals.
May I go and return in the hands of the
gods.
May I go and return under their protection.

# Commuter's Prayer

## CERNUNNOS

Remind me on my drive that my anger
harms me
more than that which angers me.
Lord of peace, in ultimate calm sitting,
pass on to me some of your beatific pose.
May even my commute be done in
beauty.[19]

# After Moving

## LAND SPIRITS

Land folk, I am here, newly arrived to this
place.
I have come from my previous home,
where I lived under the protecting gaze
of the Land Spirits there.
In this new place, then, I wish to establish
peace again
between my people and the people of the
land,
as it has been done since the
unremembered time.
I bring gifts to you, I bring offerings,
as a suppliant should when entering a
chieftain's hall.
Accept them from me and, with them, my
friendship.
Establish between us peace.

---

19    If any situation requires prayer, it's traffic. The ob-
servation of the harm done by anger is Marcus Aurelius's.

# Against Foes

Since Paganism seeks to include all life, it must include its bad parts as well as its good. That is not to say that we have to like the bad things. It is certainly okay to ask that they pass us by. But some of it is unavoidable, so we ask for the strength to deal with it. Sometimes we ask benevolent deities to protect us, and sometimes we ask the not-so-benevolent ones to deal lightly with us or to show us in what way our sufferings are necessary and even valuable.

I don't want to wax poetic about how curses can be blessings in disguise, and I don't want to insult those who suffer by implying that their suffering is a good thing. I do want to say, however, that sometimes suffering can indeed bring blessings. It shows us that the world is not all bunnies, kittens, and rainbows, which means we come face-to-face with reality, a great blessing. It both tests us and strengthens us. We learn how much we can stand and how to stand worse, if it should come. We learn that sometimes good things are born from bad things. May the gods protect the person who grows up without experiencing suffering; the first strong wind they encounter as an adult will blow them away.

Beyond all this, destruction can be positive. Sometimes the weeds need to be whacked back to let the good stuff grow. Part of us must die so the best of us can live. Deities of destruction can do this for us.

This is not easy, nor is it safe. The fire that burns away brush can get out of control and destroy the forest. It has become fashionable in neo-Paganism to worship "dark" deities—Kali, Loki, Hekate, etc. They are seen as misunderstood. They are, in fact, misunderstood but by those who see them as "fun." They are not fun. They are scary, dangerous, and difficult to deal with.

I hesitated, therefore, to include any prayers to this kind of deity. No sense in calling up trouble for people, and I have a responsibility for the use of every prayer in this book.

Yet something kept bringing me back to the need for this kind of prayer. We need to acknowledge the darker side of things in order to fill out our relationship with the universe. I compromised—a few prayers to show how they should be done and the explanation above. Not enough to rid me of responsibility, perhaps, but a slight salve to my conscience.

## CATHUBODUA

Cathubodua, fly over the field,
a crow,
seeking out, for food, my enemies.

## HEKATE

Keeper of Ravenous Dogs,
Bitch goddess,
Howler,
Bearer of Torch and Knife,

Ruler of the Dark Moon:
Hekate, I pray to you.
Turn your slaying glance from me
and direct it toward my enemies.
And if you can't turn it away,
may it be because there is something in me
   that must die.
Act with wisdom and discernment,
   destroying only what must go,
and giving me strength to endure the
   burning.

## LOKI

When the gods grew too comfortable in
   their unending life,
you stole the apples that kept them young
   and made them face age.
When they sought to cheat the giant of the
   wages for his work,
they turned to you to save themselves.
When Thor grew too sure of his strength to
   kill Chaos,
you showed him that craftiness is as
   necessary as raw power.
Loki, god of unpleasant truths, open my
   eyes to my own limits.
It is only by seeing them that I can
   overcome them.[20]

## PAN

May it be my opponents, not me,
who panic, Goat-headed God,
at the sound of your cry
in the back of their befuddled minds.

## PERUN

Perun, from galloping horseback
shoot arrows against the dangers that
   surround me.
Here is beer for you, and oats for your
   steed.

## TARANIS

Crush beneath your horse's hooves the
   ancient foe,
ride against chaos in the service of order.
Taranis, cast your rumbling wheel against
   him
and against all beings who oppose the
   sustaining of the Right Way.
Remove obstacles from growth and rains
   of prosperity.
Clear the way for fruitful creation,
god whose voice is thunder.

## THUNOR

Ruddy-bearded hammer-wielder,
Thunor, bane of the Midgard Serpent,
cast your weapon against the snakes that
   beset me.

---

20   There is no evidence that Loki was ever worshiped.
He may have existed only in myths, with the ancients
knowing better than to call out to him. There was, after all,
enough chaos in their lives. Still, I decided to include this
prayer for two reasons. First, no matter what the ancients
may have thought, neo-Pagans are going to pray to him, so
they may as well pray relatively safely. Second, today our
world is very ordered and becoming more so every day. A
little bit of chaos might do us some good, if it is channeled
into destroying pleasant lies.

*Chapter 27*

# CIVIC PRAYERS

One of the functions of ancient Paganism often overlooked by secularized neo-Pagans is how it provides a support for the social order. As citizens of a country that supports religious freedom, we, of course, do not want to establish any religion, even our own, as official. However, as citizens of a country that supports religious freedom, we should take our religion into our civic duties, and we should gladly seek to support and guide our country's institutions with prayer.

Because I'm from the US, many of these prayers are specifically American. However, some of those can be easily adapted for citizens of other countries and can serve as inspiration for prayers appropriate for them.

## INDUSTRY, COMMERCE, AGRICULTURE, WAR, PEACE, JUSTICE, LIBERTY

Industry, you have made us strong.
Commerce, you have made us rich.
Agriculture, you have fed us well.
War, you have defended our freedom.
Peace, you have given us something to
    defend.
Justice, you have enabled us to deserve all
    these.
Liberty: with these we have built a home
    for you,
and we ask you to come live with us,
continually reminding us of your gifts and
    your demands.

## JUSTICE, LIBERTY, WISDOM

We call you, Justice, to come,
no matter what the cost to ourselves.
We call you, Liberty, to come,

no matter what sacrifices you may demand.
We call you, Wisdom, to come,
no matter how wrong we may prove to be.
Bless this land with your presence.
Challenge this land with your demands.
Make all our actions prosperous and true.

## *The Land*

### LAND SPIRITS

Spirits of plants and animals,
of water and stone;
All the Spirits of this land:
Our ancestors weren't kind to your
    ancestors when they came to this land.
Today, hear our words,
taste our offerings,
so we might begin a new relationship with
    you,
a few small steps on the road to trust.

## Urban Prayers

Each building an obelisk erected in
    honor of the multitude of gods of my
    community,
the many gods of the many beliefs of the
    many people from whom it is formed.

We plant seeds in the ground and water
    them, and plants grow,
each with their own Spirit.
We quarry stone, smelt ore, and buildings
    grow,
each with their own Spirit.
A forest of trees has a Spirit.
A city of buildings has a Spirit.
Through the forests roam the gods and
    Spirits of the forest.
Through the cities roam the gods and
    Spirits of the cities.
Entering the [forest/city] I say this prayer
    to the gods and Spirits of this place
and to those of the [city/forest] I am leaving.

Every pattern is holy,
even these roads I'm driving on.
Every pattern has a Spirit,
even these roads I'm driving on.
I forget that sometimes, though,
so please forgive me,
and I'll sometime give you an offering.

### THE GOD

Mighty Horned God,
who rules as much in the city as in the
    deepest forest,
fill the spaces with your antlers,
strike the streets with your iron hooves,
come among us as we dwell with people,
not among rising trees
and wandering deer.

### THE ALL-GODS

In the midst of a busy city the gods crowd
    close,
each asking for worship,
the gods of each and all.
You are so many that I can't begin to honor
    you one by one:
take these words as a gift to you all.

### CLOACINA

Keep the pipes and fixtures of the city,
    Cloacina,
whether what they carry is pure, grey, or
    otherwise,
functioning well,
for the health of all who live here.

### ISHTAR

Ishtar, mistress of cities,
make mine strong in finances and art,
and safe for its people to enjoy.
Spread its fame and good reputation far
    through the land
so people will want to visit
and enjoy all it contains
so that it might be prosperous.

Queen of cities, protect mine,
Astarte,
from all disturbances.
May it be at peace,
its inhabitants safe and prosperous.

### XÁRYOMĒN

Lying awake in the dark of an unfamiliar
    city,
I can feel the hum that extends through it
    and holds it together.
I feel the power lines, the water mains, the
    roads.

I feel the bus routes, the subway tunnels,
the bridges.
I feel the police, the firefighters, the EMTs,
the garbagemen, the delivery trucks,
the hospitals, schools, and post offices.
I feel the network that forms the city,
its skeleton and capillaries,
supporting and feeding it.
And I feel your skeleton and capillaries,
supporting and feeding it.
And I know who you are:
You are Xáryomēn.
And I find myself familiar in an unfamiliar
city.

## THE ANCESTORS

The Works of Man are the works of
Nature,
for Man is of the World.
The towering buildings of this city stand as
nobly as ancient trees,
grown tall with age.
My praise goes out to those who built
them,
whether living or dead,
for their skill and vision,
and to the Ancestors who developed the
means to build them,
and to the Spirit of the city itself,
formed of and forming the city around us.

# Society

## THE GOD AND THE GODDESS

When I look at the people who stream by
me in the city today,
I do not see my people.
I see the other, the foreigner, the stranger,
the unknown, the barbarian.
I know that this is not right, and still I find
I am doing it.

How will I escape my trap of exclusion,
Holy Ones?
How will I learn who my tribe is?
How will I come to know that my family is
passing before me,
and·I stand by, not only not knowing,
but actually preventing that knowledge
from coming to my mind?
I pray to you, you who are the parents of
this family
of which I am a part:
open my eyes, open my ears, open my
mind,
open my heart to all the relatives that
surround me.

## DYÉUS PTḖR, GʷOUWINDĀ, XÁRYOMĒN

Open my eyes, Dyéus Ptḗr, to those around
me.
Open my heart, Gʷouwindā, with your
loving care.
Unite me with them, Xáryomēn,·
into a society of individuals,
based on reciprocal exchange.

## HERMES

Lord of travelers, unite this land.
We share one road, with many branches:
guide us along it to find each others'
homes.
And when we find them, clear our sight
so that we might see that we all live in the
same neighborhood,
that none of us lives apart.

## INDIVIDUALISM AND COMMUNITY

Individualism and Community are married,
inseparable,
neither ever found without the other.

Community without Individualism would
    be despotism;
Independence without Community,
    wandering lost.
When I pray to you, then, I will always
    pray to the both,
as two separate ones joined together.
This is how I pray to you today,
asking that you strengthen the individual
    society,
blessing us with both freedom and
    confraternity.

## MONETA

I am gifted, Moneta, by you,
with enough to live,
and extra to enjoy.
May you remind me daily
of those who do not,
of those who lack for food,
of those who lack for shelter, and for
    clothing, and for healthcare,
and for all the needs and pleasures of life.
May I give with your inspiration some of
    my excess,
whether personally or through groups that
    dispense you wisely,
or provide the things you give to those in
    need.
A just society cares for all:
may I live in such a society,
created, in some part, by what I give.
Moneta, I ask you, then, not for enough
    for me,
but for extra enough that I might help
    others.
To you I return some of what I have
    earned,
in hopes that you might give me more to
    attain this goal.

## NATURE

Here in this city, surrounded by a canyon
    of buildings that seem to block out
    Nature,
I pray to the gods of nature, who are
    present everywhere,
here no less than in the wild forest,
or the empty plains over which the storm
    winds blow,
or the ocean that hides its immense
    numbers of life in its depths.
For we human beings are not separate from
    Nature,
and have our own nature,
and this nature is above all to gather into
    communities,
and to form societies,
and to build cities.
So I stand here in this city and praise
    Nature,
present Her all around us.
How could we keep Her out?

## QUIRINUS

Amid the flow of people on this street, I
    find Quirinus, God of Peoples,
God of *my* people,
and praise him with my steps,
their rhythm blending with those of the
    others among whom I live and move.

Bring people to my group, Quirinus,
with whom we might worship,
to whom we can provide the opportunity to
    worship
in community.
Humans aren't meant to be alone,
nor are gods.
So bring us a community to worship yours,
god who brings and binds people together.

## Peace

In time of war we come together as a
  people,
as a people we must pray for peace:
Holy Ones, may there be peace.
In time of war we come together in our
  families,
as families we must pray for peace:
Holy Ones, may there be peace.
In time of war we find ourselves as
  individuals,
as individuals we must pray for peace:
Holy Ones, may there be peace.
As a people, as families, as individuals, we
  must pray for peace:
Holy Ones, bring us peace.

### THE GODDESS

Peace, sweet Peace,
bring to this divided land,
Comforting Mother of the soothing hand.

### ARES

Keep from me, Ares, your burning war,
keep peace, you who fight.
And, if it must come, may conflict be short
and lead to lasting peace.

### JANUS

Father Janus, may your gates be closed,
may your temples' doors be shut;
may all who wish to worship you
do so in their own homes,
reverently touching their doorjambs.
May peace reign,
and each family rest safely about their
  hearth,
undisturbed this day.

### PEACE

Return to us, Peace.
May our actions in this time of war not
  offend you so much
as to chase you away for good.
We do what we must,
seeking in it no pleasure,
seeking its end and your return.
We have put your way aside, Peace,
for this time,
but we would never put aside our love for
  you.
Stay with us, Peace, even in this time of
  war,
and help all to return to walk on your path.
Do not abandon those who look to you in
  hope.

On wings that light away war's shadows,
  fly swiftly to us, Peace,
to those who wait impatiently after
  praying.
We pray for Peace,
we pray to Peace.
To Peace, Goddess of Promise,
Holy and Pure One, we pray for peace.

### QUIRINUS

Quirinus who guards over people gathered
  together as a whole,
bring peace to our land,
and to anywhere in the world where people
  contend.

## The People and Government

May all the gods of my people hear my
    prayers;
as we go to the polls to choose our leaders,
may it be with wisdom.

### THE GOD AND THE GODDESS

Lady and Lord, bless my country.
Guide its governors, show them the path
    to take,
make their actions conform to the Way of
    Nature.
Knit together the many peoples into one
    tribe;
unite us, make us a family, as indeed we
    are under your loving gaze.

King and Queen of the company of the
    gods,
rulers of the ruling ones,
inspire those who govern us to do the right
    things,
the necessary things,
and not just the convenient things.
Grant them the vision to bring peace and
    justice,
drawing wisdom from the ways of the past
without being bound by them,
looking toward the future with clear eyes.

### BA'AL

Ba'al, chief of the gods,
rule, Lord on earth,
as you do in their council.
Bring harmony among those who govern
    us,
as you do among them.

### BRITANNIA

Britannia, you still rule,
still rule the waves,
the protecting moat that rings our land.
Keep us safe, and our ships as well
that ply the seas,
bringing us wealth and power.

With spear and shield protect this land,
mighty Britannia,
your lion that crouches at your feet ready
    to pounce at your command.

### DEMOCRACY

It's not your hands I'm voting with,
    Demokratia,
so don't let anyone try to tell you that.
I mean, really, what would be the point?
If my vote isn't independently given, it's
    not under your blessing.
It's only when I don't ask you how to vote
    that I can really honor you.
Freedom is your worship.

Democracy, as the voters go to the polls,
may they be wise.
May they cast their votes based not on
    what the candidates
will do for them personally,
or for a group to which they belong,
but for the people as a whole.
May they vote well for the candidate best
    for the polity.

### GENIUS OF THE PEOPLE

In times past, people prayed to the deities
    who ruled governments to bless their
    society, to ensure good government.
    They prayed to the god who guided the
    rule, or the genius of the ruler, or to the
    ruler himself.

We don't do that. We have no ruler toward whom we might pray, or to whose genius we might pray, or to whose guiding deity we might pray. Or we *do* have a ruler, but not one; we have many. For our ruler is the People. So if we are to pray for our ruler, we must pray to the genius of the polity itself, not to give power, but authority; not to ease the application of force, but its right use; to gain liberty and justice for each person, and for the People.

Make us a moral nation, Genius; that is, one in which each citizen is continually trying to both know and practice Virtue. Instill in us and encourage in us a love for the Good. This is the only way to pray for our ruler; be pleased by our knowing that.

## GOD OF WAR

Strengthen our military, God of War:
not to attack, but to defend,
not to conquer, but prevent being
    conquered,
not to be aggressive, but to battle the
    aggressor,
not to impose our will, but to allow time
    and space for our deeds to inspire.
Strengthen our military, God of War,
that we might be safe and at peace.

## INDRA, JUPITER, LUG, MIƟRA, OSIRIS

We aren't governed by kings anymore,
but those who do govern us still need the
    Truth of the King.
So, all the gods of kingship—Indra, Jupiter,
    Lug, MiƟra, Osiris—don't desert us.
In this changed time, we still look to you
    for help.

## JUPITER

Jupiter, Greatest and Best,
protect this country and make it glorious,
rightly respected by those who live
    elsewhere.

## LIBERTY

Liberty:
Our Representatives and Senators,
Our President,
Our Supreme Court,
only hold their offices to make you known.
Make this known to *them*,
so that knowing you they will be inspired
    to your service.

## LIBERTY AND MINERVA

Renew your old friendship, Minerva and
    Liberty,
create a land where creativity runs free and
    freedom possesses the skills to become
    real.
Work without freedom is enslaving;
Freedom without work, pointless.
Work without freedom is deadening;
Freedom without work, lifeless.
Renew your ancient friendship, Minerva
    and Liberty,
and inspire the citizens of this country to
    create a land where you'll feel at home.

Sweet Liberty,
whose self-evident truths can be so hard
    to see,
and so hard to establish,
and so hard to maintain:
to you, increased devotion.
Minerva, through whose wisdom the
    founding documents were composed,

and through whose martial power liberty
    has been maintained,
and through whose teachings of skill the
    People have prospered:
To you, increased devotion.
To America, ever young and learning,
ever unfolding the lessons of Liberty
    taught by Minerva:
listen to them well.
With you,
as part of you,
I worship Liberty and Minerva today,
and will each day,
with increased devotion.

## LUG

Lug, god of immigrants,
join us and those who are new to this
    country
in advancing its dream.

## MARS

With your weapons and armor, Father
    Mars,
protect our land.
With your weapons and armor, Father
    Mars,
protect our Constitution.
The one to prevent our destruction
The other to make us worthy of emulation.

## MIΘRA

Lord of a thousand pastures,
Lord of a thousand eyes:
uphold the law in this land.
May it correspond to the aša
that you well protect,
that we may be protected from the Lie,
and live safely, peacefully, and
    prosperously.

## PROVIDENCE

The founding deities, Liberty, Justice,
    Democracy, and the others,
are continually unfolded by us into a
    country more and more in accord with
    their teachings.
Liberty denied to blacks was extended to
    them with the abolition of slavery.
Justice denied to the indigent was extended
    to them by requiring public defenders
    for those who could not pay.
Democracy denied to women was extended
    to them by the ratification of the
    Nineteenth Amendment.
So even our imperfect system grows closer
    and closer to the deities' perfection,
even if it does not operate perfectly itself,
    and sometimes denies even that which
    has been extended.
These changes are created by human
    beings,
but they do this as they apprehend more
    and more the implications of the self-
    evident truths on which America was
    founded.
This apprehension is itself the result not
    just of human effort,
but its inevitability and development in
    time,
so that each new perception of truth might
    be absorbed in preparation for the next,
are in the care of Providence, the deity that
    keeps us under its special protection,
and provides the means through which the
    other deities might perform their work.
This deity is hard to know, since it is itself
    one of knowing,
and how can one know the knower?
Indeed, whether Providence is a god or a
    goddess is not even known.
So, having no shape, it is what *gives* shape.

Providence is shown in the Great Seal as
the Eye and the Pyramid:
the Eye that watches us,
and the unfinished Pyramid of the
American ideals.
It is to Providence that we pray today,
that our sight might be clear, to see the
founding principles better,
and that we might find the strength to
climb the Pyramid again and again,
carrying more blocks of stones, to place
them there, strongly cementing them
with mortar.
Providence asks us not for offerings of
things, but of words that inspire,
ideals in our minds,
and the continuing effort to defend and
protect the founding ideas.
Our vow today, then, is not to erect a stone
altar, but one that is informed of all that
is good and right,
and conducive to the extension of the Self-
Evident Truths to all,
and not just to those who pray here.
And for that we ask strength and
knowledge and wisdom,
and most of all courage:
May we both know the right and do it.

## QUIRINUS

Lord of the group,
Quirinus, god of the people,
join us now, separate individuals,
into one country,
ruled by law.

## RULE OF LAW

Rule of Law, with your rods and axe,
gather us together,
enable the State to enforce the right only
under your blessing and approval.

## SHANG TI

Shang Ti, ruler of all under heaven, rule
benevolently
through the Eastern Mother,
through the Western Mother,
through the Ruler of the four quarters.
We offer to the east.
We offer to the west.
We offer to the north.
We offer to the south.
We offer in the way of the Way.
We offer with a request for your just
governance of all.

## SRAOŠA AND MIƟRA

Aid me, Sraoša, in obeying proper laws.
Aid me, Miϑra, with courage to disobey
unjust ones.
Aid me, you two who are welcome when
you arrive,
in knowing which is which, which to be
followed eagerly,
and which to oppose in passion for the
Truth.

## TEUTATES

Teutates, god of the tribe,
strengthen, protect, and provide prosperity
to my people.
Reach out your hand in contract and
bestowal
as I reach out mine to you in offering.

## XÁRYOMĒN

It was by accident that I blew my horn,
Xáryomēn;
I meant no disrespect or insult to any other
driver.
May they be able to figure this out,

so that their attitude toward all drivers will
   be happy.
God of good social relationships,
may my accidental transgression not
   interfere with
the smooth functioning of my society,
of the connections between your people.

### THE ANCESTORS

It might be that your blood doesn't flow
   through my veins,
but your ideas flow through my mind.
Founders and Framers,
each day may I think of them,
and each day work to bring them into
   being.

On an incomprehensibly vast ocean
To an unknowably deep land;
Trusting to wood and rope and cloth,
and fickle winds,
you came from a need to live as you
   thought right.
Though I do not like all you did,
and though you would not like all *I* do,
still like calls to like.
The fire in my heart is yours.
Against obstacles you prevailed,
afraid below decks while storms shook the
   boat, you carried on.
If I, like you, set myself only to the right,
without the storms destroying my resolve,
I will consider myself truly your
   descendant.
As like calls to like, as fire to fire,
be with me and give me courage as needed.

## Deities of the Oath

President, Chief Executive, Commander-
   in-Chief:
you have sworn to preserve, protect, and
   defend the Constitution.
Gods and Goddesses of the Oath:
don't let him forget this.
And if he does, torment his dreams,
compelling him to return to his vow.

### TÝR

God of warriors, and god of oaths:
Today I am going to take my
   [commissioning/enlistment] oath
to support and defend the Constitution, a
   noble oath in honor of noble ideas.
In the times to come, I may encounter a
   situation in which it will be easier to
   break it than to keep it. If that should
   happen, Týr, prick my memory with
   your sword to remind me of today's
   words, that are more than spoken, that
   are written on my heart.
Help me keep my honor unstained, god of
   honor;
if without you I don't have the strength,
   send some to me.
The stakes are high; let me not fail.

## Liberty and Freedom

### JANUS, THOR, AGNI, AMATERASU

Open the doors, Janus.
Break down the walls, Thor.
Burn through the chains, Agni.
Show the way out, Amaterasu.
All the gods, bring freedom to those in
   your lands,

bring freedom to those in other lands,
bring freedom to all in all lands.
For by right of birth we are free,
and meant to live by Liberty's decree.

## LIBERTY

Liberty
Mother of Exiles
Hear your children as we call to you!
You have watched over our nation,
keeping it free,
keeping it independent,
for [number] years you have done this,
faithfully and carefully,
with love for your children.
Liberty
Mother of Exiles
Hear your children as we call to you!
Be with us now as you have been with us
    from our beginning.

Many and great are the gifts Liberty brings.
Many and great are the forms in which she
    comes to us.
We praise her in all of them.
Liberty of the Harbor,
may your flame shine to light the whole
    world.
Armed Freedom,
may you watch over our government.
Walking Liberty,
may it be the rising Sun of prosperity from
    which you stride.
Libertas!
Liberté!
Liberty!
We remember you in all of your forms
and worship you in all of the ways you
    show yourself to us.

Here today I would like to invoke the
    sacred name of Liberty.
It was for Liberty that our ancestors fought.
It was with her inspiration that they created
    our Constitution.
It was with her guidance that they formed
    a nation.
It was for her continuing inspiration that I
    pray today.
The Founders had a vision:
a land fit for Liberty to dwell in.
Under her guidance we will make that
    dream real.

Whether with bound-back or loose hair,
the cap of your pole bites deeper than an
    iron spear tip on any others.
Whether through images or ideas, words
    or deeds,
may you triumph throughout the world!
Praised in the past by few,
Praised today by many,
May you, Liberty, be praised in the future
    by all throughout the world,
by all nations and cultures,
your torch a light to all!

# Justice

## APOLLO

Son of Leto:
You whose chariot is the all-seeing Sun,
whose truth-knowledge sees into every
    dark corner,
whose arrows strike down liars with no
    mistakes:
today in this court may only truth be
    spoken
may only truth be heard
may only truth be decided.
Phoebus Apollo, hear my prayer.

## ČISTA AND MIθRA

Čista and Miθra,
may justice be found in my favor,
if, in fact, my cause is right.
Or, if not, let the Truth prevail,
even if it is to my detriment,
and may I accept the result.

## HEKATE

Come to me,
but don't *go* to me, Hekate.
Go instead to those who unjustly oppose
    me
and torment them.
Be relentless.
My cause is right.
If not, may it be I who feels your wrath.

## HELIOS

It is true that you see everything that
    happens under you, Helios,
great eye of the heavens.
So you know that I am blameless in this
    matter
and you know who is to blame.
Harry them with guilt.
Beat down on them relentlessly and
    mercilessly
until they right the wrong.

## JUSTICE

Not content with your blindfold's shield,
you avert your eyes from the scales by
    which you separate the false from the
    true,
and even with your unseeing eyes, the
    sword you carry will not miss,
separating the just from the unjust.
May all my deeds,
on this and other days,

be weighed as true
that I might be able to meet your piercing
    nongaze without fear.

## MA'AT

If what I'm doing is right,
a touch as light as the feather of Ma'at will
    suffice.
Goddess of Truth,
turn my feet onto the path of the Good.


May my discernment be yours, Ma'at,
as I weigh what I have heard.
In one pan of the balance, may there be
    always your feather.

## MIθRA

In this case I bring before the court,
may it be your side that I argue, Miθra.
Bring me to the truth, and show me the
    way to proclaim it.
May it not be the side of the more skillful
    that prevails,
but that of the more deserving of justice.
Great Judge, sit in judgment on this case!


I swear an oath today to Miθra, bringer of
    justice,
that I will tell only that which is true.
Whether it be to my advantage or bring me
    harm,
what I say will be what I know to be true.


Lord of the pledged word
and keeper of oaths:
Miθra, I pray to you for justice.

## MIθRA, RAŠNU, ARŠTAT

Miθra, who guards laws made by
    governments,
Rašnu, who guides judges,

Arštat, who grants justice:
be at my side in court today.

## SHANG TI

From your high mountain, dispense justice.
Impose, Shang Ti, peace-bringing order.

## TÝR

Irony of ironies, that you, God of the Oath,
have no right hand to raise in swearing.
Or perhaps just right, needing nothing to
    show for your speaking,
the speaking alone being enough.
Even thus, though I raise my hand as a sign
    of truth to others,
to you and to me the words suffice,
writing my vow into the Ørlög.

# For a Jury Member

I pray to all the gods my people worship,
    and I ask this:
May what is done be done well.
May what is done be done rightly.
May what is done be done according to
    justice.
May truth prevail, may falsehood fail,
May words and deeds and thoughts be just.

# Commerce

Commerce is not just a means, but an end.
    The buying and selling, the trade that
    Commerce is, unites people in strong
    bonds. Commerce is therefore one of the
    bases of community.
Thanks to Commerce, then, for
    establishing and contributing to our
    society. We serve you in this way:
by dealing fairly, but with an eye on profit,
    thereby contributing to human society,
    ourselves acting like you.
If imitation is the sincerest form of flattery,
    be flattered by our commerce and join
    with us,
Commerce, god of prosperous social
    relationships.

## MITRA

Grasp my hand, Mitra, as I hold it out to
    you.
I offer fairly to you, and you to me.
We are fair traders, you and I.
And I vow to you that all with whom I
    trade will be to me as you.
I will be honest in my dealings with them,
give value for value,
as you do to me.

# Chapter 28

# MISCELLANEOUS PETITIONS

I give you your proper worship, Holy One,
and pour this libation for you.
I ask that you in return bless this day,
removing obstructions and the bad,
bringing freedom of action and the good.
My gift for yours is what I offer:
may we be friends doing each other a favor.

With this libation,
with its pouring,
with its offering to the gods of peace,
we establish our friendship,
we confirm agreement between our groups,
we form a bond between us.
We swear this oath with this offering.

May I find just the book I need that will
    convey the knowledge and insight
I most need at this moment.
This is my prayer as I enter the bookstore,
these are my words, all you gods of
    knowledge,
to whom all words are precious.

## THE GOD

Lord of strength, give me strength;
to your faithful friend, strength.

God of transformation, reach into me for a
    piece of treasure

I am best without.
Accept this beloved fault as an appropriate
    offering,
presenting me in return with the perfect
    gift of your gift's removal:
precious gain from precious loss,
Transforming God.

A deer knows the ways of the forest's edge,
and you who wear a crown of antlers,
know the way between our world and the
    wild.
May I cross the border between all worlds
safely, with you beside me, Lord.

Your antlers are branches as you fade into
    the forest,
or as you come out of the trees into my
    sight.
Horned God, come and leave as you will;
I ask only that you continue to leave your
    blessings behind,
the life and death that you grant.

## THE ALL-GODS

I was the one who erred,
and I must be the one to fix the problem.
I am the one who did what should not have
    been done,

and I am the one who must make things
right.
The responsibility is mine, All-Gods,
and I will live up to it.
All I ask of you is the wisdom to know the
right way to fix things
and the strength of mind, body, and
character to do it.
If I don't find these on my own,
I ask that those of you proper to the way
aid me.
We will all then share in the honor of the
rightly done,
and I will offer to you in thanks.

## AENGUS ÓG

Aengus Óg, young lad, young son,
Though I am no longer young,
may love grow in my old heart.

## ANUBIS

Prepare my soul with sweet smelling
unguents,
anointing it for the tomb, preparing it,
Jackal-headed Lord,
to come to judgment in the hall of Osiris,
that I might be found worthy,
that I might stand before the scales,
saying, "I did not do this, I did not do that,
I did not do anything that would disturb the
feather's weight,
that rests in the other pan of the scales,
opposite my heart, my soul."
Through you, Anubis, I will be made ready,
by living a worthy life through your help.

Anubis who prepares the dead,
who guides them into the presence of
Osiris,
guide me, while living,
into the presence of the gods.

May I not be found wanting to stand before
them.
Guide me in the right way
in this world and the next.

## APHRODITE

Born of foam, where water and air meet,
you bring together man and woman in
loving embrace.
Lovely Aphrodite of golden sandals,
bring someone to love to me.
My happiness will be as great as that which
is right to mortals
if you answer my prayer,
that of me, who burns this incense in your
honor:
sweet smell for the sweetest one.

Foam-born Cypriot goddess,
bring me love
as I have brought you this gift.
Pour it out for me as I pour this wine for
you.

The love you bring, Aphrodite, is a
blessing to all who receive it.
And yet it can be a curse, bringing pain to
those bereft.
May it come to me in all its goodness,
a balm to my aching soul.

## ARTIO

Artio, who brings the wild bear,
tame, into the city,
fill me with wild and tame, both at the
same time,
bringing power into my day,
rebuilding what has become dry and
lifeless.

## ATHENA

May I find beautiful clothes
that fit well
that look good on me,
on today's shopping trip,
Lady of Weavers.

Athena, who guides weavers,
guide me as well as I knit this
[sweater/pair of mittens/garment/etc.],
my needles clicking happily,
the yarn under the right tension,
to end up with something that you might
    wear with pride.
Not as good as something you might make,
but made with the arete appropriate to a
    human being.

## AUSTÉJA

Be a goddess, Austéja,
through whose actions flowers are brought
    to fruit.
Bring mine to successful ends.
May I be productive and fertile,
reliably bringing forth new creations.

Bless the bees, Austéja.
Bless their goings out that they may find
    flowers
in abundance
Bless their returns that they might be
    accomplished safely,
burdened with pollen and nectar.
Bless their lives together in their hives.
May their children and their honey be
    plentiful.

## BRIGID

The hammer on the anvil
creates delicate beauty.

The fire in the forge
creates delicate beauty.
May the force and fire within which I live
create delicate beauty,
beautiful Brigid.

## ČISTA

Čista, I pray to you,
with words I hope you will find welcome,
to guide me on the straight path.

## DIWÓS SUNÚ

Sons of the God, I see your glory in the
    light
of the Morning Star.
Horsemen, I see you ride through the sky.
Sailors, I see you travel on the sea of its
    light.
Saviors, I ask you to come into my life,
bringing health and prosperity and freedom
    from troubles,
as it is within your power to do,
as it has been your practice in the past,
as I look for it in the future.

## EARTH MOTHER

Spread your hips
and let Him enter.
Wide extending,
let the rain come
Be fertile, be fruitful,
under his giving,
Mother Earth,
Great Mother.

## FREYJA

Dear One, Freyja,
whose love is boundless,
strong to give:
send love my way,
to me, who loves you.

Cat-driven Lady,
bring love to your dear one
who prays to you in the night.

## GUAN YIN

On your lotus-petal way,
strewn by your gentle hands,
Guan Yin, may I travel throughout my life.

## HERAKLES

With arrows you killed the snake of the
    Hesperides,
With a torch the Hydra,
With your own hands the Nemean lion.
I don't care what weapon you use, as long
    as my difficulties
fall before you.

## HERMES

Trickster whose cleverness defeated
    Apollo, the wisest of gods,
except for Zeus,
and amused Zeus himself, father of men:
show me the way out of this predicament,
bring me a clever solution.


Strength in my limbs, Heroic Herakles,
give me for the task ahead,
for successful labors.

## HORAE

Horae, may I be aware of each enjoyable
    hour,
of each moment as it comes to be,
and then passes by.
May my lifetime be filled with joy,
and may I not fail to notice it.

## IRIS

Most beautiful of the goddesses,

who conveys the messages of the king of
    the gods,
through you may I learn the speaking of
    Fate,
that I might live rightly by divine will.

## IRMIN

Irmin, whose pillar holds firm the world,
continue to uphold the Natural Law,
of which you are protector and king.

## ISIS

Queen who in love traveled far,
across and again,
to recover the body of Osiris,
your slain and dismembered husband,
victim of the traitor Set:
Isis, knit together with divine magic
my fragmented marriage
and bring it to life again.

## JUNO

Juno, goddess of marital peace,
Sweet and strong, gentle wife,
Queen and Savior and Pure,
who reigns beside your husband Jove
    there,
high above the celestial vault,
reach down, I pray, your soothing hand,
and smooth away the discord in my blesséd
    marriage.
Juno, wife, marriage goddess,
to you this prayer;
to you I will utter grateful words.


Juno Seispes Mater Regina,
bring purity, prosperity, and power to me
as I burn these [grains/sticks/cones] of
    incense for you,
sweet smells to ask for your loving
    concern.

## KHNUM

As a potter on a wheel,
turning the clay with shaping fingers,
conform me to Ma'at,
Potter god,
Creator god,
Crafter of worlds,
Khnum whose name is glorified,
who is worshiped throughout the lands,
who, if beheld, is regarded with awe:
[Name], your worshiper, from out of his
    confusion,
prays to you.
It is from your guidance that I am made right
to follow the True,
and through which my soul is made equal
    to Ma'at's feather.

## LADY OF THE ANIMALS

Lady of Beasts,
I speak of one of your charges that I want
    to stay far away.
They're small, these ticks, but they can do
    great harm.
They can bring sickness,
which would require me to turn to your
    brother,
with his healing arrows.
Better just to keep them away from me,
in the wild, their natural home,
that is in your special care.

## LESHY

Leshy, don't lead me astray today when I
    go into your forest.
I want to be friends with you.
See this pretty necklace I'm hanging on
    this tree. It's for you, happily given.
Take it, and don't lead me lost.

## LUG

May the electricity flow, your long spear
    of Gorias,
through this recalcitrant computer,
Lug, who fixes the broken.

At the second battle of Mag Tuired,
    Samildánach,
you gathered together the skills of the
    Túatha Dé Danann,
each contributing their ability to the
    victory.
You coordinated their talents, forging a
    successful team,
which won the battle.
You who know the way to knit disparate
    skills into one plan,
help me to do the same in my work,
to bring this project to a successful
    conclusion.

## MA'AT

The justice that you rule, Ma'at,
O Queen of the Feather,
is not just that of the courtroom,
is not, in fact, *primarily* that of the
    courtroom.
It is, rather, the justice of the life well
    lived.
The slightest ill-wrought deed disturbs the
    balance.
May my life be such that it matches your
    justice perfectly;
may none of my actions be such that I
    would be ashamed for my heart to be
    placed in the pan of your scale,
opposite your feather of the truly acted life,
Ma'at whose judgment is true.

Against all that is, balances the feather of
    truth;

Ma'at sits in the balance,
I sit in the other pan.
What I will do will be what is right,
What I will do will equal the truth.

Ma'at, purest of all,
in words, in thoughts, in deeds:
I have not fulfilled your commands.
But it is hard to do so in an imperfect
    world,
with an imperfect soul,
and I have done the best I could.
I ask you to stand with me before Osiris
when I come into his world.
May I not fall into the maw of Ammut,
but come to be enthroned,
an Osiris myself.

A life that is balanced is as light as a
    feather,
one that I can place with confidence into
    one pan of the scale
opposite that feather of yours upright on
    the other.
My own life is not that way, not yet, Ma'at,
but can be if you will help.
Show me each time the right action to take,
and push, and pull, and prod me to take it.
Most of all, mold me into someone who
    can see
the right way myself.
May I be myself a righteous person,
someone whose life is as light as a feather,
as *your* feather,
Ma'at, whose name is reverenced by those
    who wish to live an ethical life.

## Manannán mac Lir

Your cloak, Manannán, mist of the sea,
which separated Fand from Cú Chulainn,
removing from the pains of a doomed love;

place it between my lately loved one and
    me,
from whom I am now parted forever.

## Marduk

This is a story of what happened before
    anything happened,
when Tiamat rose against the gods,
the great emptiness threatening to swallow
    them all.
The gods, defeated, huddled fearfully in
    their shining halls.
Desperate, they turned to the great
    champion,
the caster of the thunderbolt,
supreme in war:
Marduk!
They prayed to him for help.
Can you imagine it, the gods praying?
In fear the great ones came to him,
asking him to save them from the Great
    Deep.
The Roaring One, with lightning playing
    around his head,
the Arrogant One,
agreed with their prayer.
He promised to save them,
but asked something in return.
(He deserved it, he who was to set his face
    against all-encompassing darkness.)
This is what he asked:
the kingship of all, gods and men.
He did not, actually, ask this:
he *demanded* it, as would only be fair for
    one who could stand up to the Abyss.
And how could the gods refuse him?
They of great might were cowering in fear,
dreading the smothering sea,
greatly fearing Tiamat;
how could they say no?

They gave it to him, then,
the kingship,
the lordship over gods and men.
With relief they put it into his hands,
singing in joy for the strength of Marduk.
He took up his mace and set forth.
Terrible was he to see.
Humans could not have borne the sight,
so strongly did the light of heaven shine
    from him.
His mace was lightning, his feet shook
    heaven.
With his quick-striking mace he lashed out.
He killed Apsu, who foolishly sought to
    stand in his way,
seeking to protect Tiamat.
Cruelly she had sent him out to face the
    world-ruling hero,
and Marduk slew him, quickly and easily.
It was no great work for the Great One;
a little thing, like brushing aside an insect
    that sought to bite him.
Then, with her hero gone (Could he really
    be called a hero? Marduk showed what
    a hero really was),
Tiamat herself came against Marduk,
putting herself at risk.
Stretching wide her mouth, he killed her,
    too.
The one who had cast dark fear on the
    hearts of the gods
died under the flashing power of Marduk.
He made short work of her, the Great
    Champion.
He split her wide open and formed from
    her earth and sky, and all between it.
He formed land and water, and men to
    serve the gods.
From emptiness he formed presence,
from Chaos, there rose Cosmos under his
    extended hand.

The gods, seeing his complete victory over
    she whom they had feared,
gladly put into his keeping the lordship
    over all,
over gods and men.
They made him willingly, with gratitude
    for the great deed he had done,
the great king, to rule forever.
Those who know this,
those people, those lands,
that recognize his power,
are given his protection and blessings.
His mace is withheld from them,
and turned instead against their enemies.
That is why we turn with confidence to
    Marduk.
We have poured out beer to the Great
    Champion,
dutifully worshiped him,
and he will place his hand over us.
Marduk! King! Champion! Warrior! Hero!
If our words today have pleased you
If the offered beer has enflamed your heart
Remember us.
May our names not pass from your mind.
When you distribute blessings, hold us in
    your thoughts.
When you seek to punish, though,
when your mace urges you to cast it,
then forget us.
May we be hidden from your sight and
    from your memory.
Marduk,
we have been loyal servants to you:
Be a good king over us.

I praise Marduk, mighty in battle,
who slew menacing Chaos,
yes, even Tiamat of the gaping jaws,
and her lover Apsu, when they rose against
    the gods.

Surely no disorder can withstand him,
surely not the small ones of my day.
A faithful servant to a well-disposed and
    powerful king,
I ask for this deserved reward.

Marduk, with your mace you rule all:
rule my actions
and rule the actions of those who oppose me
so that I may accomplish my goals.

## MERCURY

I haven't been able to find [item] for sale,
so I ask you, Mercury, for your help,
you who watch over and aid commerce and the
exchange of goods
as well as guiding those who search.
Mercury, I would be grateful for your help.

Mercury, who holds the purse,
who travels with the merchant,
may I find what I want as I shop today,
and at a good price, too,
a steal, even, god of thieves:
to you these prayers
and for you coins upon my success.

God of speech
and speaking teacher,
master of ways,
guide of souls on their last journey,
god of ever-flowing purse,
enabler of trade:
Lord who guides between one thing and
    another,
help me to transform myself,
to awaken who I can be.

## MIΘRA

With the shaking of hands,
with promises spoken aloud,

I establish this covenant,
this contract, this agreement,
under your view, Miϑra.
Upholder of the Aša,
I swear it, I enter it into our law,
I will uphold it, and you as well.
So I say, so I pray, so I will do.

## MITHRAS

Mithras Soter,
Mithras Pater,
Mithras of the Ever-Descending Knife:
Through your obedience to Sol Invictus
you rose to be with him,
to grasp hands with him,
to feast with him.
May I be as obedient to you.
May you alone be my crown.
May I come to sit beside you in the
never-ending feast,
there among the stars.
Through Mercury may I rise.
Through Venus may I rise.
Through Mars may I rise.
Through Jupiter may I rise.
Through the Moon may I rise.
Through the Sun may I rise.
Through Saturn may I rise.
Through the agency of the salvific bull-
    slaying,
May I rise,
May I be made immortal.

## MITRA

Good friend, Mitra,
look with fondness on your worshiper
who turns to you in fondness.
Protect all those who keep the way
from the snares of Varuṇa.
Grant me a peaceful life
surrounded by friends.

## The Norns

Each act of mine is a knot in the web of wyrd,
each one a pass of the shuttle.
Keep me aware of this, Norns,
as you work your threads,
so that my contribution to the weaving of
    the world's tale
might be worthy.

## Perkūnas

Directly, accurately,
may my rounds fly,
like your lightning seeking the short route
and hitting the intended target,
Perkūnas who strikes hard.

## Poseidon

Earthquake-bringer, destroyer of cities,
whose horse's hooves shatter the shores on
    which they land,
bring down the walls that surround me,
powder to dust their supporting stones,
view with the derision fit for a god their
flaunted strengths:
free me from even my most beloved prisons;
release me to the widely extending world that
awaits liberated souls.

## Saturn

Golden god of a golden age,
bringer of great harvests,
provider of peace:
Saturn, may my time be glorious and
    productive
and full of beauty.
You who bring such things, I pray to you.

## Silenus

Silenus, god of laughter and pleasure,
may my visit to [this amusement park/
    theme park] today be a good one.
May the lines be short, may all the rides be
    working,
may the people with and around me be
    filled with happiness,
and may I be filled with happiness, too,
giving myself over to the joy this place can
    bring.
May I be especially happy in this happy
    place, happy Silenus,
and return home delightfully tired.

## Tiwaz

Tiwaz, though you may have lost your
    place in the pantheon
to that upstart Woðanaz,
you have not lost it in my heart, which
    values truth above all.
And so I pray to you, god of clarity,
and dedicate to you and to truth my actions
    and words.

## Varuṇa

Lord of Order, Varuṇa, of the Ṛta,
Enforcer of the Sacred Law,
whose snares await those who violate your
    Ordinances:
inspire in me devotion to the rules of the
    game
I am about to play.
If my acts are not fair, they can never be
    excellent,
and instead of glory will bring down
    on me
your deserved punishment.

From the noose that ensnares those who
    violate the Ṛta,
protect me, Varuṇa.

From the noose that ensnares those who
   live by untruth,
protect me, Varuṇa.
From the noose that ensnares those to
   whom their Dharma is nothing,
protect me, O Varuṇa.

## VEDIC DEITIES

Difficult as it may be for me to make
   friends,
teach me, Vāc, the words to say in this
   social situation.
Connect me, Aśvins, to others closely,
you who are connected closely to each
   other,
whose horses' gaits brings people together.
Mitra, whose name is "friend,"
may I be seen as a friend to those I will
   meet.

## VELES

Veles, from your underground cave
bless and enliven all that has been
   committed to the earth,
seed and dead alike.
Enliven them through your power.

## WIND

Winds, fill the sails of my life's small boat,
propelling it safely across shoal-filled seas,
to safely rest in welcome port.
No gales, no calm, only a canvas-filling
   breeze,
I ask of you.

Carry in blessings,
giving wind.
Carry away ills,
cleansing wind.
Bring all that is good.
Remove all that is bad.
Leave me behind, happy and healthy.

## LAND SPIRITS

With the help of the Land Spirits,
whom I will continue to honor,
may this construction project run smoothly.
May it be finished on time and within
   budget.

# *Appendix 1*

# OFFERINGS

Appropriate offerings will vary from deity to deity. Gods have personal tastes just as we do. If you're going to be having a dinner guest, and you know they don't like peas yet you serve them, how rude is that? You're not likely to develop a relationship that way. It can be worse; serving pork to an observant Jew isn't just offending, it's an offense. The same is true with deities. Some are offended by certain offerings (most commonly meat, which is particularly bothersome to some domestic deities).

It is sometimes possible to find out what to offer through research. Cultures often have traditions: water mixed with wine for Greek deities, sake for Japanese kami, etc. Individual deities may have preferences. For instance, we know from Apuleius (Golden Ass 3.27) that Epona liked roses. Other times, you will need to experiment, starting with what seems best and seeing what happens.

There are some patterns linking deity type and offerings that help with this. The following list gives some of them. They are not meant to be taken as hard-and-fast rules—a deity from a culture that does not drink milk might be confused by a milk offering—but they are a point from which to start experimenting.

**Ancestors:** Food and drink from the family table, bread (especially dark), beer, legumes, caraway, hair. If you are offering to a particular Ancestor, then use their favorite foods.

**Birth deities:** Bread, eggs, cookies, sandalwood, mint, roses, hair from a first haircut.

**Border guardians:** Pigs, eggs, honey, cakes, milk, wine, flower garlands.

**Culture deities:** Songs, poems, prepared food, articles of culture such as handiworks.

**Death deities:** Pork, dogs, beer. This is one exception to the rule of sharing; you don't want to share with death. Make the offering, but don't consume any part of it.

**Deities in general:** Bread, butter or oil (burned), wine, beer, mead; incense (particularly frankincense).

**Earth deities:** Bread, pigs, beer.

**Fire deities:** Flammable items, especially liquids such as vegetable oils, melted clarified butter, whiskey, or other distilled liquors. (Note: Be careful with distilled drinks. Make sure you pour safely, either with a long spoon or while wearing a fire glove, since they will flare up. Also, when the alcohol and any sugar are all burned, you're left with essentially water, so don't pour too much at a time, or you will extinguish the fire).

**Garden Spirits:** Bread, grain, fruit, water, milk, honey, bay leaf incense, flowers.

**Hearth guardians:** Bread, butter (especially if clarified), milk, pine incense, rosemary. Generally not meat.

**House Spirits:** Bread, salt, wine, milk, food from the family table, butter, wine, beer, frankincense, rosemary.

**Lunar deities:** Milk, white bread, white flowers, silver.

**Nature Spirits (in general):** The local grain (cornmeal in America, wheat or barley in England, etc.), bread, cheese, sage, beer, flowers, shiny things.

**Nature Spirits (American):** Cornmeal, sage, tobacco, shiny things.

**Solar deities:** Horses, white wine, mead, gold, butter.

**Storm deities:** Cattle, beer, meteorites, sledgehammers, axes, flint, stone tools.

**Technology deities:** Tools, products of labor.

**Threshold guardians:** Barley, bread, wine, juniper.

**War deities:** Cattle, goats, iron, weapons.

*Appendix 2*

# GLOSSARY OF DEITIES

A ll Pagan deities are far more complex than I can describe here. If one interests you, don't limit yourself to what is said in this glossary; do further research, especially into their myths.

**Aengus Óg:** Irish. God of youth, love, and inspiration.

**Agni ("Fire"):** Vedic. God of fire, priest of the gods, intermediary between us and the gods.

**Airmed:** Irish. Goddess of healing, especially with herbs.

**Airyaman ("God of the People"):** Vedic. God of society, healing, and marriage; of bringing things together happily.

**Amaterasu ("Shining in Heaven"):** Japanese. Sun goddess.

**Anahita (possibly "Pure"):** Iranian. Goddess of purity, wisdom, nurturing, and the waters.

**Andraste:** British. A war goddess favored by the famous queen Boudicca.

**Anna:** The Proto-Indo-European word for "old woman, grandmother." I use it in this book as a name for the Crone (the waning Moon). It is a nice name for the hag goddess, almost a euphemism; as if by using such a pleasant name, we might keep away the fearsome side of her.

**Anubis:** Egyptian. A psychopomp and god of mummification.

**Apąm Napāt ("Close Relative of the Waters"):** Iranian. God of the Waters, and thus of purity, he also is in charge of the afternoon.

**Apām Napāt ("Close Relative of the Waters"):** Vedic. God of fire hidden in water; often identified with Agni (q.v.).

**Aphrodite:** Greek. The Greeks translated her name as "foam born," but it probably has its origin in "Ashtoreth," the Phoenician version of "Astarte" (Ishtar, q.v.). Goddess of love, beauty, and passion.

**Apollo:** Greek and Roman. God of healing, truth, civilization, music, and the Sun.

**Ares ("Strife"):** Greek. God of war.

**Arianrhod ("Silver Wheel"):** A possible Welsh goddess who cursed Lleu Llaw Gyffes (q.v) into not having a name, weapons, or a human wife. She was tricked by Gwydion (q.v.) into giving him the first two; Gwydion then made a wife for him out of flowers.

**Ariomanus:** Roman. A god in Mithraism depicted with a lion's head and wings. He likely was a god of fire who served to purify the soul on its journey toward the celestial realm.

**Arštat:** Iranian. Goddess of justice.

**Artemis:** Greek. Goddess of the wild, the hunt, virginity, and the Moon.

**Artio ("Bear"):** Romano-Gaulish. A goddess, most likely connected with both the wild and the city.

**Asherah:** Near Eastern. Chief goddess, represented in worship by poles.

**Asklepios:** Greek. God of healing. (In Rome he was called "Aesculapius.")

**Aśvins (also "Ashvins") ("Horsemen"):** Vedic. Savior gods, close to mankind. Also called the Nāsatyas (q.v.), which was the name of one of them, applied to both.

**Athena ("Of Athens"):** Greek. Goddess of wisdom, communication, and the practical arts (especially weaving); also of politics and protection.

**Attis:** Greek and Phrygian. God who died in the spring; small plots of lettuce, which grew quickly and then died, were planted in his honor.

**Aurora ("Rising"):** Roman. Dawn goddess.

**Aušrine (also "Aushrine") ("Rising"):** Lithuanian. Goddess of the dawn and spring.

**Austėja:** Lithuanian. Bee goddess, associated with honey and weddings.

**Ba'al ("Lord"):** Phoenician. Chief deity.

**Bast (also "Bastet" or "Ubesti"):** Egyptian. Cat-headed goddess of protection and fertility. In modern times, she has become especially a protector of cats.

**Bes (possibly "Guardian" or "Protector"):** Egyptian. Protector god, especially of pregnancy and children, he was portrayed as a gnome with a lion's face.

**Boand ("White Cow," or perhaps, "Giver of Cows"):** Irish. The goddess of the river Boyne in Ireland. She unwittingly let loose the fiery water from the well of her husband, Nechtan (q.v.). Since this was the water that inspired poets, she may be prayed to for inspiration.

**Brigid (also "Brighid") ("Exalted," "High One"):** Irish. Hearth goddess, mothering goddess. As patron of poets, smiths, and healers, she is also a goddess of inspiration.

**Britannia:** British. Goddess of the British Isles. Depicted as similar to Minerva (q.v.), only with a lion at her feet and a Union Jack on her shield.

**Cardea:** Roman. Goddess of hinges.

**Castor and Pollux:** Greek and Roman. Twin gods, protectors, especially of sailors, soldiers. Patrons of cattle and horse ranchers.

**Cathubodua (possibly "Battle Crow"):** Gaulish. A goddess of war.

**Ceres ("Grower"):** Roman. Goddess of growing things, especially grain, and of prosperity.

**Cernunnos ("Antlered God"):** Gaulish. The one who goes between opposites; god of prosperity, especially that acquired through trade. The name is also sometimes used for the Wiccan God, who is a completely different deity.

**Charon:** Greek. Ferryman who carries the souls of the dead across the river Styx to the Underworld.

**Čista ("Teacher"):** Iranian. Goddess connected with justice who shows the right way to go, in both the physical sense (e.g., roads) and the moral sense.

**Cloacina ("Cleanser"):** Roman. Goddess of sewers and, oddly enough, marital sex.

**Coyote:** American Indian. Trickster figure. He plays a lot of practical jokes, and a lot of practical jokes are played on him, but he is the giver of useful skills to humanity.

**Cybele:** Phrygian. Mother goddess.

**Dagda Mor (also "Daghda Mor" or "An Dagda") ("Great Good God"):** Irish. Not good in a moral sense, but good at things. His title "Eochu Ollathair" means "Stallion All Father," so he was most likely a chief god, but one who is presented in a rather comical sense, with a tunic that doesn't really cover his rump, and as a glutton. He mated with the Morrígain (q.v.), the war goddess, at Samhain (Halloween).

**Demeter:** Greek. Earth goddess. Her daughter, Persephone (q.v.), was stolen by Hades, god of the dead. Demeter mourned, and the Earth, deprived of her power, started to die. Nothing grew, and mankind was on the verge of starvation. Finally, Zeus made a deal with Demeter. Persephone could return only if she had eaten nothing in the land of the dead. Unfortunately, she had eaten a few pomegranate seeds. From then on, she was required to spend a certain amount of time each year in the dark land as its queen. During that time, Demeter mourns again, bringing on winter. When Persephone returns, however, so does life in this world, in the form of spring.

**Dian Cécht:** Irish. God of healing.

**Diana:** Roman. Goddess of the Moon and the hunt; protector of children.

**Dievas ("Shining"):** Lithuanian. God of the bright sky, order, and fate.

**Dionysos:** Greek. God of wine, the vine, ecstasy, and faithful marriage.

**Dioskouroi ("Zeus's Boys"):** Greek. The name for the Greek Castor and Pollux (q.v.) when seen together; gods of horses, sailors, healing; saviors in general.

**Diwós Sunú ("Sons of God"):** Proto-Indo-European. Gods of horses, sailors, healing; saviors in general; of all the gods, the ones closest to people. The "god" who is their father is Dyéus Ptér (q.v).

**Domovoi:** Russian. House guardian who lives behind the stove.

**Dyéus Ptér ("Shining Sky Father"):** Proto-Indo-European. Chief god, dispenser of wisdom and justice, enforcer of the natural order of things.

**Eos ("Rising"):** Greek. Goddess of the spring and dawn.

**Eostre ("Rising"):** Germanic. Goddess of the spring and dawn.

**Epona ("Horse Goddess"):** Protector of horses and cavalry; possibly goddess of sovereignty and protector of children.

**Eris ("Strife, Discord"):** Greek. Goddess of chaos and disruption.

**Firebird:** Russian. A bird that dwells in a faraway land, guarding the tree of life. It may bring blessings or disaster on those who encounter it.

**Flora ("Flower"):** Roman. Goddess of flowers.

**Fortuna:** Roman. Goddess of luck. Her emblem was the wheel, which is, of course, the wheel of fortune.

**Freyja ("Lady"):** Norse. Goddess of love, life, and death. Her cart is pulled by cats.

**Freyr ("Lord"):** Norse. God of friendship, fertility, and sexuality.

**Gabija ("Coverer"):** Lithuanian. Goddess of the hearth, protector of the family.

**Gaea:** Greek. The earth goddess.

**Gaṇeśa (also "Ganesha") ("Lord of Categories"):** Hindu. An elephant-headed god, overcomer of obstacles.

**Genius ("One Who Gives Birth"):** Roman. A divine being who is intimately connected with a certain thing—a person, an area, a group of people, etc.

**God:** Wiccan. The male principle personified, with attributes such as death, power, and sexuality.

**Goddess:** Wiccan. The female principle personified, with attributes such as birth, fertility, and sexuality.

**Green Man:** Modern Pagan. A personification of the forces of the wild, especially of forests.

**Guan Yin ("Perceiver of Prayers"):** Buddhist. A divine being (technically a bodhisattva) of mercy and compassion. Also spelled "Kwan Yin," but pronounced the same way.

**Gʷouwindā ("Giver of Cows"):** Proto-Indo-European. A goddess of prosperity; a mother goddess.

**Gwydion (possibly "Born of Wood[s]"):** A magician in Welsh literature who may have been a god.

**Hathor ("House of Horus"):** Egyptian. A very complicated goddess, mixing motherhood, sexuality, fertility, death, and protection. She was often depicted with a cow's head.

**Heimdall:** Norse. God who guards the road to the realm of the gods.

**Hekate:** Greek. Goddess of witchcraft and the crossroads.

**Helios ("Sun"):** Greek. God of the Sun, as the great "eye in the sky," he sees the deeds of men and is thus a god of justice, truth, and sight.

**Hephaestus:** Greek. God of smiths and potters, thus of artisans in general.

**Hera:** Roman. Queen of the gods; patron of marriage and children.

**Herakles ("Glory of Hera"):** Greek. Hero god; originally half-human, he knows what it's like to be us. Because he had to wander so far in his Twelve Labors, he protects travelers and also merchants.

**Hercules:** Roman. Version of Herakles.

**Hermes:** Greek. Messenger of the gods, leader of the soul to the land of the dead. Also a god of magic, commerce, travel, thieves, and skills.

**Herne ("Horn"):** English. A hunting god, leader of the Wild Hunt (the procession of the dead across the sky or through the world, especially at Samhain); the name is sometimes used by Wiccans for their God. The "horn" refers to one he blows, not ones on his head, and he is therefore not related to Cernunnos (q.v.).

**Hestia:** Greek. Goddess of the hearth. Her priestesses were chosen from among widows.

**Horae ("Seasons"):** Greek goddesses of time.

**Horus ("Distant [or "Superior"] One"):** Egyptian. God of the Sun, hero god, destroyer of evil.

**Iðunn (also "Idunn") (possibly "Ever Young"):** Norse. Keeper of the apples that keep the Norse gods immortal and young.

**Inanna ("Lady of the Sky"):** Sumerian. Goddess of sexuality, life, death, and kingship. Famous for descending to the land of the dead to recover her lover Dumuzi.

**Indra ("Man," "Hero"):** Vedic. Protector, warrior, god of the thunderstorm; with his lightning weapon (*vajra*) he killed Vṛtra, the great serpent of Chaos. As Indravayu, he has been combined with the wind god, emphasizing his storm nature.

**Iris:** Greek. Goddess of the rainbow and, in early times, the messenger of the gods.

**Irmin:** Possible Germanic god of the world pillar.

**Ishtar:** Akkadian, Assyrian, and Babylonian. Goddess of cities, sexuality, and war.

**Isis ("Throne"):** Egyptian. Mother goddess, sovereignty goddess, wife of Osiris, mother of Horus.

**Janus ("Doorway," or possibly "Going"):** Roman. God of beginnings and of doors; he was depicted with two faces—one looking one way, one looking the other—showing that he was the god of the moment between one thing and another.

**Juno:** Roman. Goddess of marriage. That she was also Juno Seispes Mater Regina, "Purifier, Mother, Queen," shows that she was much more.

**Jupiter ("Shining Sky Father"):** Roman. Head of the gods, wielder of the thunderbolt, and a god of justice. Sometimes referred to as "Jupiter Optimus Maximus," "Jupiter Best and Greatest."

**Kali ("Dark"):** Hindu. Goddess of destruction. She also has a motherly side, but to find it, you have to deal with her scary side.

**Kami:** Japanese. The term for any spiritual being; it can be used for either the singular or the plural.

**Kanaloa:** Hawaiian. God of sailing and the Underworld.

**Kane:** Hawaiian. Ancestor, creator, and fertility god.

**Kane-kuaana:** Hawaiian. A Moʻo (a sacred water lizard), originally a woman, who brings or withholds fish and pearls.

**Khnum ("Builder"):** Egyptian. A god who creates the world and people by forming them from clay.

**Kindreds:** The sacred figures seen as a whole, encompassing the deities, the Ancestors, the Land Spirits, etc.

**Kirnis:** Slavic and Baltic. God of cherries.

**Ku and Hina:** Hawaiian. God and goddess, respectively, of fertility and the continuation of mankind.

**Ku-ka-ohia-laka:** Hawaiian. God of canoe-making, but also of hula.

**Kupa-ai-ke'e:** Hawaiian. Craft god.

**Laima:** Baltic. Goddess of fate, pregnancy, birth, and childhood.

**Leshy ("Of the Forest"):** Russian. Shape-changing god of the forest.

**Liber:** Roman. God of wine and freedom.

**Liberty:** Throughout the history of the United States, Liberty has been called upon as the country's protecting goddess. Her image is found on coins, and she has been celebrated in song. Her most famous image, the one seen by immigrants entering New York harbor, has become the symbol of the dreams of our country. She is thought of more as a metaphor than as an actual goddess, of course, but, as Pagans, we can invoke her in a literal way, just as the Romans did, under the name Libertas.

**Lleu Llaw Gyffes ("Bright One with the Steady Hand"):** Welsh. Champion god, god of kingship and justice.

**Loki:** Norse. A figure in Norse mythology who spends most of his time working against the gods. Indeed, in the final battle at the end of the world, he will be one of the leaders of the army opposing the gods. There is no evidence that he was ever worshiped.

**Lug (also "Lugh") ("Shining," or perhaps "Champion"):** Irish. God of lightning, kingship, protection, and agriculture. He is called "He of many skills," and is a patron of artisans.

**Ma'at ("Truth, Order"):** Egyptian. Goddess of justice, not in the legal sense but in that of doing the right thing. It is by her that the rightness of our actions is determined.

**Manannán mac Lir ("Little One of the Isle of Man, son of the Sea"):** Irish. A god of the sea and of wisdom. "Mac Lir" means "Son of the Sea," which is probably not meant to indicate who his father was but what he was associated with. His earliest name was probably Oirbsen.

**Marduk (possibly "Bull Calf of the Sun"):** Babylonian. A god of lordship, protection, and war, he fought against Chaos and created the Cosmos from her body.

**Mari:** Proto-Indo-European word for "maiden," used here as a title for that aspect of the triple goddess.

**Mars:** Roman. God of war and agriculture; likely originally one of thunder.

**Maruts:** Vedic. A warrior troop that accompanies Indra (q.v.) and may originally have been connected with thunder.

**Mater:** Proto-Indo-European word for "mother," used here as a title for that aspect of the triple goddess.

**Mater Dea:** Roman. The name means "mother goddess."

**Mati Syra Zemlja:** Russian. Earth Goddess.

**Matronae ("Mothers"):** Celto-Germanic. Deities who appear in groups of three on a large number of images from Britain, Gaul, and Germany. They are often shown with babies and seem to have been protectors of children.

**Ménōt ("Moon, Measurer"):** Proto-Indo-European. God of the Moon and, because the Moon measures out time, of measurement and right thinking.

**Mercury:** Roman. A go-between—messenger of the gods, protector of merchants (and thus a god of wealth), guide to the land of the dead. Also a god of knowledge.

**Minerva (possibly "Thought"):** Roman. Goddess of wisdom, communication, and the practical arts; also of politics and protection. Equivalent to the Greek Athena (q.v.).

**Miðra (also "Mithra") ("Contract"):** Iranian. God of the human laws, protector from the vagaries of the divine. In later Sanskrit, his name becomes the everyday word for "friend."

**Mithras:** Roman. The god at the center of a mystery cult that seems to have been based on the idea of the development of the soul into a level of divinity. Not the same god as either Miðra or Mitra.

**Mitra ("Contract"):** Vedic. Enforcer of agreements, god of justice, protector of friendship.

**Mitravaruṇa:** Vedic. A combination of the gods Mitra and Varuṇa (q.v.), both gods of law, the former of social law, and the latter of the Ṛta, the order of the cosmos.

**Moneta:** Roman. A title applied to Juno as protector of money; she may have been a separate goddess.

**Morpheus ("Shaper, Molder"):** Greek. God of sleep.

**Morrígain ("Nightmare Queen"):** Irish. Goddess of sovereignty, war, and sexuality. The accent is on the second syllable.

**Nāsatyas:** Vedic. Nāsatya is one of the Aśvins, whose name is applied to both.

**Nechtan (possibly "Nephew" and/or "Wet"):** Irish. Guardian of the Well of Wisdom from whom only the worthy could drink.

**Nike ("Victory"):** Greek. Goddess of victory.

**Ninurta:** Mesopotamian. God of agriculture, healing, and war.

**Norns:** Norse. Three goddesses who water the World Tree and determine people's fates.

**Nuit:** Thelemic. Goddess of the stars, of infinite possibility, and of the great Void.

**Nut ("Sky"):** Egyptian. Goddess of the night sky.

**Odin ("Ecstatic One"):** Norse. God of war, wisdom, magic, and inspiration.

**Ogma (also "Oghma") ("Writing"):** Irish. God of writing and thought.

**Ogmios:** Gaulish. Version of Ogma.

**Osiris:** Egyptian. Lord of the Underworld, husband of Isis, father of Horus. One version of his original name is Asar.

**Pan ("Nourisher, Protector"):** Greek. God of the pastures; that is, of the land in between the domesticated and the wild. Bringer of divine madness.

**Pele:** Hawaiian. Goddess of the volcano.

**Perkons:** Latvian. Version of Perkūnas.

**Perkūnas ("Striker"):** Baltic. Hero god, protector of the common people.

**Perkʷúnos ("Striker"):** Proto-Indo-European. Protector, warrior, god of the thunderstorm. Patron of farmers.

**Persephone:** Greek. Goddess of the spring and of new growth, but also the queen of the dead.

**Perun ("Striker"):** Russian. Protector, warrior, god of the thunderstorm.

**Pomona ("Fruit"):** Roman. Goddess of fruit and fruit trees.

**Poseidon (possibly "Lord of Earth"):** Greek. God of the ocean, earthquakes, and horses.

**Pṛthivi (also "Prithivi") ("Wide Extending One"):** Vedic. An earth goddess.

**Pūṣan ("Nourisher"):** Vedic. God of travel and marriage; also a psychopomp. He was given offers at the beginning of sacrifices.

**Quetzalcoatl ("Feathered Serpent"):** Aztec. Wind, Sun, and creator god; a culture hero who, after giving the Aztecs corn and the practical arts, left, promising to return.

**Quirinus ("God of the Assembly"):** Roman. God of the people as a whole.

**Rán (possibly "Robber"):** Norse. Goddess of the sea; she pulls down ships with her net.

**Rašnu (Also "Rashnu"):** Iranian. God of justice and truth; one of the judges of the dead.

**Rātri:** Vedic. Goddess of night, sister of the dawn goddess Uṣas (q.v.).

**Re-Horakhty ("Re, Horus of the Horizon"):** Egyptian. Sun god, defeater of enemies.

**Rhiannon ("Great Queen"):** Welsh. Goddess of sovereignty and of wisdom.

**Rosmerta ("Great Provider"):** Gaulish. God identified by the Romans with Fortuna (q.v.), often represented holding a rudder, thus guiding us in our actions. More commonly, she stands next to a vat and holds what may be a strainer for what is in the vat. Possibly had a sovereignty role.

**Rudra ("Howler"):** Vedic. God of the jungle, and not in the nice sense.

**Sarasvati ("Marshy"):** Vedic, Hindu. Goddess of speech, eloquence, poetry, the arts, and music.

**Saturn:** Roman. God of the Golden Age and harvest.

**Saulė ("Sun"):** Lithuanian. Sun goddess.

**Scythian Ares:** Scythian. According to Herodotus (4.61–2), the Scythians worshiped Ares in the form of a sword stuck into a pile of brushwood.

**Selene ("Moon"):** Greek. Goddess of the Moon.

**Sequana:** Gaulish. Goddess of the Seine river.

**Shang Ti (also "Shangdi") ("Celestial Lord"):** Chinese. The creator god, the divine version of the Emperor.

**Silenus:** Greek. Follower of Dionysos. Usually shown as drunk, often on a donkey.

**Silvanus ("Lord of the Forest"):** Roman. Originally a god of the forest, he came to be seen as also the protector of the land that had been carved out of the forest, and thus of property and those who inhabited it.

**Skaði:** Norse. Goddess of winter, snow, and skiing.

**Soma ("The Pressed Out"):** Vedic. Personification of a drink that brought ecstasy; in later Hinduism, god of the Moon.

**Spider Woman:** American Indian. Plains and southwestern culture hero.

**Sraoša (Also "Sraosha") (possibly "Obedience"):** Iranian. God of prayer and the victory that comes from it.

**Sūrya ("Sun"):** Vedic. Sun god.

**Svantevit:** Slavic. God of protection; depicted with four heads/faces, he can therefore see danger approaching from any direction.

**Tahuti:** Egyptian. Original name of Thoth (q.v.).

**Taranis ("God of Thunder"):** Gaulish. God of the thunderstorm.

**Telepinu:** Hittite. God of farmers.

**Terminus ("God of Borders"):** Roman. God of borders and border stones.

**Teutates (also "Toutatis") ("Of the People"):** Gaulish. God who protects a group of people.

**Thor ("Thunder"):** Norse. Protector, warrior, god of the thunderstorm, patron of farmers, enemy of the forces of Chaos, whom he fights with his lightning hammer Mjǫlnir.

**Thoth:** Egyptian. God of wisdom, magic, and writing; he is pictured with the head of an ibis.

**Thunderbird:** American Indian. Spirit/god of the storm, especially of the beginning of the rainy season in desert areas.

**Thunor ("Thunder"):** Anglo-Saxon. God of lightning, thunder, and farming.

**Tiwaz ("Shining"):** Proto-Germanic. God of the sky and oaths.

**Tvaṣṭṛ (also "Tvashtar"):** Vedic. God of crafts, maker of miraculous weapons.

**Týr ("Shining"):** Norse. God of the oath and of war.

**Uṣas ("Rising"):** Vedic. Goddess of the dawn, the sister of night. Often found spelled "Ushas."

**Vāc ("Word"):** Vedic. Goddess of speech.

**Varuṇa ("Encloser"):** Vedic. Enforcer of the moral order, both social and cosmic.

**Veles:** Slavic. God of cattle and perhaps the Underworld; possibly an opponent of Perun.

**Velnias:** Lithuanian. God of the Underworld and the earth.

**Venus ("Desire"):** Roman. Goddess of love and beauty.

**Vesta (possibly "Burning"):** Roman. The hearth goddess. She was believed to be present in the fire on the hearth, where she was given some of the food from each day's main meal.

**Viṣṇu (also "Vishnu"):** Hindu. Creator of the extent of the world, and its sustainer.

**Vulcan:** Roman. God of smiths and potters, and thus of artisans.

**Westyā ("She of the Household"):** Proto-Indo-European. A hearth goddess.

**Weyland (also "Wayland"):** Anglo-Saxon. A smith who, among other things, fashioned a winged cloak.

**Woden ("Ecstatic One"):** Anglo-Saxon. God of wisdom, magic, inspiration, and travel; related to the Norse Odin (q.v.).

**Xápōm Népōt ("Close Relative of the Waters"):** Proto-Indo-European. Protector of a well of fiery water that inspires and enlivens but is dangerous to those who aren't worthy to drink from it.

**Xáryomēn ("God of Our People"):** Proto-Indo-European. God of society, healing, and marriage; of bringing things together happily.

**Yama ("Twin"):** Vedic. God of death.

**Žemepotis:** Lithuanian. Protector of the household and its land.

**Žemyna ("Earth"):** Lithuanian. Earth goddess; goddess of life and death. She is also appealed to for knowledge.

**Zeus ("Shining Sky"):** Greek. Chief of the gods; lord of justice, lightning, and hospitality.

**Zorya:** Slavic. Goddesses of the morning and evening stars.

**Zurvan Akarana ("Time Who Is Alone"):** Zoroastrian. The god of eternal time in a heretical form of Zoroastrianism.

# ANNOTATED BIBLIOGRAPHY

## *General References*

Adkins, Lesley, and Roy A. Adkins. *Dictionary of Roman Religion*. New York: Oxford University Press, 1996. Descriptions of not just Roman deities, but many Gaulish ones.

*www.avesta.org* Includes translations of all the Zoroastrian hymns.

*Book of Common Prayer. www.eskimo.com.* Although Christian, its style has sunk in to such an extent that it has become much of what we expect from prayers. The imagery is wonderful, and the prayers are good examples of how noble spoken English can be.

Boyce, Mary, ed. and trans. *Textual Sources for the Study of Zoroastrianism*. Manchester, UK: Manchester University Press, 1984. Includes translations of a number of the Zoroastrian hymns, different from *avesta.org,* and perhaps more reliable.

Budge, E. A. Wallis. *The Gods of the Egyptians* (2 vols.). New York: Dover Publications, 1904. His translations are out of date, as are his commentaries, but they are all suggestive of the style of Egyptian prayers. Particularly valuable is that he gives many titles by which each deity might be called.

Carmichael, Alexander. *Carmina Gadelica: Hymns and Incantations Collected in the Highlands and Islands of Scotland in the Last Century*. Edinburgh: Lindisfarne Press, 1992 (1909). Originally published in four volumes in the late 19th/early 20th centuries. The original version included the Scottish Gaelic; this edition does not. Christian, but with a Pagan appreciation for nature. Many Pagans have used prayers from this, with the substitution of Pagan deities for the Christian God and saints. It has been questioned as to how much Carmichael simply recorded the prayers and how much he "improved" them.

Dangler, Michael J., ed. *The Fire on Our Hearth: A Devotional of Three Cranes Grove, ADF*. Columbus, Ohio: Three Cranes Grove, 2008. Rituals of a modern druidic grove. Available from *www.threecranes.org.*

Dumezil, George. *Archaic Roman Religion* (2 vols.). Translated by Philip Krapp. Baltimore: Johns Hopkins University Press, 1996 (1966).

Eliade, Mircea. *Essential Sacred Writings from Around the World.* San Francisco: HarperSanFrancisco, 1967. Contains many prayers, as well as excerpts from scriptures.

——— *The Sacred and the Profane.* New York: Harcourt Brace Jovanovich, 1959. The classic work on sacred space.

Evelyn-White, Hugh G., ed. and trans. *Hesiod, the Homeric Hymns,* and *Homerica.* Cambridge, Massachusetts: Harvard University Press, 1936 (1914). Besides being a major source of information on Greek mythology, the Homeric Hymns are beautiful prayers.

Fitch, Ed, and Janet Renee Fitch. *Magical Rites from the Crystal Well.* St. Paul: Llewellyn, 1984. Neo-Pagan rituals with some beautiful prayers.

Gantz, Jeffrey, trans. *The Mabinogion.* New York: Penguin Books, 1976.

Grant, Frederick C., ed. *Ancient Roman Religion.* New York: Liberal Arts Press, 1957. Roman texts, including prayers.

Graves, Robert. *The White Goddess.* New York: Farrar, Straus, and Giroux, 1948. Just don't believe a word it says, and you'll be all right.

Griffith, Ralph T. H. *The Rig Veda.* New York: Book of the Month Club, 1992. Completed in 1896, it is dated. It's easy to find, and is even available online at *http://www .sacred-texts.com.*

Hayakawa, S. I. *Choose the Right Word: A Modern Guide to Synonyms.* New York: Harper and Row, 1968.

Heiler, Friedrich. *Prayer: A Study in the History and Psychology of Religion.* Edited and translated by Samuel McComb. New York: Oxford University Press, 1932.

Hollander, Lee M., trans. *Poetic Edda.* Austin, Texas: University of Texas Press, 1962. One of our major sources of information on Norse religion. Hollander limits himself to words with Germanic roots, which makes the poems sometimes difficult to understand but still beautiful.

Jackson, Kenneth Hurlstone, ed. and trans. *A Celtic Miscellany.* Harmondsworth, UK: Penguin Classics, 1975. A collection of Celtic tales and poems.

Jamaspasa, Kaikhusroo M. *Acta Iranica 24 (Papers in Honour of Professor Mary Boyce)* (1985), 335–356. "On the Drōn in Zoroastrianism."

Lady Sheba. *The Book of Shadows.* St. Paul: Llewellyn, 2002. A presentation of the Gardnerian *Book of Shadows.*

Laurie, Erynn. *A Circle of Stones: Journeys and Meditations for Modern Celts.* Chicago: Eschaton, 1995. A rosary using Irish texts. Purchasable as a pdf file at *www.sanet .com.*

Lincoln, Bruce. *Death, War, and Sacrifice: Studies in Ideology and Practice.* Chicago: University of Chicago Press, 1991.

Lyle, Emily B. "Dumezil's Three Functions and Indo-European Cosmic Structure." *History of Religions,* 22:1 (Aug 1982), pp. 25–44.

Macdonell, Arthur Anthony. *Vedic Mythology.* New York: Gordon Press, 1897 (reprinted 1974). The more important Vedic deities, short summaries of their myths, and titles.

Marcus Aurelius. *Meditations.* Translated by Maxwell Staniforth. Harmondsworth, UK: Penguin Classics, 1964.

McMahon, Gregory. *The Hittite State Cult of the Tutelary Deities (Assyriological Studies) 25.* Chicago: University of Chicago Press, 1991. Hittite rituals and prayers.

Modi, Jivanji J. *The Religious Ceremonies and Customs of the Parsees*. New York: Garland Publishing, 1979 (1922). *avesta.org* (accessed 12/5/18).

Nelson, John K. *A Year in the Life of a Shinto Shrine*. Seattle: University of Washington Press, 1996.

Nicolson, Adam. *God's Secretaries*: *The Making of the King James Bible*. New York: HarperCollins, 2003.

O'Flaherty, Wendy Doniger, ed. and trans. *The Rig Veda*. London: Penguin Books, 1981. The oldest of the Vedic prayers. This is a translation of about one tenth of the original. Good inspiration and useful as examples.

Ovid. *The Metamorphoses*. Translated by Horace Gregory. New York: Penguin Books, 1960.

Panikkar, Raimundo. *The Vedic Experience*: *Mantramañjarī*. Berkeley: University of California Press, 1977. Collection of excerpts from Vedic prayers and other texts. Available online at *www.himalayanacademy.com*.

Polomé, Edgar C. "Old Norse Religious Terminology in Indo-European Perspective." In *Language, Society, and Paleoculture: Essays by Edgar C. Polomé*, selected and introduced by Anwar S. Dil. Stanford, California: Stanford University Press, 1982.

Propp, V. J. *Down along the River Volga*: *An Anthology of Russian Folk Lyrics*. Edited and translated by Roberta Reeder. Philadelphia: University of Pennsylvania Press, 1975.

Rananujan, A. K., trans. *Speaking of Śiva*. New York: Penguin Books, 1973. Hymns to Śiva.

Redford, Donald B., ed. *The Oxford Essential Guide to Egyptian Mythology*. New York: Oxford University Press, 2003.

Regardie, Israel, ed. *Gems from the Equinox*. Newburyport, Massachusetts: Red Wheel/Weiser, 2007. Ceremonial magical rituals, with some lovely prayers.

Roberts, Elizabeth, and Elias Amidon, eds. *Earth Prayers from around the World: 365 Prayers, Poems, and Invocations Honoring the Earth*. San Francisco: HarperSanFrancisco, 1991. Prayers from around the world, in a number of religious traditions, all roughly associated with what might be called "Earth Spirituality."

Serith, Ceisiwr. *Deep Ancestors*: *Practicing the Religion of the Proto-Indo-Europeans*. Tucson, Arizona: ADF Publishing, 2009.

Staal, Frits. *Agni: The Vedic Ritual of the Fire Altar* (2 vols.). Delhi: Motilal Banarsidass, 1983. A description, with photographs and interpretation, of a performance of the Vedic Agnicayana ritual.

Virgil. *The Aeneid*. Translated by Allan Mandelbaum. New York: Bantam Books, 1981.

Willis, Garry. *Lincoln at Gettysburg: The Words that Remade America*. New York: Simon and Schuster, 1992. Contains an analysis of the Gettysburg address that demonstrates well-elevated speech.

Watts, Alan. *The Way of Zen*. New York: Vintage Books, 1957.

# Poetry

Benveniste, Emile. *Indo-European Language and Society.* Translated by Elizabeth Palmer. Coral Gables, Florida: University of Miami Press, 1969. Much on Indo-European poetic structure.

Frost, Robert. *The Poetry of Robert Frost: The Collected Poems, Complete and Unabridged.* Edited by Edward Connery Lathem. New York: Holt, Rinehart and Winston, 1979. A master of American poetic style, Frost uses nature imagery as metaphors for human life, linking us to the natural world. He was a close observer of seasons.

Haiku. There are many books on haiku and related verse forms, as well as many websites.

Heaney, Seamus, trans. *Beowulf: A New Verse Translation.* New York: W. W. Norton, 2000. A translation of this Old English classic that keeps to the Old English alliterative scheme, but loosely enough to correspond to modern English poetic sensibilities.

Matasović, Ranko. *A Theory of Textual Reconstruction in Indo-European Linguistics.* New York: Peter Lang, 1996. Indo-European (primarily Vedic and Greek) poetic metaphors and structures.

Shakespeare, William. Naturally. He demonstrates the thin line between prose and poetry.

Sturluson, Snorri. *Edda.* Norse poetic theory, including kennings.

Tolkien, J. R. R. *The Legend of Sigurd and Gudrún.* Edited by Christopher Tolkien. Boston: Houghton Mifflin Harcourt, 2009 A modern version of a medieval Germanic tale, told in the alliterative style. Good discussion of Germanic poetic style.

Watkins, Calvert. *How to Kill a Dragon: Aspects of Indo-European Poetics.* New York: Oxford University Press, 1995. An analysis of Indo-European poetry, especially meters. Most of the texts are prayers from ancient cultures. Very technical.

West, M. L. *Indo-European Poetry and Myth.* New York: Oxford University Press, 2007. Deals with the form and imagery of Indo-European poetry, as well as basic religion. Many excerpts from prayers and hymns. Technical, but not as technical as Watkins.

Whitman, Walt. *The Complete Poems.* One of the prime inventors of American poetic style. The tendency of his poems to dissolve into lists is actually a good model for prayers.

Yeats, W. B. *The Poems: The Collected Works of W. B. Yeats.* Edited by Richard J. Finneran. New York: Simon and Schuster, 1997. The most famous poet of the Celtic Revival, Yeats nevertheless wrote in English. This gives us a feel for how Irish rhythms and imagery can be adopted by English writers.

# ABOUT THE AUTHOR

Ceisiwr Serith (David Fickett-Wilbar) is a writer and teacher in the Pagan community. His interest in prayers and rituals grew naturally as a result of working in the Wiccan and Druidic traditions, as well as writing books such as *A Book of Pagan Prayer* and *Deep Ancestors: Practicing the Religion of the Proto-Indo-Europeans.* He is a member of Ár nDraíocht Féin, a Druid fellowship, and is priest and liturgist for Nemos Ognios grove in Durham, New Hampshire. He has been published in the *Journal of Indo-European Studies* and *Proceedings of the Harvard Celtic Colloquium.*

# TO OUR READERS